Palgrave Series in Indian Ocean World Studies

Series Editor
Gwyn Campbell
Indian Ocean World Centre
McGill University
Montreal, QC, Canada

This is the first scholarly series devoted to the study of the Indian Ocean world from early times to the present day. Encouraging interdisciplinarity, it incorporates and contributes to key debates in a number of areas including history, environmental studies, anthropology, sociology, political science, geography, economics, law, and labor and gender studies. Because it breaks from the restrictions imposed by country/regional studies and Eurocentric periodization, the series provides new frameworks through which to interpret past events, and new insights for present-day policymakers in key areas from labor relations and migration to diplomacy and trade.

More information about this series at
http://www.palgrave.com/gp/series/14661

Steven Serels • Gwyn Campbell
Editors

Currencies of the Indian Ocean World

palgrave
macmillan

Editors
Steven Serels
Martin Luther Universität
Halle-Wittenberg
Halle, Germany

Gwyn Campbell
Indian Ocean World Centre
McGill University
Montreal, QC, Canada

Palgrave Series in Indian Ocean World Studies
ISBN 978-3-030-20972-8 ISBN 978-3-030-20973-5 (eBook)
https://doi.org/10.1007/978-3-030-20973-5

Cover illustration: Michele Burgess / Alamy Stock Photo

This Palgrave Macmillan imprint is published by the registered company Springer Nature Switzerland AG
The registered company address is: Gewerbestrasse 11, 6330 Cham, Switzerland

Contents

Notes on Contributors

Gorah Beebeejaun was the former Chairman of the Mauritius Research Council, Port Louis, Mauritius. An avid collector of coins, he curated an exhibition on the currencies of Mauritius in 2010.

Gwyn Campbell is the Canada Research Chair in Indian Ocean World History and the founding Director of the Indian Ocean World Centre at McGill University, Canada. He is also the General Editor of the Palgrave Series in Indian Ocean World Studies and the Editor-in-Chief of the *Journal of Indian Ocean World Studies* (JIOWS). Born in Madagascar and raised in Wales, he holds degrees in Economic History from the universities of Birmingham and Wales and has taught in India (Voluntary Service Overseas) as well as at universities in Madagascar, Britain, South Africa, Belgium and France. He served as an academic consultant for the South African Government in a series of inter-governmental meetings which led to the formation of an Indian Ocean regional association in 1997. He has written widely on the history of Madagascar, Africa and the wider Indian Ocean world. He holds a Humboldt Award (2017–2019) for his research and teaching in Indian Ocean world studies.

John S. Deyell is an independent researcher into the pre-modern money of greater India. A former postdoctoral fellow of the University of Wisconsin, he has written extensively on numismatics and monetary history. Recently a visiting professor at Jawaharlal Nehru University, he is now settled in Ottawa, Canada.

Catherine Eagleton is Director of Museums at the University of St Andrews, where she continues to research trade and currencies in a global context. She was previously Associate Director of Curatorial Affairs at the Smithsonian's National Museum of American History, and before that Head of Asian and African Collections at the British Library, London. The majority of the research for this chapter was carried out while she led the Money in Africa research project in the Department of Coins and Medals, British Museum, London, and was supported by a Research Project Grant from the Leverhulme Trust.

Amenah Jahangeer Chojoo is an associate professor at the Mahatma Gandhi Institute (MGI), Mauritius. Her thesis was published as "La Rose et le Henné. Une étude des Musulmans de Maurice", MGI, 2004. She has written several book chapters and articles and her present research interest is in the Mauritian Diaspora.

Johan Mathew is Assistant Professor of History at Rutgers University, New Brunswick, and is the author of *Margins of the Market: Trafficking and Capitalism Across the Arabian Sea* (2016). He is working on a new project tentatively entitled "Opiates of the Masses: A History of Humanity in the Time of Capital", which explores how human bodies adapted to the demands of industrial labour through the consumption of narcotics.

Karin Pallaver is Associate Professor of African History at the Department of History and Cultures, University of Bologna, Italy. Her research interests lie in the social and economic history of nineteenth-century and early colonial East Africa, with special reference to pre-colonial and colonial currencies.

Angela Schottenhammer (蕭婷) is Professor of Non-European History at the University of Salzburg, Austria, and the research director and adjunct professor at the Indian Ocean World Centre, History Department, McGill University, Canada. She is the chief editor of an academic journal (*Crossroads*) and of two book series and has widely written on East Asian and Chinese history and archaeology, with a focus on historical exchange relations.

Steven Serels holds a joint appointment as a research officer at the Zentrum für Interdisziplinäre Regionalstudien at Martin Luther Universität Halle-Wittenberg, Germany, and as a visiting scholar at Harvard University's Center for Middle Eastern Studies. He holds a Master's degree (2007) and a PhD in History (2012), both from McGill University. He is the author of *Starvation and the State: Famine, Slavery, and Power in Sudan, 1883–1956* (Palgrave Macmillan, 2013) and *The Impoverishment of the African Red Sea Littoral, 1640–1945* (Palgrave Macmillan, 2018).

List of Images

List of Maps

List of Tables

CHAPTER 1

Introduction: The Indian Ocean World Currency System

Steven Serels

The development of sustained trans-regional connections across the Indian Ocean was made possible through the invention of a number of key technologies and the adoption throughout East Africa, the Middle East and South Asia of a set of shared social practices. One key technology around which a set of social practices converged was money, a human invention whose value is socially constructed. The Indian Ocean World (IOW) currency system was highly complex and comprised a number of competing currencies, each with its own range of circulation and depth of penetration. The list of currencies that, at one point or another, were widely circulated included, but in no way was limited to, gold, silver and copper coins, salt bars, cloth squares, grain, beads, shells, heads of cattle, promissory notes and bills of exchange. These currencies had a wide variety of provenances. For example, precious metal coins that circulated in the IOW were minted in India, China, the Middle East, Europe and the Americas. Similarly, cloth was manufactured throughout the IOW and,

S. Serels (✉)
Martin Luther Universität Halle-Wittenberg, Halle, Germany

Harvard University, Cambridge, MA, USA

S. Serels, G. Campbell (eds.), *Currencies of the Indian Ocean World*, Palgrave Series in Indian Ocean World Studies,
https://doi.org/10.1007/978-3-030-20973-5_1

following the introduction of mechanization, imported from Britain, France, Germany and the United States. Cowry shells were harvested primarily in the Maldives, though their range as a currency extended from Southeast Asia all the way to West Africa.[1]

In the IOW, currencies served a number of economic, spiritual, aesthetic and affective functions. As a result, their use was fraught with the tensions between the global/universalist and the local/particularist. On the one hand, currencies were a medium of exchange employed to settle market transactions and, therefore, were a technology that bridged differing cultures. Historically, a significant portion of trade in the IOW took place over long distances. This was true both of high-bulk, low-value commodities and of luxury goods. For example, in the nineteenth century, Indian grain fed Red Sea communities,[2] and enslaved peoples from the African interior were sold in Persian Gulf markets.[3] For these Indian grain merchants, Red Sea grain purchasers, African enslavers and Persian Gulf elites, as well as the many others in the IOW who depended in some measure on market transactions, currencies were key to participating in long-distance trade. Currencies were by definition commodities to which purchasers had access that sellers accepted in direct exchange for their goods. As a result, their circulation represented a commonality of ideas that transcended local understandings. On the other hand, the creation and circulation of currencies were guided by culturally specific considerations. Currencies were, at times, used for adornment and, therefore, subject to the vagaries of shifting local fashions.[4] Additionally, they were used in specific religious rituals. For example, in China coins have traditionally been used as a medium for communication with the spirit realm and, therefore, sometimes play a prominent ritualistic role in divination ceremonies.[5]

The case studies in this collection demonstrate that the IOW currency system was shaped by the tension between the local and the trans-regional.

[1] Jan Hogendorn, *The Shell Money of the Slave Trade* (Cambridge, Cambridge University Press, 1986).

[2] Steven Serels, 'Famines of War: The Red Sea Grain Market and Famine in Eastern Sudan, 1889–1891,' *Northeast African Studies* 12:1 (2012) 73–94.

[3] Matthew Hopper, *Slaves of One Master: Globalization and Slavery in Arabia in the Age of Empire* (New Haven, Yale University Press, 2015).

[4] This was the case with glass beads in Africa, see: Ila Porkonowski, 'Beads and Personal Adornment,' in *The Fabrics of Culture: The Anthropology of Clothing and Adornment*, Justine M. Cordwell and Ronald A. Schwarz, eds. (New York, Mouton Publishers, 1979) 103–18.

[5] Hill Gates, 'Money for the Gods,' *Modern China* 13:3 (July 1987) 267–8.

By examining the ways that conditions in the IOW impacted the local use of currencies in India, China, the Red and Arabian Seas, Madagascar, East Africa and Mauritius, these studies show that the IOW currency system was not simply created and propagated by economic forces. Rather, this system was, in no small part, structured by the moral economy shared by market actors throughout the IOW. This moral economy was, as E. P. Thompson defined it in another context, "grounded upon a consistent traditional view of social norms and obligations, of the proper economic function of several parties within the community".[6] In turn, this moral economy was structured by the tensions between local and trans-regional social, political and religious forces. The community of market actors in the IOW was cosmopolitan by nature, and comprised members of a number of religious denominations, ethno-linguistic groups and social classes. Nonetheless, this diverse community shared, to varying degrees, a common understanding of the role of the state in shaping market exchanges. In particular, this community accepted that sovereign states had the exclusive right to mint silver, gold and, in some cases, copper coins, but not the right to determine the currencies used to settle transactions. This latter right was seen as the traditionally inalienable prerogative of the participants in the market. As was the case in other realms of the IOW economy, the set of "social norms and obligations" that underpinned the IOW currency system was undermined by political innovations introduced from the end of the nineteenth century as a direct result of or challenge to European imperial rule. Though this process was contested, states ultimately wrested control of the currency system away from market participants. In asserting the right to determine the currency denomination of market transactions, states introduced new territorial currencies and demonetized all others within their borders. By the last third of the twentieth century, the trans-regional IOW currency system had been replaced by a system of national currencies and official currency exchanges. Nonetheless, the use and circulation of currencies throughout the IOW continued to be shaped by non-economic factors because currencies are by nature social inventions.

[6] E. P. Thompson, 'The Moral Economy of the English Crowd in the Eighteenth Century,' *Past and Present* 50 (February 1971) 79.

The Nature of Money

Currencies must be understood in terms of what they represent—money. Within the field of economics, an analysis of what money *is* generally grounds itself in an analysis of what money *was*, that is how money came into being. In classical economics, money is a social convention that was spontaneously invented by participants in primitive barter economies. Within the typical classical economic narrative, the exchange of goods in early societies was structured by direct barter. When these societies became more complex, they ran into the problem of what William Stanley Jevons in 1875 labelled the double coincidence of wants.[7] As economic specialization deepened and the list of in-demand goods widened in these societies, it became unlikely that two people would each simultaneously have the goods that the other needed. This barrier to barter led people to spontaneously use the most readily in-demand good as a medium of exchange because everyone recognized that it could be easily re-traded at a later date. The development of a universal medium of exchange marks the transition away from barter to a money economy. Though Jevons is credited with naming the problem that classical economists believe money solves, he did not originate the barter theory of money. This theory dates back to Aristotle.[8] However, it was first elaborated in its modern form by Adam Smith in his chapter "Of the Origin and Use of Money" in *The Wealth of Nations* (1776).[9] Subsequent classical economists have slightly modified Smith's original definition of money as a medium of exchange to recognize money's ability to act as both a common measure and a store of value. Nonetheless, economists continue to repeat Smith's formulation that the nature of money was shaped by its history—that is by the transaction difficulties that historically arose in early barter-based societies.[10]

Though the barter theory of money is fundamentally a theory about both the history of money and the way exchange works in non-money

[7] See: William Stanley Jevons, *Money and the Mechanism of Exchange* (New York, D. Appleton & Co, 1875) 3–5.

[8] Aristotle, *Politics*, Part I, Book IX.

[9] Adam Smith, *The Wealth of Nations* (New York, Bantam Dell, 2003) 33–42.

[10] For some examples of this pervasive conceptualization see: Joseph Stiglitz and John Dariffill, *Economics* (New York, W. W. Norton, 2000) 251; Michael Parkin and David King, *Economics*, 2nd edition (London, Addison-Wesley, 1995) 65; Peter Maunder, Danny Myers, Nancy Wall and Roger LeRoy Miller, *Economics Explained*, 3rd edition (London, Harper Collins, 1991) 310; Karl Case, Ray Fair, Manfred Gärtner and Ken Heather, *Economics* (London, Prentice Hall, 1996) 564.

societies, the economists who have advanced this theory have offered little historical, archaeological or anthropological evidence to back it up. Instead, economists often resort to imploring their readers to "imagine" a pre-monetary past or a barter society that the economist posits *must have* existed. This paucity of mustered evidence has led historians, archaeologists and anthropologists to search out the missing evidence. However, scholars in these fields generally have found evidence that fundamentally contradicts the assumptions underlying the barter theory. Anthropologists have not found pure barter economies, such as the one described by Adam Smith in which, according to the example he gives, the butcher trades his surplus meat to the baker in exchange for the latter's surplus bread.[11] This kind of simple barter has only been found in formerly money societies that have experienced a currency crisis and therefore reverted to direct exchange.[12] In societies that are not governed by the logic of money, the redistribution of goods tends to work on the principles of hospitality, obligation and reciprocity.[13]

Similarly, archaeologists and historians have found no evidence that money developed spontaneously as a means of reducing transaction costs.[14] Instead, a number of scholars have convincingly demonstrated that money appeared as a measure of value centuries before it emerged as a medium of exchange. This is exemplified by the evolution of the command economies of ancient Egypt and Mesopotamia. The emergence of these ancient societies was characterized by a shift away from egalitarianism characterized by communal control of production and equal rights to output. As a hierarchy emerged in these societies, the new elites introduced the concept of money as a means of recording the value of the taxes owed by their respective subaltern population. Though elites introduced the concept of a money of account, money in the form of currencies was used neither to pay taxes (which could be done in kind) nor to settle market transactions. Currencies were only introduced in Egypt and

[11] Caroline Humphery, 'Barter and Economic Disintegration,' *Man* 20 (1985) 48–72; Anne Chapman, 'Barter as a Universal Mode of Exchange,' *L'Homme* 22:3 (1980) 33–83.

[12] For an example of this, see: Jean-Michel Servet, 'Démonétisation et remonétisation en Afrique-Occidentale et Équatoriale (XIXe-XXe siecles),' in *La Monnaie Souveraine*, Michel Aglietta and André Orléans, eds. (Paris, Odile Jacob, 1998) 289–324.

[13] For a concise outline of the difference between exchange and hospitality, see: Stephanie Bell and John H. Henry. 'Hospitality versus Exchange: The Limits of Monetary Economies,' *Review of Social Economy* 59:2 (June 2001) 203–26.

[14] Geoffery Ingham, *The Nature of Money* (Cambridge, Polity Press, 2004) 89.

Mesopotamia centuries later.[15] Scholars studying early Anglo-Saxon and Germanic societies have also showed that the widespread assessing of *wergild*, that is the value of damages owed for injuring or killing a person, preceded the use of money as a medium of exchange. Philip Grierson goes so far as to state that the process of developing the practice of *wergild* "would appear to satisfy, much better than any market mechanism, the prerequisites for the establishment of a monetary system. The tariffs for damages were established in public assemblies, and the common standards were based on objects of some value which a householder might be expected to possess or which he could obtain from his kinfolk."[16] These conclusions suggest that money emerged first as a means of measuring the value of debts, whether to other members of society or to emerging states, and only later was adopted to be used as a medium of exchange.

The connection between debt and the development of money was first identified by A. Mitchell Innes in 1913. In his seminal article "What is Money", Innes argued that money as a medium of exchange is not necessary to solve the problem of the double coincidence of wants. Rather, debt can easily solve this problem. If, in Adam Smith's classic example, the butcher wants bread at a time that the baker does not want meat, then the butcher can receive the bread in exchange for an acknowledgement of debt. Money was invented as a means of measuring and recording this debt. As a result, money was created first as a measure of value. Once debt had a measurable value, it could be traded. This allowed, to continue the example, the baker to trade 100 coins, shells or whatever measuring convention was adopted of the butcher's debt to the shoemaker for 100 currency units of shoes. In the end of this chain of transactions, the butcher has bread, the baker has shoes and the shoemaker owns 100 units of the butcher's debt. The butcher's debt has become circulating money that is it is now a currency. Therefore, Innes concludes "credit and credit alone is money. Credit and not gold or silver is the one property which all men seek, the acquisition of which is the aim and object of all commerce."[17]

[15] John H. Henry, 'The Social Origins of Money: The Case of Egypt' Money,' in *Credit and State Theories of Money: The Contribution of A. Mitchell Innes*. L. Randall Wray, ed. (Cheltenham, UK, Edward Elgar, 2004) 79–98.

[16] Philip Grierson, 'The Origins of Money,' *Research in Economic Anthropology* 1 (1978) 13.

[17] A. Mitchell Innes, 'What is Money,' in *Credit and State Theories of Money: The Contribution of A. Mitchell Innes*, L. Randall Wray, ed. (Cheltenham, UK, Edward Elgar, 2004) 31.

Though the debt theory of money laid out by Innes was initially marginalized within mainstream economics, this theory influenced John Maynard Keynes's *A Treatise on Money* (1930) and has gained wider traction since the 1990s.[18] Scholars in a number of disciplines have explored the implications of Innes's insights and, in particular, have demonstrated that, as Geoffrey Ingham puts it, "money *is* itself a social relation".[19] The recognition of the social nature of money is a radical departure from the understanding of money within classical economics, which asserts that money is a neutral and transparent medium of exchange. Scholars have shown that in order for money to exist as both a measure of value and a medium of exchange a number of conditions must also exist. Stephanie Bell and John H. Henry have shown that money cannot exist within societies organized around the "principle of hospitality" in which each member "had an equal right to the output produced by all on the means of production controlled by all". According to Bell and Henry, within hospitality societies there may be private property, however "such property allowed no control over others; in particular, personal property could not be used to extract the produce of another's labor. Further, as long as the community controlled the productive equipment, no property-based constraints could be placed on the production of personal goods held by the population."[20] The kinds of debt that leads to the creation of money can only exist in societies that already conceptualize a relationship between property ownership and control over others. In order for debts to have value, they must be enforceable. There must be social institutions that give creditors power over debtors. Though these institutions may exist within a moral economy that limits the power of creditors, their existence suggests a stratified, hierarchical society.

Scholars have argued that the debt theory of money recognizes a place, previously denied by the barter theory, for the state in the creation and circulation of money. States can levy taxes and taxes are a form of debt obligation owed by subjects to the state. In addition, states determine which currencies will be accepted in discharge of tax obligations. This creates a special demand for tax-currencies because, as long as the state routinely collects

[18] R. Randall Wray and Stephanie Bell, 'Introduction,' in *Credit and State Theories of Money: The Contribution of A. Mitchell Innes*, L. Randall Wray, ed. (Cheltenham, UK, Edward Elgar, 2004) 1–3.

[19] Italics in original. Geoffrey Ingham. *The Nature of Money* (Cambridge, Polity Press, 2004) 12.

[20] Bell and Henry, 11–12.

taxes, people will need to regularly acquire them. The ready demand for tax-currencies has spillover effects for private market exchanges. This demand allows market participants to have confidence that any tax-currencies they accept will be easily discharged in exchange for other goods and services. This special role of the state in shaping monetary systems was first identified by George Knapp in *The State Theory of Money* (1924), who termed it the chartalist theory of money. Though Knapp did not explicitly connect the chartalist and debt theories, other scholars have done so for him. These scholars have argued that the only difference between tax-currencies and private-debt currencies is the power of enforcement. Money created by the state is more universally acceptable only because it is directly backed by the power of the state to levy and collect taxes. Whereas, money created by private debt is backed indirectly by the social institutions and judicial structures that, generally, force respect for debt obligations. The difference between the powers of the state and of non-state actors creates a differential in confidence. Market participants can be more certain that taxes will be paid than that non-state actors will respect their debt. As a result, they will prefer accepting tax-currencies over private-debt currencies.[21]

While the chartalist theory helps explain the influence of contemporary states over the currency systems within their borders, it does not reflect the role of the state in the IOW currency system. Not all states in the IOW operated in the fashion assumed by Knapp. Similarly, the social institutions that enforced repayment of debts were at some times and in some places within the IOW stronger than the coercive abilities of the state. As a result, the disparity in demand between tax-currencies and private-debt currencies in the IOW could run in the reverse direction and "official" currencies were at times less desired than their "unofficial" counterparts. The flexibility that merchants, peddlers and consumers had in shaping their transactions meant that they routinely assessed the relative strength or weakness of each circulating currency. The choice of currency did not, simply, reflect an evaluation of the relative merits of local state institutions. Rather, market participants throughout the IOW were required to simultaneously think locally and globally. Currency valuations fluctuated from market to market depending on both local conditions and the whole chain of exchanges that structured the IOW currency system.

[21] Stephanie Bell, 'The Role of the State and the Hierarchy of Money,' *Cambridge Journal of Economics* 25 (2001) 160–1.

The IOW Currency System

With the notable exception of parts of the East Asian Mediterranean, the role of the state in currency markets was generally circumscribed throughout much of the IOW. Instead, the IOW currency system was, primarily, maintained by merchants, peddlers and *sarrafs* (Arabic, moneychangers). Traditionally, IOW merchants owned the capital that was invested in long-distance trade. K. N. Chaudhuri has shown that, with just a few notable exceptions, these merchants "earned no more than a modest living". Their economic position was uncertain because they needed to reinvest profits back into their commercial enterprises, which always ran the risk of failing. In addition, they were vulnerable to "arbitrary expropriation" by "unpredictable" states. The real power of these merchants came not from their wealth, but from their important position within the IOW currency system. As Chaudhuri writes, "the most immediate and powerful means of self-protection available to merchants was in their command over money. Commercial understanding of international currencies complemented the ability to move precious metals over long distances and make payments separated by time and space."[22] This position was supported by the *sarrafs* who exchanged the various currencies. Professional moneychangers were necessary in the IOW because Islamic law prohibits *riba* (Arabic, lit. "increase" but generally translated as "interest"). This restriction is understood to apply both to loans and to currency exchanges. As a result, certain kinds of profits from currency exchanges are forbidden. The various schools of Islamic jurisprudence developed complex sets of regulations on currency exchange contracts. A. Zysow notes that this complexity "made it difficult for those engaged in frequent exchanges to avoid violating the prohibition of *riba*, which put the profession of money-changing in a bad light".[23] From the fifteenth century onwards, the commercial activities of merchants and *sarrafs* in the IOW became increasingly more sophisticated and complex. In response to the development of new kinds of trading partnerships and arrangements, Muslim *sarrafs* and their Hindu counterparts created new kinds of banking arrangements, such as bills of exchanges,

[22] K. N. Chaudhuri, *Trade and Civilisation in the Indian Ocean: An Economic History from the Rise of Islam to 1750* (Cambridge, Cambridge University Press, 1985) 212–14.

[23] A. Zysow, '*Ṣarf*' *Encyclopedia of Islam. Volume XII: Supplement* (Leiden, Brill, 2004) 706.

that allowed for an intensification and an increase in the velocity of the flow of currencies and credit throughout the IOW.[24]

For gold and silver currencies, the direction of the flow was, generally, from Europe through the Middle East towards China and India. Some scholars have claimed that Asia was a precious metal sink because gold and silver were overvalued in these markets. However, Najaf Hadler has argued that the flow of silver and gold in the IOW was directed by the currents of trade. India and China simultaneously had a limited demand for foreign products while also manufacturing goods that were highly desired abroad. Gold and silver were the means of settling the structural trade imbalance.[25] In her contribution to this volume, Angela Schottenhammer further complicates this dynamic by demonstrating that metal currencies did not always flow into China. From the ninth to the twelfth century, China had a negative balance of trade with the East Asian Mediterranean that was settled through the export of large quantities of copper coins. By the twelfth century, the intensity of the rate of export of copper coins destabilized the Chinese economy and harmed the state's treasury. The introduction of paper currency exacerbated the currency crisis and, ultimately, led to the further export of metal coins and silver ingots. The flow of currencies out of China was only reversed because of the sudden and sustained growth in demand in Europe for Chinese goods. By the sixteenth century, China had become an importer of foreign precious metal currencies.

India's conventional image as a precious metal sink is also more complicated than conventionally depicted because, as John S. Deyell's contribution demonstrates, India was not historically a single currency zone. For the period between the twelfth and fifteenth century, India was divided into a number of maritime facing currency zones, each employing a different constellation of metallic coins. All of these zones were dependent on imported metal to meet their currency needs. Nonetheless, the ratio of gold to silver to copper coins in circulation varied greatly from zone to zone. Additionally, India's East Coast and Bay of Bengal imported cowry shells from the Maldives for use as a medium of exchange. Other scholars have shown that the increased importation of silver into India with the

[24] Patricia Risso, *Merchants and Faith: Muslim Commerce and Culture in the Indian Ocean* (Boulder, CO, Westview Press, 1995) 68.

[25] Najaf Hadler, 'The Network of Monetary Exchange in the Indian Ocean Trade, 1200–1700,' in *Cross Currents and Community Networks: The History of the Indian Ocean World*, Himanshu Prabha Ray and Edward A. Alpers, eds. (Oxford, Oxford University Press, 2007) 182–6.

Spanish exploitation of South American mines did not lead to the development of a single, unified silver currency system throughout the subcontinent. Rather, coins of various weights and qualities continued to circulate throughout India.[26] In addition, silver that was imported into India did not simply stay there. Some of it was reminted into rupees and re-exported. Starting in the seventeenth century, European mercantile trading companies began using Indian rupees to engage in trade throughout the Indian Ocean World and, subsequently, made it the official currency of some of their newly established colonies, as the Dutch did in Java and the British did in Ceylon.[27]

The Indian rupee was one of a number of currencies that served in the IOW as, to borrow Akinobu Kuroda terminology, complementary interfaces between multiple markets. Kuroda, in describing the circulation of Maria Theresa Thalers in the Red Sea, located "three layers of monetary circulation" in the region. The top layer was comprised of currencies that "flowed in the international and inter-regional circuits". These were high-value currencies that were universally in demand. They comprised silver or gold coins, minted by established powers and recognized as having a uniform fineness and weight. The bottom layer was comprised of "a variety of smaller monies" that "were in circulation with significant and greatly varying regional preferences". They were used in day to day exchanges between peddlers and end consumers and, therefore, were of low value. Between these two layers stood the *sarrafs* and traders who "were competing for profits through speculation".[28] Though Kuroda located just two classes of trade currencies, Karin Pallaver's contribution finds that there were a large number of currency exchange "interfaces" that facilitated the movement of goods into and trade profits out of the East African interior. As goods made their way from Indian Ocean ports to East African markets, traders utilized silver coins, cloth, glass beads, cowries, iron and brass wires. Each of these currencies was unique in range and their use necessitated crossing

[26] R. J. Barendse. *Arabian Seas: 1700–1763. Volume 3: Men and Merchandise* (Leiden, Brill, 2009) 879.

[27] Shailendra Blandare, 'Money on the Move: The Rupee and the Indian Ocean Region,' in *Cross Currents and Community Networks: The History of the Indian Ocean World*, Himanshu Prabha Ray and Edward A. Alpers, eds. (Oxford, Oxford University Press, 2007) 210–15.

[28] Akinobu Kuroda, 'The Maria Theresa Dollar in the Early Twentieth Century Red Sea Region: A complementary Interface between Multiple Markets,' *Financial History Review* 14:1 (April 2007).

a currency "interface". Successful traders wanting to export ivory and slaves had to navigate a dizzying array of currency zones and regional currency exchanges. At times, the geographic scope of a currency zone could be just a few days' journey along the caravan route.

States played circumscribed, though important roles in the IOW currency system. Throughout the IOW the right to mint precious metal coins was the exclusive prerogative of sovereign rulers and the designs of coins typically included inscriptions that reflected this.[29] This right was so bound up with conceptions of sovereignty that ambitious local rulers would sometimes mint their own coins as a sign of their amassing power, as was the case in the Hadramaut in the nineteenth century.[30] Many of the coins minted by lesser rulers were not struck in sufficient quantities to widely circulate. Instead, as Edward Alpers has shown for the Swahili kings of the East African coast, they "were a form of royal regalia that gave prestige to the rulers".[31] Though many coins were just symbols of power, some circulated widely. To ensure their widespread acceptance, the rulers who commissioned them had to work tirelessly to ensure the quality of the coins they commissioned. Om Prakash has shown that Indian rulers went to great lengths to guarantee the uniform fineness of Indian rupees. As a result, trust in the rupee was widespread, enabling it to circulate throughout the IOW.[32]

Traditional conceptions of sovereignty and state power in the IOW came under increasing pressure over the course of nineteenth century as strengthening economic ties to Europe laid the foundation for a new wave of European imperial expansion. As European interest in the region increased, local rulers throughout the IOW also sought to minimize the harm and maximize the benefit from innovations in the trans-regional economy. These efforts were often hindered by currency crises characterized by high rates of inflation or monetary devaluations, as was the case in

[29] For an illustrated general survey of coin designs in the IOW, see: Catherine Eagleton and John Williams, *Money: A History* (London, British Museum Press, 2007) 86–161, 193–217.

[30] Ulrike Freitag, *Indian Ocean Migrants and State Formation in Hadhramaut: Reforming the Homeland* (Leiden, Brill, 2003).

[31] John Middleton. *African Merchants of the Indian Ocean: Swahili of the East African Coast* (Long Grove, IL, Waveland Press, 2004) 84.

[32] Om Prakash, 'Foreign Merchants and Indian Mints in the Seventeenth and the Early Eighteenth Century,' in *The Imperial Monetary System of Mughal India*, J. F. Richards, ed. (Delhi, Oxford University Press, 1987) 171–92.

Sudan, the Ottoman Empire and large parts of the cowry zone.[33] Nonetheless, local rulers were reluctant to challenge the traditional moral economy of the market that limited state interference in an increasingly unstable currency system. Gwyn Campbell's contribution to this collection highlights the negative consequences of the tension between the traditional moral economy and the new economic realities. During the nineteenth century, the Merina rulers of Madagascar territorially expanded and modernized their state as part of a broad effort to curtail European designs on the island. Unfortunately, the reforms implemented by these rulers not only failed to deliver their promised economic benefits but set off a currency crisis throughout the island. To cope, the Merina state intensified the exploitation of its subject's labour to mine previously untapped gold deposits. However, the state was unable to compel its subjects to comply with new regulations on the gold trade. The state was also unwilling to challenge the traditional moral economy of the market and, as a result, the island's economy continued to be dependent on increasingly scarce imported currencies. The instability caused by this dependence, ultimately, laid the groundwork for the French conquest of the island.

European commercial penetration and imperial expansion in the IOW did not initially directly challenge the prevailing notion that states should not interfere in the currency system because this notion was shared by many European imperial agents. Catherine Eagleton's case study in this volume demonstrates that understandings of the rights and obligations of states vis-à-vis the currency system were shared by the Omani rulers of Zanzibar, French merchants, British officials and German commercial interests that were competing with each other on the East African littoral at the end of the nineteenth century. These four groups had a common understanding that only sovereign states could mint currencies and that currencies should, under normal conditions, freely flow across state borders. Nonetheless, they did not collectively share a unified definition of sovereignty. Specifically, they disagreed as to the circumstances under which a ruler can be considered sufficiently sovereign so as to be able to claim the right to mint currencies. As a result, the right to mint was used as a tool by the Sultan of

[33] H. S. Job, 'The Coinage of the Mahdi and the Khalifa,' *Sudan Notes and Records* 3:3 (1920) 164–71; Sevket Pamuk, *A Monetary History of the Ottoman Empire* (Cambridge, Cambridge University Press, 2000) 193–200; Jan Hogendorn and Marion Johnson, *The Shell Money of the Slave Trade* (Cambridge, Cambridge University Press, 1986) 64–79.

Zanzibar to assert his independence, by a French merchant to advance his commercial interests, by the British to claim protection over the Sultan and by the Germans to limit the sphere of British influence on the East African coast.

The moral economy that structured the IOW currency system was not seriously challenged until well into the twentieth century. My own contribution to this volume links this challenge to structural problems caused by the First World War. These problems destabilized currencies in Europe and led many European imperial planners to search for fixes in their colonial possessions. As a result, officials that had been content to allow pre-colonial currency systems to persist began taking active measures to demonetize local currencies and replace them with new, imperial ones. In the Red Sea region, this effort was stymied by the weakness of colonial states, which prevented officials from seriously challenging the prevailing moral economy. Nonetheless, local communities were pushed into a cycle of poverty that weakened their resistance to imperial innovations, compelled them to abandon pre-colonial currencies and led them to seek out newly introduced imperial currencies. Though these new currencies eventually garnered a wide circulation throughout the IOW, European imperial agents continued to remain incapable of gaining complete control over the regional currency system. Johan Matthews's contribution to this volume shows that the merchant networks that controlled maritime currency flows were able to use smuggling and arbitrage to circumvent those currency regulations that countered their commercial interests well into the second half of the twentieth century. The intensity of these activities was such that they forced colonial officials and their post-independence successors to further expand the right of the state to intervene in the currency system. In an effort to prevent black market currency movements from destabilizing domestic markets, officials introduced a system of independent, national currencies during the second half of the twentieth century that marked the ultimate demise of the IOW currency system.

As the IOW currency system was dismantled over the course of the middle third of the twentieth century, communities throughout the region reinscribed many of its longstanding features within continuously evolving cultural practices. In their contribution to this volume, Amenah Jahangeer Chojoo and Gorah Beebeejaun explore the ways that demonetized currencies in Mauritius continue to structure certain economic, cultural and religious practices on the island nation. Nonetheless, the continuation of some of these practices has necessitated a change in understanding of their rationale. Mauritius, like all of the countries in the IOW, has abandoned the use of trans-nationally circulating precious metal coins in favour of paper money issued by the local authority for domestic circulation. However, in Mauritius the Spanish silver dollar is still used as a money of account in auctioneering. While, previously, the use of the Spanish dollar was an act of defiance by the planter class against the British rulers of the island, now the Spanish dollar is seen as an integral part of the spectacle of the public auction. Similarly, wearing necklaces made out of silver coins had been a way for Indian indentured labourers to safely store their earnings on their bodies during a time when they did not have access to banks. Though Mauritius has a developed banking system, these coin necklaces have been refashioned as tokens of family heritage and integrated into life-cycle rituals.

The IOW is now fully integrated into a global currency system characterized, generally, by national currencies that are traded on international exchanges and that are the exclusive currency within the territorial boundaries of the issuing authority. This transformation went hand in hand with a radical redefinition of state power. The new global system was developed initially in Europe and therefore treats money, first and foremost, as a legal institution.[34] Currencies within this system are created, regulated and controlled by the state. Nonetheless, state control is not complete. Merchants, peddlers, *sarrafs* and consumers have not given up all of their power. The legacy of the old system can still be seen in the alternate, black market currency exchanges that take place routinely throughout the region.

[34] For the fullest argument for treating money within the global currency system and its progenitor European national systems as a legal institution, see: Christine Desan, 'Money as a Legal Institution,' in *Money in the Western Legal Tradition: Middle Ages to Bretton Wood*, David Fox and Wolfgang Ernst, eds. (Oxford, Oxford University Press, 2016) 18–35.

CHAPTER 2

Major "International" Currencies of China and Japan: The Use of Copper Coins, Silver Ingots and Paper Money

Angela Schottenhammer

In common with most regions in medieval and early modern times, East Asia was characterized by a multi-currency system. There, too, existed competition between state and private mining and the minting of coinage, and counterfeiting that mostly arose when the value of the metal content of a coin rose above the coin's value. In addition, we have to take into consideration that highly developed, globally integrated regional markets co-existed with less developed ones. In China, for example, some regions maintained barter or commodity currencies, such as grains or cowries, far into the nineteenth century.[1] This chapter will concentrate on Chinese

[1] This study is part of the MCRI (Major Collaborative Research Initiative) project "The Indian Ocean World—The Making of the First Global Economy in the Context of Human-Environment Interaction", sponsored by the Social Sciences and Humanities Research Council of Canada and carried out at McGill University under the supervision of Gwyn Campbell. See, for example, Hans-Ulrich Vogel, 'Cowry Trade and Its Role in the Economy of Yünnan: From the Ninth to the Mid-Seventeenth Century,' *Journal of the Economic and Social History of the Orient* 36:3 (1993) 211–52.

A. Schottenhammer (✉)
University of Salzburg, Salzburg, Austria

S. Serels, G. Campbell (eds.), *Currencies of the Indian Ocean World*, Palgrave Series in Indian Ocean World Studies,
https://doi.org/10.1007/978-3-030-20973-5_2

and Japanese currencies that were used in Asian "international maritime trade". It focuses on copper, silver and paper money and will also briefly discuss the use of gold that played a less important role in trade than in Europe, as an international currency in East Asia.

To correctly understand the historical flow of "moneys" in contemporary Asia, it is, firstly, important to understand that "although the movement of the money is merely the expression of the circulation of commodities, *yet the contrary appears to be the actual fact*, and the circulation of commodities seems to be the result of the movement of the money".[2] This means that the use of currencies in cross-border exchanges is, thus, a result of vivid commercial exchange relations and not vice versa. Secondly, we will observe that during some epochs, China was a great exporter of money metals, especially copper cash (actually bronze and, in later periods, brass coins, see below) but also silver, whereas the situation changed dramatically in the early modern period when China started to import large quantities of money metals. In the sixteenth century, Japan became the major source of silver and subsequently, notably in the eighteenth century, a source of copper for China. Consequently, the second section of this chapter will also examine Japan's role in the currencies of the region.

A striking particularity of China's monetary system was the relatively marginal role of gold as a general equivalent of value and medium of exchange. Whereas over long periods of time, gold and silver were the dominant currencies in the Western world, the major currencies in East Asia after the unification of China under the Qin 秦 dynasty (221–206 BCE), and especially from Han 漢 times (206 BC–220 CE) on, were Chinese copper or bronze coins (i.e. an alloy of copper, lead and tin; both terms, that means, copper and bronze coins, are in use interchangeable, but, strictly speaking, one should make a distinction). However, the composition of metals changed over time. Whereas, for example, during Northern Song times a standard bronze coin consisted of an alloy of normally approximately 65 per cent copper, 25 per cent lead and 10 per cent tin, much higher quantities of lead were used during the Southern Song regime (Image 2.1). Moreover, in the seventeenth century such significant quantities of zinc were added to the alloy instead of tin that we can actually

[2] Cf. Karl Marx, *Capital. A Critique of Political Economy*, Chapter III, Section 2, Online version available under https://www.marxists.org/archive/marx/works/1867-c1/ch03.htm#S2b (accessed December 22, 2015). Italics are mine.

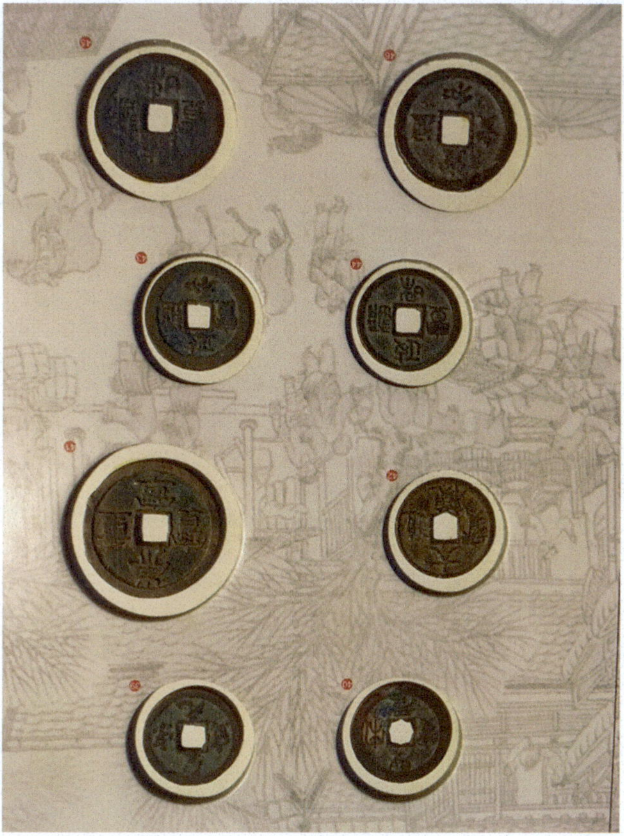

Image 2.1 Song copper coins (original Shanghai Museum, author's photo)

speak of brass coins (see discussion below).[3] A second distinctive feature of East Asia's currency system was that it was for long periods dominated by Chinese money. Chinese bronze coins were shipped widely across East Asian and Indian Ocean waters, especially following the upswing in traffic along the maritime silk route in Tang 唐 times (618–906). This is attested to by various shipwrecks found in the Asian waters. From Song 宋 times

[3] For an excellent study of the role of zinc in Qing Chinese economy, see Chen Hailian, *Zinc for Coin and Brass Bureaucrats, Merchants, Artisans, and Mining Laborers in Qing China, ca. 1680s–1830s* [Monies, Markets, and Finance in East Asia, 1600–1900, vol. 11] (Leiden, E. J. Brill, 2018). The author argues that zinc played a far greater role in Qing economy than has hitherto been assumed.

(960–1279), when China emerged as the "motor of Asia's economy", both as a producer of commodities such as porcelain and as a major consumer of incense, aromatics and various other Southeast Asian goods,[4] huge quantities of coins were smuggled out of China and shipped to various destinations in the eastern Indian Ocean World (IOW) and beyond.

Silver ingots also played an essential role in supra-regional trade and commerce. It is noteworthy that in China, silver currency circulated officially as bullion only in the form of ingots and not, as a rule, as coins. The exception was foreign silver coins such as the Spanish "real de a ocho" peso imported from New Spain (Mexico) and Peru. This means that, except for foreign coins, silver coins did, as a rule, not serve as an official means of circulation in China. However, special official memorial or anniversary coins, as well as private silver coins, were minted from time to time and were especially popular during Qing times (1644–1911). The Jurchen Jin introduced a silver coin in 1197, but this immediately inspired counterfeiting of cheaper silver-copper forgeries, so that the initiative was soon abandoned.[5]

Larger amounts of silver coins started to circulate only in the second half of the nineteenth century. Nonetheless, as Richard von Glahn has shown, China's monetary system shifted gradually from a bronze coin to a silver standard long before significant quantities of foreign, mainly Japanese and South American, silver entered the country.[6] During most of the medieval era and the beginning of early modern period, China exported large quantities of bronze coin, while silver was used as a means of payment in supra-regional trade or offered as a gift in, or tribute to, neighbouring countries. From the late eleventh to the early fourteenth centuries, in particular during the Song and Yuan 元 epochs (1279–1368), large quantities of bronze coin and silver ingots flowed from China to Japan, Korea, Southeast Asia, Central Asia, the Middle East and Europe. Two hundred years later, in the late sixteenth century, the situation had changed. China suffered increasingly from a lack of monetary metals and started to import these, first silver, then copper. Indeed, in the sixteenth century, China emerged as the world's biggest recipient of silver bullion, especially from Japan, but also from Europe and Spanish America. Spanish

[4] Cf. Janet Abu-Lughod, *Before European Hegemony: The World System A.D. 1250–1350* (Oxford, Oxford University Press, 1991).

[5] Cf. Richard von Glahn, *Fountain of Fortune. Money and Monetary Policy in China, 1000–1700* (Berkeley, Los Angeles, University of California Press, 1996) 53.

[6] "The monetary system of Ming-Qing China conventionally is described as a type of 'parallel bimetallism,' in which uncoined silver and bronze coin were relatively discrete forms of money." Richard von Glahn, *Fountain of Fortune*, 8.

galleons brought great quantities of silver from the New World to the Philippines where Chinese traders purchased it with Chinese commodities and shipped it back to China. Japan emerged in the late sixteenth century as China's major source of silver, great quantities of which it continued to export far into the seventeenth century when copper took its place. This chapter focuses on the role of copper/bronze coins, silver ingots and paper money as currencies and commodities in Asian waters from mediaeval to early modern times (approximately the seventh to eighteenth centuries). During this period, China played a pivotal role in providing the coinage that underwrote economic developments in East Asia. In the early modern era, Japan also emerged as a significant player in the regional currency system. Korean gold and silver were also exported (as bullion), as was copper, but did not play a major role in this period, despite the fact that from the time of the Silla 新羅 state (57 BC–935), it gained a reputation as far away as the Middle East as being rich in precious metals.[7]

Gradual Integration of China into the Indian Ocean World

It is important to distinguish between domestic or local and "international" long-distance and cross-border use of currencies. Metal monies constituted one of the major items of East Asian supra-regional exchange, as currencies and commodities. They thus had both use and exchange value. Iron, for example, was of major importance in the manufacture of weapons, agricultural tools and knives. Gold and especially copper and bronze played important roles in Asian religions, notably in Buddhism, in the manufacture of religious images and ritual implements. However, metals also possessed intrinsic worth, and thus a particular exchange value, functioning as monies in local and supra-regional currencies.[8]

In this respect, it is important to examine the role of Iranian/Persian (Chin. Bosi 波斯)[9] and Arab (Chin. Dashi 大食, i.e. Tajik) traders who

[7] Michael J. Seth, *A Concise History of Premodern Korea: From Antiquity through the Nineteenth Century* (London, Rowman & Littlefield, 2016) 70.

[8] See Angela Schottenhammer, 'The Role of Metals and the Impact of the Introduction of Huizi Paper Notes in Quanzhou on the Development of Maritime Trade during the Song Period,' in *The Emporium of the World. Maritime Quanzhou, 1000–1400* [Sinica Leidensia, 49], Angela Schottenhammer, ed. (Leiden, E. J. Brill, 2001) 95–176.

[9] Although the term "Bosi" may also refer to Malay people, I would argue that we should probably understand the designation of Bosi as a diaspora with communities spread all over

arguably initiated the long-distance maritime trade of China, in which Chinese merchants started to become actively involved only in the late eleventh century.[10] While barter governed much of Chinese foreign trade, Arab traders used gold and silver, possibly even gold dinārs of the Islamic world (?), in the local trade of Guangzhou,[11] which Sulaymān, a merchant from Sīrāf who was active in the mid-ninth century, described as the major entrepôt for Arab and Chinese merchandise.[12]

Silver and gold were not used as currencies in the domestic Chinese economy except for silver in Lingnan (the Guangnan region) where, as Edward Schafer notes,

> the metal was more common than elsewhere, it passed freely as a medium of exchange, as salt and silks did on the Tibetan marches, and cinnabar and quicksilver in mountainous central China. Indeed, beyond "the Five Mountain passes [which divide Lingnan from the rest of the country] buying and selling is wholly done with silver",[13] and so important was silver to the commercial life of the Canton region that when the mining of silver was outlawed in 808 (the emperor urging that, while copper is useful, silver is not), Lingnan was specifically excepted.[14]

By contrast, in long-distance maritime trade, as both textual and archaeological evidence suggest, silver appears to have been the major currency. The importance of silver as an international currency is attested to

the Indian Ocean region, as Claudine Salmon has recently suggested. Personal communication 04.11.2008; cf. also Claudine Salmon "Srivijaya, la Chine et les marchands chinois (Xe–XIIe s.). Quelques réflexions sur la société de l'empire sumatranais", *Archipel* 63 (2002) 57–78.

[10] Angela Schottenhammer, *Das songzeitliche Quanzhou im Spannungsfeld zwischen Zentralregierung und maritimem Handel. Unerwartete Konsequenzen des zentralstaatlichen Zugriffs auf den Reichtum einer Küstenregion* (Wiesbaden, Otto Harrassowitz, 2000) 57. Arab merchants also reached Korea around 11024/25.

[11] Edward H. Schafer, *The Golden Peaches of Samarkand. A Study of T'ang Exotics* (Berkeley, University of California Press, 1963) 257.

[12] Gabriel Ferrand, *Voyage du marchant arabe Sulayman en Inde et en China* (Paris, Ed. Bossard, 1922), 37.

[13] Edward H. Schafer, *The Golden Peaches of Samarkand*, 256, with reference to Han Yu 韓愈 (768–824), 'Qian zhong wu qing zhuang' 錢重物輕狀, in *Quan Tangwen* 全唐文, Dong Gao 董誥 et al., eds. (Beijing, Zhonghua shuju, 2001), 549.7b.

[14] Edward H. Schafer, op.cit., with reference to *Jiu Tangshu* 舊唐書, by Liu Xu 劉昫 [887–946] (Beijing, Zhonghua shuju, 1977), 48.3272b. Accordingly, most imported silver came from Silla or Tibet.

by finds from the Intan shipwreck, representing possibly a Śrīvijayan vessel, found off South Sumatra in 1997. From this wreck archaeologists brought to light 97 silver ingots, as well as coins and ceramics. These finds strongly suggest that it was a ship returning from a trading voyage to Guangzhou, capital of the Southern Han 南漢 Kingdom (917–971), where the silver seems to have been used to pay for the vessel's original cargo. Most of the recovered ingots were of extraordinary purity (between 93 and 98.1 per cent silver). The silver had originally been used as revenue from the government's salt tax monopoly in the neighbouring state of Chu 楚.[15] It was deposited in the Nan Han treasury, and probably used to purchase very valuable Southeast Asian commodities, such as incenses, spices and religious art objects.[16] The silver suggests that the Nan Han court possessed great quantities of silver.[17]

Chinese silver was probably of greater importance as a currency and equivalent of value than bronze coins in Chinese long-distance overseas commerce, especially in seventh- to tenth-century trade with Southeast Asia and the Indian Ocean. However, China also continued to export bronze coins, as is evident in finds from the wrecks of at least three ocean going vessels: the Belitung (an Arab-Iranian or Arab-Indian ship wrecked off Belitung Island, Indonesia), dating to around 826,[18] the above-mentioned Intan and the mid- to late tenth-century Cirebon wreck (salvaged from the Java Sea).[19] Objects salvaged from the Belitung include 29 Chinese bronze mirrors—one of the largest assemblies of Tang mirrors ever found, several hundred Chinese bronze coins, over 2 kilogrammes of gold foil and 18 Chinese silver ingots. These amount to the largest amount

[15] Denis Twitchett and Janice Stargardt, "Chinese Silver Bullion in a Tenth-century Indonesian Shipwreck", *Asia Major*, 3rd Series, 15:1 (2004) 23–72, 46.

[16] Op. cit., 41.

[17] See Angela Schottenhammer, 'China's Gate to the South: Iranian and Arab Merchant Networks in Guangzhou During the Tang-Song Transition (c.750–1050), PART II: 900–c.1050,' *AAS Working Papers in Social Anthropology/ÖAW Arbeitspapiere zur Sozialanthropologie* 29 (2015) 1–30.

[18] According to the dating of a bowl from the Changsha kilns, which was inscribed with a year equivalent to 826 on the bottom. Cf. Regina Krahl, John Guy, J. Keith Wilson and Julian Raby (eds.), *Shipwrecked: Tang Treasures and Monsoon Winds* (Washington and Singapore, Arthur M. Sackler Gallery and the National Heritage Board Singapore and Singapore Tourism Board, 2010) 19–20, 20 (fig. 12).

[19] Angela Schottenhammer, 'China's Gate to the South,' 13.

of Tang silver bullion discovered to date.[20] Moreover, items recovered from all three wrecks attest to the widespread use of both copper and silver in trade.

Chinese bronze coins were used as a means of circulation, that is as a local tender (even if locally recast), in neighbouring countries such as Japan, and parts of Vietnam and Korea, and additionally were accepted as a general equivalent of value, generally accepted and exchangeable, in Southeast Asian countries such as Majapahit Java and Cambodia. Neighbouring countries sometimes used Chinese bronze coins in trade even though they possessed their own copper deposits. This was partly due to the lack of appropriate technologies, although some did cast their own coins. In 986, for example, the local Vietnamese ruler Lê Đại Hành 黎大行 (r. 980–1005) cast bronze coins, termed the Thiên-phúc, the first locally cast currency outside China.[21] Copper coins also developed as a major currency in East Asian waters in the tenth to eleventh centuries. However, textual and archaeological evidence makes it clear that, for much of the medieval period up to early Song times, copper and bronze were used more as base metals in the manufacture of religious items, such as stupas, Buddha statues and tiles, rather than in the casting of coins.

China's Emergence as the Economic Motor of Maritime Trade in East Asian Waters

With the consolidation of the Song dynasty, China emerged as a much more important participant in international trade. Indeed, John Chaffee, following Janet Abu-Lughod, claims that it became the motor of Asian foreign commerce.[22] The reason for active Chinese government sponsorship of foreign, especially maritime, trade has to be sought for, first of all, in contemporary geopolitical circumstances, specifically the influence of the northern states of Liao 遼 (907–1125), Xi Xia 西夏 (1038–1227) and later the Jurchen Jin 金 (1115–1234). The gradual shift in long-distance exchange from traditional overland routes to maritime

[20] Francois Louis, 'Metal Objects on the Belitung Shipwreck,' in *Shipwrecked*, Regina Krahl, John Guy, J. Keith Wilson and Julian Raby, eds., 85–91.

[21] Lê Tành Khôi, *Histoire du Vietnam des origines à 1858* (Paris, Sudestasie, 1981) 142.

[22] John Chaffee, 'Song China and the Multi-state and Commercial World of East Asia,' *Crossroads: Studies on the History of Exchange Relations in the East Asian World* 1/2 (2010) 33–54.

routes can, thus, be explained first by the political instability in Central, North and East Asia, and last not least in China itself. Because overland routes were blocked or dominated by states like the Liao and the Jin, many of the tenth-century Chinese kingdoms and later the Song dynasty were forced to redirect their foreign trade onto maritime routes. The upswing in maritime trade was also encouraged by the enforcement of a new official policy that laid greater importance on the development of trade and commerce in consolidating its political power. Maritime commerce, especially, came to be considered to a larger extent than ever before, as a source of state revenue.[23] This, in turn, underscored the importance of copper which, as both archaeological and textual evidence confirms, was one of the most important metals in Asian international trade (from the tenth to thirteenth centuries), because of its quality both as a currency (exchange value) and as a commodity (use value)—mainly in the production of religious, mostly Buddhist artefacts.[24]

Song China's Domestic Currency and Its Role in International Trade

During the Song dynasty, prices were generally expressed in terms of bronze coins, although regionally, iron, lead or tin coins, as well as commodity moneys, were used, while the Southern Song also introduced paper money. Silver was only employed for large business transactions and was not normally used to denominate local prices.[25] Consequently, bronze coins formed the standard currency in all economically developed regions of China, functioning as both domestic means of circulation and equiva-

[23] See Angela Schottenhammer, 'The Emergence of China as a Maritime Power,' in *The Cambridge History of China*, vol. 5, part Two, *The Five Dynasties and Sung China, 960–1279*, John W. Chaffee and Paul J. Smith, eds. (Cambridge, Cambridge University Press, 2014) 437–525, 464–5 *et seq.*

[24] *Jingkou qijiu zhuan* 京口耆舊傳 (1844), 71.4b, in Shoushangge congshu 守山閣叢書; Ma Duanlin 馬端臨 [1254–1325], *Wenxian tongkao* 文獻通考 (completed c. 1308; reprint Taibei, Shangwu yinshuguan, 1987) 332.566.

[25] The regions, in which circulated silver-denominated notes of account during Southern Song, could have been exceptions to this rule. Cf. Peng Xinwei, *Zhongguo huobi shi. A Monetary History of China*, translated by Edward H. Kaplan, Vol. 1. [East Asian Research Aids and Translations, vol. 5] (Western Washington University, 1993), 426 (Original, 502). This is a translation of Peng Xinwei 彭信威, *Zhongguo huobi shi* 中國貨幣史 (Shanghai: Shanghai renmin chubanshe, 1958).

lent of value.[26] As a rule, one Song coin or *qian* 錢, that is a solid copper coin weighing roughly 4g, was equivalent to 1/10th of an ounce (*liang* 兩).[27] In later times, the term "*qian*" simply designated one "cash", being the equivalent to one coin. Classical Chinese still gives evidence of the double meaning and understanding of the monetary units of measurement, namely that they originally represented a fixed weight unit, which developed historically into an independent, arithmetical money unit. This can also be seen in the double meaning of the character "*zhong*" 重, meaning both the weight and the value, later also the purchasing power, of a unit.

Solid bronze coins were in high demand outside China. Copper was scarce in all parts of insular and peninsular Southeast Asia except the Philippines and Sumatra. Thus, China constituted an ideal source of copper for foreign merchants. Substantial numbers of Northern Song coins, notably those dating to the mid-eleventh century, and secondarily Tang coins, have been excavated from archaeological sites in Southeast Asia, India, Sri Lanka, East Africa (Mogadishu, Mozambique and Zanzibar), in the Persian Gulf and on the Malabar Coast.[28]

The outflow of copper coins grew steadily after the late eleventh century:

> Foreign ships and wagons loaded with copper coins were busy on their way out and military personnel and commoners alike were allowed to take coins across the border as long as they paid duties.[29]

In return, China received medicines, spices, ivory and rhinoceros horn imported from regions such as Śrīvijaya, Brunei and Champa.[30]

[26] For price examples, see Peng Xinwei, *A Monetary History of China*, 407 *et seq*. A *qian* originally seems to have indicated one metal piece of a hoe or a spade, for which there is evidence in the *Books of Odes*. See Yang Lien-sheng, *Money and Credit in China: A Short History* [Harvard Yen-ching Studies, vol. 20] (Cambridge, MA, Harvard University Press, 1952) 24.

[27] See *Song huiyao jigao* 宋會要輯稿, by Xu Song 徐松 [1781–1848] *et al.* (comp.) (Taibei, Shijie shuju 1964), Shihuo 11.3a.

[28] Peng Xinwei, *A Monetary History of China*; Robert S. Wicks, *Money, Markets, and Trade in Early Southeast Asia. The Development of Indigenous Monetary Systems to A.D. 1400* (New York, Cornell Southeast Asia Program, 1992).

[29] Li Dao 李燾, *Xu zizhi tongjian changbian* 續資治通鑑長編, 269.16a, reprinted in Siku quanshu, fasc. 318.

[30] *Song huiyao jigao*, Shihuo 55.1b–2b; *Xu wenxian tongkao*, 7.8b.

When the drainage of copper coins accelerated in the mid-twelfth century, the authorities proclaimed numerous severe measures to stop the outflow of copper with, however, little effect. Thus the scholar-official Li Xinchuan 李心傳 (1166–1243), for instance, complained that few people from Guangdong and Fujian observed the strict prohibitions, and local officials in Quanzhou failed to report clandestine exports.[31] The revenue officer, Bao Hui 包恢 (1182–1268), complained that all money from Fujian and Guangdong flowed to Quanzhou and Canton respectively, to be exported aboard foreign ships.[32] He also observed that foreign vessels brought cargoes of silver to Canton and Quanzhou to exchange for copper coins at the extremely favourable price of one *liang* of silver for one string of cash.[33] This raises the issue of supra-regional price differences (discussed further below).

An imperial edict of 1182 illustrates how serious the situation had become, and that it involved both private merchants and officials. The edict blamed the Canton, Quanzhou, Mingzhou 明州 and Xiuzhou 秀州 authorities for the leakage of cash abroad. The *Song History* states that even officials of the two Maritime Trade Offices (*shibo si* 市舶司) in Canton and Quanzhou and the two Money Casting Offices (*quansi* 泉司; unofficial reference to the *kangye zhuqian si* 坑冶鑄錢司 that were established in Southeast and South China in the early Song), who were supposed to implement the prohibition on the export of coinage, secretly despatched ships to foreign countries to trade in Chinese coins.[34] The Southern Song era thus represented a peak of bronze coin exports—which explains why underwater archaeologists have found so many coins dating from this period. Many regions in Southeast Asia and the eastern Indian Ocean World sought copper coins to use not as a currency but for religious purposes, such as for the casting of bronze Buddha statues, as the following example may display—in other words, they were interested in the use value of the metal. In 1172, for example, the king of Śrīvijaya asked Quanzhou for authorization to receive copper in order to have 30,000 copper tiles (*wa* 瓦) produced to take them back home to decorate their Buddhist

[31] Li Xinchuan 李心傳, *Jianyan yilai chaoye zaji* 建炎以來朝野雜記, (Originally 1202, 1216; reprint Beijing, Zhonghua shuju, 2000) 150.2422.

[32] Bao Hui 包恢, *Bizhou gaolue* 弊帚稿略, 1.19b and 20a, reprinted in Siku quanshu zhenben sanji 四庫全書珍本三集 (Taibei, Shangwu yinshuguan) fasc. 246.

[33] *Bizhou gaolue*, 1.19b and 20a.

[34] Tuo Tuo (Toghto) 脫脫, *et al.*, *Songshi* 宋史, (Beijing, Zhonghua shuju, 1985) 180.4396.

temples. But, after the prefect of Quanzhou, Wang Dayu 汪大猷 (1120–1200), sent a petition to the emperor that the export of copper was at any rate prohibited, the copper was eventually not delivered.[35] A Śrīvijayan merchant chief (*Sanfoqi fanshou* 三佛齊番首) then asked again for permission to get copper tiles. The Song court finally approved this request, although the emperor later asked for a recompensation of the copper.[36] Seen against the Buddhist background of societies, the assurance that the copper was to be used for the decoration of Buddhist temples may in some cases perhaps also have served as an excuse to obtain permission to export copper even under political circumstances that prohibited its export from China.

By contrast, Japan used Chinese coins both for religious objects and as a currency. In Japan, the production of domestic coins had ceased in the tenth century, but from the middle of the twelfth century a steady growth in the agrarian economy and local commerce stimulated demand for a general measure of value as a means for exchange. As a consequence, more and more Song coins entered the country.[37] By the end of the twelfth century, the private melting down of Song coins to be recast as local money had apparently become so popular that a Japanese edict of 1193 officially prohibited private business from using Song coins, which "mandated the conversion of loans previously contracted in coin to payments in rice".[38] The ample use of these foreign coins had disrupted an officially established set of exchange values (*kokahō* 沽價法) for gold, rice and silk (in order to equalize tribute payments of local officials) and, consequently, effected the values of rice and silk. This prohibition, however, could not efficiently restrict the diffusion of Chinese coins. Huge quantities of Song coins have been discovered on the Japanese islands. Archaeologists have so far excavated several dozen hoards of over 10,000 coins. For example, in the 1930s 554,714 coins were unearthed on Tsushima 對馬 Island, 553,802 of which came from China. Indeed, Song coins alone have been accounted for 456,086 of the coins.[39] Large quantities of Song coins have

[35] Lou Yue 樓鑰, *Gongkui ji* 攻媿集, 88.1200, in Wenyuange Siku quanshu 文淵閣四庫全書 [= Siku quanshu] (Taibei, Shanwu yinshuguan, 1984) fasc. 1152.

[36] *Jingkou qijiu zhuan* 京口耆舊傳 (1844), 71.4b, reprinted in Shoushangge congshu 守山閣叢書; also *Wenxian tongkao*, 332.566; *Gongkui ji*, 88.1200.

[37] Richard von Glahn, 'The Ningbo-Hakata Merchant Network and the Reorientation of East Asian Maritime Trade, 1150–1350,' *Harvard Journal of Asiatic Studies* 74:2 (2014) 249–79, 258.

[38] Richard von Glahn, 'The Ningbo-Hakata Merchant Network,' 259.

[39] Peng Xinwei, *A Monetary History of China*, 543.

also been found in Hakata 博多, a major port of settlement for Song merchants, especially from Ningbo 寧波. Many of the largest hoards were found in the north, which might suggest that they were shipped via Korea: The largest one at Sinori 志海苔 in Hokkaidō originally consisted of 450,000 coins. A very mixed iron and bronze coin assemblage has also been excavated from the Sinan 新安, a ship that sank off the Korean coast in 1323 while sailing from Ningbo to Japan. In all, it carried 8.1 tonnes of coinage (amounting to some 8,100,000 coins).[40]

In many cases the majority of coins discovered were Tang and Northern Song coins, the *Kaiyuan tongbao* 開元通寶—those cast during the Kaiyuan period (713–741)—comprising more than 10 per cent of the total hoard. In 1199, in order to stem the outflow of bronze coins, the Song government banned their export to Japan and Korea,[41] and prohibited Korean and Japanese merchants from dealing in copper cash.[42] However, continued complaints about the clandestine export of cash indicate that such measures were largely ineffective.

As Richard von Glahn has argued, the zenith of Song coin imports into Japan was between 1250 and 1350.[43] Kuroda Akinobu 黑田明伸 and Ōta Yukio 大田由紀夫 have shown that the increasing demand for copper coins in Japan at this time cannot be explained simply by an expansion of market activities that required coins as a medium of exchange and circulation. Rather, the rise in Song coin imports coincided with a thirteenth-century increase in tax on landed estates in the form of copper cash.[44] In

[40] Jeremy Green and Zae Geun Kim, 'The Shinan and Wando Sites, Korea: Further Information,' *The International Journal of Nautical Archaeology and Underwater Explorations* 18:1 (1989) 33–41; Carla M. Zainie, 'The Sinan Shipwreck and Early Muromachi Art Collections,' *Oriental Art* 25:1 (1979) 103–14. In Korea, copper was increasingly used as an equivalent of value, although, for example, on the domestic Korean markets rice and cloth remained as ever the medium of exchange and standard of value and doubtlessly barter was the chief means by which people traded with each other. M. Ichihara, 'Coinage of Old Korea,' *Transactions of the Korea Branch of the Royal Asiatic Society*, 4:2 (1913) 45–74, 54.

[41] Richard von Glahn, *Fountain of Fortune*, 54.

[42] Peng Xinwei, *A Monetary History of China*, 415–16.

[43] Richard von Glahn, 'The Ningbo-Hakata Merchant Network.'

[44] Ōta Yukio 大田由紀夫, '12–15 seiki shotō Higashi Ajia ni okeru dōsen no ryufu: Nihon, Chūgoku o chūshin toshite' 12–15 世紀初頭東アジアにおける銅錢 の流布:日本中國を中心として, *Shakai keizaishi gaku* 社會經濟史學 (1995) 61–2; Kuroda Akinobu, 'Between Money and Material. Old Chinese Bronze Coins Dominated Medieval Japan,' Paper presented at the international conference Currencies of Commerce in the Great Indian Ocean World, IOWC, McGill University April 24, 2015, 4.

addition, recent isotope analyses of religious bronze objects from Japan, including Buddha statutes, indicate that they must have been cast with Chinese copper cash. This would also correspond to the increase in the use of Song copper coins during this period. Apparently few Buddha statues were moulded in the ninth and twelfth centuries when the imports of copper cash were still much lower.[45] We consequently see that trade in Chinese bronze (or copper) coins was triggered by an interest both in their function as currency, as money, and in the use value of their copper content.

In China, the growing export of copper cash coincided with an increased use of paper money in the Southeast coastal regions. According to von Glahn, the widespread substitution of paper money for bronze coin in China triggered a massive export of Chinese coins to Japan—one that started from as early as 1170 and peaked in the 100 years from 1250 to 1350. In Japan, these imports stimulated a rapid monetization of the domestic economy. The gradual disruption of the inflow of Chinese coins into Japan, on the other hand, led to the appearance of gold and silver coins in Japan. In the 1570s even rice was used for larger payments, including taxes. Subsequently, the mining and production of both gold and silver was actively promoted by the Japanese ruling elites, especially Toyotomi Hideyoshi 豊臣秀吉 (r. 1585–1598) and later Tokugawa Ieyasu 德川家康 (r. 1603–1616) (see below).

The Introduction of Privately and State-Issued Paper Money

Recapitulating the history of paper money, we have to distinguish between privately issued paper notes and state-issued paper money. Historically speaking, paper exchange or credit notes emerged from the necessity within supra-regional trade and commerce to separate purchase and payment temporally and geographically and to raise credit from each other. Long distance trade, whether by land or by sea, very early led to an elementary form of credit on the basis of the requirements of private trade – merchants, privately, gave each other credit and postponed their payment in cash. Merchant A, for example, wanted to purchase commodities from merchant B, but had a temporary cash flow problem because he had invested his money in a ship's cargo on which he had not yet received the return, so merchant B accepted from him a "promise to pay". This

[45] Kuroda Akinobu, 'Between Money and Material,' 4, 6 and 7.

arrangement emanated from personal relations of trust. As noted by Shiba Yoshinobu 斯波義信, such paper exchange notes were originally issued in China by private merchant associations, generally of wealthy merchants. The basis on which they trusted each other and raised credit was the speculation on their future business success plus interest. Paper notes facilitated their trade activities by enabling them to separate purchase and payment—which constituted a credit arrangement—both temporally and geographically. In China, promissory notes also emerged as a means to avoid transporting heavy quantities of cash over long distances. State authorities subsequently copied such practices.[46]

An early example of money orders or payment cheques that resulted in a simple form of credit can be traced back to the emergence in the Tang dynasty of so-called flying money (*feiqian* 飛錢). This basically constituted a paper draft, authorizing the transfer of accounts, or entitlements to certain amounts of money, to distant places. They were used by Sichuan tea merchants who wished to transfer to South China the profits they had made from the sale of tea in North China, without incurring the cost and risk of physically transporting to the south large quantities of cash. Provincial authorities were confronted with the same problem when having to transfer tribute or taxes in the form of money to the imperial court in Chang'an 長安. Some district authorities also wished to prohibit the export of cash beyond their borders. Consequently, authorities and money shops were established where private merchants and local governments could deposit their cash in exchange for paper vouchers that guaranteed reimbursement in a designated location. By the mid- to late Tang eras, money shops started to accept paper claims in exchange for money, or as a savings account deposit, while merchants could use them to take out a mortgage. In other words, such paper notes performed functions of real money.

In the early Song dynasty, promissory notes called "*jiaozi*" 交子 started to circulate as a substitute for heavy iron coins, and at the end of the tenth century the state granted a group of 16 rich merchants in Sichuan exclusive management of them.[47] These merchants did not always reimburse their clients promptly, which aroused popular protests and many legal cases, and eventually obliged the government to establish an "Exchange

[46] Shiba Yoshinobu 斯波義信, *Sōdai shōgyōshi kenkyū* 宋代商業史研究 (Tōkyō, Kazama shobō, 1968) 78–132.

[47] See Yang Lien-sheng, *Money and Credit in China*, 52 *et seq.*; Peng Xinwei, *A Monetary History of China*, 368–71 discusses the character of these exchange notes.

Note Authority" (*jiaozi wu* 交子務) in Yizhou 益州 to manage the issue of promissory notes. From government or state perspective, it was historically the insight into the necessity for the divergence of coin representing real value on the one hand and its function as a mediator of commodities, as a means of circulation, on the other, that resulted in the practice of minting smaller fractions of bigger money units in less valuable metals. This divergence eventually resulted in replacing them with tokens of other material serving the same function. Everyday use and thus erosion of metallic coins effected a separation between their nominal value as a circulation medium and their real weight. This in turn led to the possibility that metallic coins might be replaced as a circulating medium by tokens that represented the desired value but which were of intrinsically valueless content. In this way valuable coins were substituted as a circulating medium by mere tokens of value.[48] The ultimate consequence of this substitution of metallic coins by tokens of value was the issuing of paper money.

During the Song and Yuan periods, state authorities increasingly used paper money. In the twelfth century, the Song government issued paper money in large quantities to replace coins and to solve its financial problems.[49] However, during Song times, these paper notes were temporary with a limited period of validity and remained geographically restricted to certain areas. In order to explain how paper money functioned in the Song and Yuan eras, it is first important to note that, by contrast to modern credit money which is no longer linked to a stock or treasury of metals with intrinsic value, in historical times, the credibility of paper money depended on a stock of treasury or metallic moneys with intrinsic value and on their possible convertibility into valuable money. Given the sum of prices of commodities and the average turnover velocity, the quantity of metallic coins functioning as money depended on the value of the metal content—in this case, copper or silver. If, according to the general law of commodity circulation, the metallic money in circulation was replaced by token money, the quantity of the latter in circulation should not exceed the quantity of the metallic money it represented. If the quantity of token money in circulation exceeded this specific quantity, it depreciated

[48] For a detailed analysis see Karl Marx, *Capital*, vol. 1, Chapter III, Section 1, especially 125–30 (coin and symbols of value): "The fact that the currency of coins itself effects a separation between their nominal and their real weight, creating a distinction between them as mere pieces of metal on the one hand, and as coins with a definite function on the other—this fact implies the latent possibility of replacing metallic coins by tokens of some other material, by symbols serving the same purposes as coins" (p. 126).

[49] See Richard von Glahn, *Fountain of Fortune*, 35.

in relation to currencies with intrinsic value.[50] Merchants started to notice this phenomenon precisely when the fiat moneys started to depreciate in relation to valuable moneys and when they were no longer redeemed. The central government thus had to ensure, first, that it did not issue too many tokens and, second, that it backed tokens with reserves of real value. As long as the government guaranteed the convertibility of paper notes into valuable metallic currency, those notes could function as a means of circulation. However, faced with growing financial deficits and a growing inability both to finance the military campaigns they were waging against their northern neighbours and to meet official expenses generally, the government raised taxes, forced tax-paying households to hand over valuables such copper utensils and stopped redeeming paper notes—with the result that the value of such notes, and public willingness to accept them, declined. In other words, the Song government started to issue paper money in the twelfth century in order to attract wealth in the form of bronze cash and precious metals from its economy, transferring it into the state coffers and, in this way, attempting to solve its financial difficulties.

An early example of the use of a *state-issued* fiat currency occurred under the Han Emperor Wudi 漢武帝 (r. 141–187 BC) who in 113 BCE introduced a deerskin money in an unsuccessful attempt to pay for his ruinous campaigns of foreign conquest. The Song rulers similarly introduced paper notes in an attempt to resolve their fiscal problems. However, these caused major problems, as noted by the famous Chinese literati, Lu Jiuyuan 陸九淵 (1139–1193), with reference to a time when, due to the shortage of copper coins in circulation, the state introduced "Huizi" 會子 paper notes yet obliged subjects to pay their taxes in copper money, although hardly any copper cash was circulating any more. They occasionally issued copper cash in order to redeem the Huizi paper notes at interest rates of 30 per cent; sometimes they even obliged people to pay silver in exchange for cash. The net result was that officials grew rich at the expense of the general population who became increasingly impoverished.[51] Von Glahn notes that "ironically" the "crisis of confidence in the value of paper money spurred a flight from bronze coins as well".[52] The introduction of

[50] "If the paper money exceed its proper limit, which is the amount in gold coins of the like denomination that can actually be current, it would, apart from the danger of falling into general disrepute, represent only the quantity of gold, which, in accordance with the laws of the circulation of commodities, is required, and is alone capable of being represented by paper". Karl Marx, *Capital*, vol. I, 128.

[51] See: Lu Jiuyuan 陸九淵, *Xiangshan xiansheng quanji* 象山先生全集, in Sibu congkan, fasc. 1159–68.

[52] Richard von Glahn, 'The Ningbo-Hakata Merchant Network,' 262.

paper money did indeed accelerate the export of copper coins by merchants who may have feared that otherwise government authorities would seize them in exchange for paper money. Great quantities of copper coins were exported abroad, notably to Japan (Hakata). There, the merchants exchanged them for gold, handicrafts and especially sulphur, timber and mercury, bulk commodities that were essential for military and architectural purposes in China.[53]

To assess the role and impact of paper money in China's national and regional economies, it is, thus, important to distinguish between the economic dealings of state authorities and those of private trade. While Chinese maritime trade continued to flourish in certain regions, and local merchants made great profits by exporting ever-greater quantities of coins, the state treasury increasingly suffered from a lack of money metals and its major metal currency. Moreover, while private traders habitually used paper money as a form of credit, or a promise to pay in expectation of future profits, state authorities generally used it to raise credit, either as a means of extorting metal coins from its subjects or simply by paying them, through their authority, with promises to pay (although they were not a commercial enterprise that could calculate with future profits) that were consequently only partly or never cashed, in order to meet state expenses.

Generally speaking, before the sixteenth century the international currency exchange between China and Japan consisted of an exchange of Chinese bronze coins for Japanese gold, as Richard von Glahn has emphasized.[54] Starting in the sixteenth century, gold was, as a rule, exported from China, and in Japan, the falling price of silver that resulted from the growth of silver mining and the increasing availability of silver encouraged a rush to gold. Great quantities of gold were exported from China to Japan and other markets overseas.[55] At the same time, it is clear that the sudden increase in the production of both gold and silver, although particularly of silver, after the sixteenth century, was closely related to the expansion of foreign trade.[56]

[53] See Richard von Glahn, 'The Ningbo-Hakata Merchant Network,' 251, 262, 269, who quotes Yamauchi Shinji 山内晋, a Japanese historian who forged the term "sulphur road" in the context of contemporary Sino-Japanese trade (p. 269).

[54] Richard von Glahn, 'Myth and Reality of China's Seventeenth-Century Monetary Crisis,' *The Journal of Economic History* 56:2 (1996) 429–54, here 433–4.

[55] Richard von Glahn, *op.cit.*, 434–5.

[56] For the production of gold and silver in early Tokugawa Japan, see Kobata Atsushi, 'The Production and Uses of Gold and Silver in Sixteenth- and Seventeenth-Century Japan,' *The Economic History Review* 18:2 (1965) 245–66.

The Mongol Period: Silver and Paper Currency

Bronze coins constituted the primary currency of petty commerce,[57] while silver, as a rule generally used for larger business transactions and long-distance trade, was accepted as a means of payment everywhere in the IOW where it helped to underwrite the expansion in maritime trade from the ninth century onwards. Typically, silver ingots (Image 2.2) constituted part of the cargo of a Chinese vessel engaged in overseas trade. Also, merchants wishing to exploit supra-regional price differences sometimes imported silver into China to exchange, for example, for copper cash.[58] In the home countries of some overseas merchants the price of coins in relation to silver must have been considerably higher. Otherwise, it would not have been profitable for these foreign merchants to offer one *liang* of silver, expressed in copper cash, for three times the silver price prevailing in China. Conversely, from at least Song times, large quantities of silver flowed out of China westward—a development that reached its peak on both overland and maritime routes during the Mongol Yuan period (1279–1367).[59] Indeed, from the tenth to thirteenth centuries the westward flow of Chinese silver helped to alleviate silver shortages in the

Image 2.2 Yuan period silver ingot from Zhending 真定路 Circuit, Hebei 河北

[57] Richard von Glahn, *Fountain of Fortune*, 8; cf. also Angela Schottenhammer, "Chūgoku keizaishi no kenkyū ni okeru kahei to kahei seisaku: futatsu no jiri to sore ni kansuru kenkai 中国経済史の研究における貨幣と貨幣政策: 二つの事例とそれに関する見解" (Money and Monetary Policy in the Study of Chinese Economic History: Two Examples and Some Related Observations), in 宋銭の世界』 [*The World of Song Money*], Ihara Hiroshi, ed. (Tōkyō, Bensei shuppansha, 2009) 219–50.

[58] *Bizhou gaolue*, 1.20b.

[59] Cf., for example, Yokkaichi Yasuhiro 四日市康博, 'Chinese and Muslim Diasporas and the Indian Ocean Trade Network under Mongol Hegemony,' in *The East Asian Mediterranean—Maritime Crossroads of Culture, Commerce, and Human Migration* [East Asian Maritime History, 6], Angela Schottenhammer, ed. (Wiesbaden, Otto Harrassowitz, 2008) 73–102.

Islamic world.[60] The importance of silver as a currency in international trade grew steadily with China's increasing integration into the larger Asian world, von Glahn terming the period from 1550 to 1650 China's "silver century".[61]

The 97 Chinese silver ingots recovered from the Intan wreck (noted above) originated from the Southern Han Kingdom, where silver was used to pay for the original cargo of this vessel, consisting probably of incense and other Southeast Asian products. Again, 14 silver ingots were salvaged from the Cirebon, another tenth-century wreck lost in the Java Sea, which probably had taken on board considerable part of its cargo at Guangzhou. A large quantity of coagulated iron and silver ingots were also discovered on the Nanhai 南海 I wreck, from Taishan 台山 off the Guangdong 廣東 coast (Image 2.3). It is significant that a Danish archaeological team found evidence of Chinese silver ingots as far away as Bahrain in the Middle East.[62]

Image 2.3 Song silver ingot recovered from the Nanhai no. 1 Southern Song shipwreck (picture courtesy of Dr Li Qingxin)

[60] Robert P. Blake, 'The Circulation of Silver in the Moslem East Down to the Mongol Epoch,' *Harvard Journal of Asiatic Studies* 2 (1937) 291–328.

[61] Richard von Glahn, *Fountain of Fortune*, 113 *et seq.*

[62] According to the *Hong Kong South China Morning Post* (27 February 1958); Peng Xinwei, *A Monetary History of China*, 414–15, and note 28.

During the Song period, silver played a central role in China's foreign trade, a role that increased during the Mongol Yuan dynasty when there occurred a new development in the history of international currencies: The Mongol court, namely, introduced a *countrywide* circulation of paper money as domestic currency, then insisted that taxes were paid in silver, which they subsequently stored in state treasuries to back the paper money.

The paper currency was fully convertible into silver through specific exchange bureaus set up in major cities. As archaeological evidence suggests, the paper money circulated throughout the Mongol Empire,[63] and Yuan rulers also tried to get their trading partners to use it. All of China's trading or political partners were at least supposed to accept and to circulate these notes, although not always willing to do so. The value of paper money was obviously sustained by the large volume of exports from China.[64] Thus, initially, Mongol era paper money was also accepted in overseas countries. As Marco Polo observed, "Yuan paper notes were as good and pure as gold. All his [the khan's] subjects receive it without hesitation … because the holder can use it to purchase gold and silver or jewels."[65] However, over time, the government steadily increased the quantity of circulating notes and at the same time stopped their full convertibility. This was done to finance, for example, their military campaigns and the construction of a new capital in Beijing. As a result, the value of the paper currency depreciated and, by the end of the Mongol Yuan period, people commonly rejected paper notes. Despite several attempts at reform, such as the issue of a new paper currency, or even issuing coins of small denominations, the central government had insufficient metallic money in its treasuries to reintroduce full convertibility of its paper currency. The system eventually collapsed, forcing the government to investigate means of reintroducing a metallic currency. As already noted, the ongoing outflow of bronze coins and silver from China accelerated the government's financial distress and scarcity of money metals. To pay for all the incense, aromatics, spices and scented woods that entered China through maritime trade, great quantities of silver were exported to the Middle East, Southeast Asia, India and even as far west as the Red Sea.

[63] Cf. the examples introduced by Hans-Ulrich Vogel in his *Marco Polo Was in China New Evidence from Currencies, Salts and Revenues* [Monies, Markets, and Finance in East Asia, 1600–1900] (Leiden, Brill, 2013).

[64] Lo Jung-pang, *China as a Sea Power, 1127–1368*, edited with commentary, by Bruce A. Elleman (Hong Kong, Hong Kong University Press, 2011) 316–17.

[65] Marco Polo etc., *The Travels of Marco Polo* (New York, Liveright Publication Corporation, 1953) Book II, 159–60.

The international trade in and transfer of currencies was, however, also influenced by price differences of gold, silver and copper across the Indian Ocean World. The price of silver relative to gold was, for example, low in China compared to Japan and the Muslim world. As von Glahn has shown, while the gold-silver ration was approximately 1:12 in Europe, 1:10 in Iran and 1:8 in India, it was about 1:4 in the late fourteenth and 1:6 in early sixteenth-century China, and even a little bit lower in Japan. This meant that merchants who brought their silver from Europe or the Middle East (Iran) to China to exchange it for gold with which they returned home, could enhance their profits by making use of these international price differences.[66] After 1543, Portuguese merchants, for example, initiated a lively trade between Ningbo 寧波 in China and Kyūshū 九州 in Japan, exchanging silk products for Japanese silver.[67] Traders from Southeast Asia brought both gold and silver to China, but a considerable proportion of the silver taken to China from Southeast Asia was probably later re-exported by Arab merchants to the Indian Ocean region. A sudden rise in the price of silver in China from as early as 1015 was blamed on the outflow of silver to both Central and Southeast Asia.[68] As India and the wider Indian Ocean World were fully integrated into the domain of the gold dīnar and the silver dirham, the universal gold and silver coinage of the early medieval world, these Muslim coins naturally also affected other countries and areas involved in the Muslim trade system.

The evidence indicates that silver was preferred as the general measure and equivalent of value in Southeast Asia, the Indian Ocean and the Middle East, while bronze coins were preferred in Japan, and increasingly also in Korea. Moreover, independently of local monetary systems, Chinese copper coins were in demand in almost every country with which it traded by sea. The continuous outflow of Chinese valuable money had far-reaching long-term consequences for China and supra-regional trade in the Indian Ocean World.

[66] Richard von Glahn, *Fountain of Fortune*, 127–8.

[67] Kobata Atsushi, 'The Production and Uses of Gold and Silver in Sixteenth and Seventeenth Century Japan,' *Economic History Review* 18:2 (1965), 245–66; Richard von Glahn, *Fountain of Fortune*, 115.

[68] Richard von Glahn, *Fountain of Fortune*, 54.

The Ming Scenario

As a result of the continuing outflow of money metals during the Yuan era, the subsequent Ming regime (1368–1644) was left with little copper and silver in the treasury. Gu Yanwu 顧炎武 (1613–1682), a famous contemporary Chinese scholar-official, noted: "Short of old copper coins, the Mint Commission (*Baoyuan ju* 寶源局) had no material to fill its smelting furnace. The Deputy Minister of Works proposed a compulsory collection of artifacts made in copper from its people to cast the designed *Dazhong tongbao* 大中通寶 (Hongwu copper coin)."[69] He commented further that: "In the early Ming years, people old and young in a village seldom saw a silver ingot, and there was not a single silver-scale available in the whole village".[70] As a result, China, once the greatest supplier of copper and silver in the Asian world, gradually ran out of the copper and silver resources required to provide for its own currencies.

Consequently, the Ming tried to reintroduce paper money as a domestic currency. In order to secure its acceptance, the government declared it the only legal tender. However, the government vacillated between the circulation of metal currencies and paper. Initially, paper money was internationally appreciated and was used as a gift to foreign envoys and rulers. For instance, during the famous Zheng He 鄭和 (1371–c. 1433) expeditions, chieftains of Palembang who came to Court to offer tribute of horses and local products, were offered a total of 150 ding of paper money as well as 12 *biaoli* of patterned fine silks and 70 bolts of thin silks.[71] Nevertheless, paper money showed signs of depreciation already by the late fourteenth, early fifteenth centuries.

Thereafter, despite all government efforts, paper notes experienced severe inflation. In contrast to the Song and Yuan dynasties, the Ming did not build up sufficient silver, gold and copper reserves to redeem their paper notes. When problems of inflation became more and more evident,

[69] Cao Renhu 曹仁虎, *Qinding xu wenxian tongkao* 欽定續文獻通考, 10.1a, in Siku quanshu, fasc. 62; Gu Yanwu 顧炎武, *Rizhi lu* 日知錄, "Qianfa zhi bian" 錢法之變, 11.30b, in Siku quanshu, fasc. 858.

[70] Gu Yanwu, Fujian 福建, *Tianxia junguo libing shu* 天下郡國利病書, 26.121a, in Xuxiu Siku quanshu 續修四庫全書 (hereafter Xuxiu) (Shanghai, Shanghai guji chubanshe, 2002) fasc. 597.

[71] *Taizong shilu* 太祖實錄, in *Ming shilu* 明實錄 (Taibei, Zhongyang yanjiu yuan, 1966), 48.3b. This reference stems from Geoff Wade, translator, *Southeast Asia in the Ming Shi-lu: An Open Access Resource, Vol 10* (Singapore, Asia Research Institute and the Singapore E-Press, National University of Singapore) 734.

the government tried to resume the issue of copper coins. As coins were scarce, the authorities tried, once again, to stop the export of copper coins, as well as clandestine counterfeiting and debasement. Despite this, by the Jiajing 嘉靖 period (1527–1567), official Ming coins were heavily adulterated with lead, zinc and tin.[72] During the Wanli 萬曆 period (1576–1621), the amount of zinc increased so significantly that the alloy in coinage was almost totally brass.[73] Generally speaking, coins issued before the sixteenth century comprised leaded bronze, and those of later periods, brass.[74] Consequently, the value of copper relative to silver coins fell ultimately by a factor of 6 or 7. Both the Ming paper notes (*Da Ming baochao* 大明寶鈔) and counterfeit copper coins suffered from serious inflation and were not accepted as "international currencies".

Finally, silver was the only hope of the Ming government and merchants. Zhang Tingyu 張廷與 (1672–1755), author of the official history of the Ming dynasty, *Mingshi* 明史, describes the situation as follows: "Paper notes were out of use, copper coins were slow in circulation, only silver was treasured as the best alternative."[75] Fortunately for China this period of monetary crisis coincided with the advent of the Europeans who seemed to have access to the almost limitless supplies of New World silver and had an insatiable demand for Chinese products. Even more important, Japan emerged as China's most important source first of silver and later also of copper (see below). In Japan, a great demand existed for Chinese silks, satins, raw silk and medicinal drugs which were exchanged for silver (and later copper).[76] Silver actually became a favourite money metal for larger business transactions in both China and large parts of maritime Asia from approximately the mid-sixteenth century. The uncoined silver (and silver circulated basically uncoined in China) was, of course, not suitable for the every-day small commodity circulation and trade on local markets.

[72] Zhang Tingyu 張廷玉, et al., *Mingshi* 明史, (Beijing, Zhongua shuju, 1974) 81.7a.

[73] Helen Wang, Michael Cowell, Joe Cribb and Sheridan Bowman, 'Metallurgical Analysis of Chinese Coins at the British Museum,' *British Museum Research Publication Number* 152 (2005) i–v, 1–61, 3, cf. https://www.britishmuseum.org/pdf/RP%20152%20Metall%20Analysis%20Chinese%20coins-Prelims-Appendix.pdf (accessed October 30, 2015). See also Hailian Chen, *Zinc for Coin and Brass.*

[74] *Op. cit.*, 6.

[75] *Mingshi*, 81.6b.

[76] For the importation of copper into China, see, for example, Angela Schottenhammer, 'Brokers and 'Guild' (*huiguan* 會館) Organizations in China's Maritime Trade with her Eastern Neighbours during the Ming and Qing Dynasties,' *Crossroads—Studies on the History of Exchange Relations in the East Asian World* 1/2 (2010) 99–150, esp. 126 *et seq.*

In order to understand China's demand for and the subsequent influx of silver, not only the European search for Chinese products,[77] but also domestic monetary political developments, such as the centuries-old outflow of copper coins and silver, are of central importance. Over the centuries, huge quantities of money metals were legally and illegally exported from China, so that by Ming times at the latest the Chinese government was in urgent need of metals to support the domestic circulation of metallic money.

It is in this context that from 1522 to 1566, a pilot programme, the "*yitiao bianfa*"一條鞭法 (single-whip-tax reform) was implemented to convert labour services into payments in silver. By the late sixteenth century, the government had converted land tax, labour service and all other miscellaneous levies into a single silver tax payment.[78] However, there were insufficient quantities of silver in circulation to sustain the system. As the high-ranking official Gu Yanwu noted:

> There is not enough silver to pay the land tax. ... In Dengzhou 登州 and Laizhou 萊州 people sold their children to get silver ... there is no silver in the mountain area and on the coast in Shandong. Even in years of rich harvests peasants still have no way to meet their tax obligations ... whenever the due day approaches, people sell their sons to the army to get the metal ... what the peasants harvest from their parcels of land is useless in paying tax. Silver does not come from the sky and the existing silver resources have already been exhausted.[79]

Hao Jing 郝敬 (1558–1639), a Supervising Secretary during the Wanli reign, commented on the contradiction between attempting to maintain the silver system in the face of insufficient supplies of the metal:

> It is no wonder that we lack silver when the whole country is using the rarest metal as currency. The military has consumed most of the silver, little of which is circulating and returning to society, and the Treasury is reluctant to

[77] Dennis O. Flynn and Arturo Giráldez, 'Born with a 'Silver Spoon': The Origin of World Trade in 1571,' *Journal of World History* 6:2 (1995) 201–21, 212.

[78] Li Kangying, 'A Study on the Song, Yuan and Ming Monetary Policies within the Context of Worldwide Hard Currency Flows during the 11th–16th Centuries and Their Impact on Ming Institutions,' in *The East Asian Maritime World 1400–1800. Its Fabrics of Power and Dynamics of Exchange*, Angela Schottenhammer, ed. (Wiesbaden, Otto Harrassowitz, 2007) 99–136, 123, with reference to *Tianxia junguo libing shu*, 17b (原編七冊); *Mingyi daifang lu*, 26b.

[79] Gu Yanwu, *Tinglin wenji* 亭林文集, 1.13a–13b, in Xuxiu, fasc. 1402.

> release silver from the state coffers. As silver neither rains from the sky nor is a product that can be manufactured, it is not surprising that supplies are exhausted. We know there is little silver in circulation, but we still demand that everything has to be paid in silver; how then can we not harm the interests of our people? Without the possibility of revenue being collected in silver, how can we not harm our state?[80]

However, as Quan Hansheng, William Atwell and others have shown, after the Ming proscription on maritime trade was lifted in 1567, ever-increasing quantities of silver flowed into China. Consequently, Ming government silver receipts increased significantly, especially between 1576 and 1628, when large quantities of silver were also collected in fees for licences, poundage and tonnage from the port of Yuegang 月港 in Fujian.[81]

From the 1530s to the early 1600s, China's most important source of foreign silver was Japan which, following the discovery of rich silver mines, notably in Iwami 石見 (Silver Mountain [*ginzan* 銀山] of Iwami) in 1526, became one of the world's leading silver producers and the chief exporter of silver to China. A second major source was the New World, from where silver flowed to China in part through trade with Europe, but chiefly via the Manila galleon trade from Acapulco via Manila. Scholars disagree about when exactly Latin American silver became more important than Japanese silver. According to Richard von Glahn, except for a few years in the early 1600s Japanese silver accounted for approximately 75 per cent of Chinese imports of silver during the seventeenth century.[82] American silver sources may have become dominant in the early eighteenth century, although Lin Man-houng argues that it was paramount only in Fujian and Guangdong.[83] Nevertheless, an estimated 33–40 per cent of the silver output of Mexico and Peru, which combined accounted for approximately 85

[80] Sun Chengze 孫承澤, *Chunming mengyu lu* 春明夢餘錄, 47.9b, in Siku quanshu, fasc. 868.

[81] Quan Hansheng 全漢昇, '"Ming Zhongye hou taicang suiru yinliang de yanjiu" 明中葉後太倉歲入銀兩的研究, *Zhongguo wenhua yanjiusuo xuebao* 中国文化研究所学报' 1 (1972) 136–39; William S. Atwell, 'International Bullion Flows and the Chinese Economy, circa 1530–1650,' *Past and Present* 95:1 (1982) 68–90, 80–1.

[82] See Table 23 in Richard von Glahn, *Fountain of Fortune*, 232.

[83] Lin Man-houng, 'The Shift from East Asia to the World: The Role of Maritime Silver in China's Economy in the Seventeenth to Late Eighteenth Centuries,' in Maritime China in Transition 1750–1850, Wang Gungwu and Ng Chin-Keong, eds. (Wiesbaden, Otto Harrassowitz, 2004) 77–96, 96.

per cent of global production between 1500 and 1800, flowed to China.[84] Indeed, so familiar did Mexican pesos become in the Chinese coastal provinces of Fujian and Guangdong that the Chinese created special names for them. Manila, located on the Philippine island of Luzon, was the main distributive centre for Latin American silver. Chinese merchants shipped silk, ceramics and other manufactures to Manila in exchange for some local marine and forest products, but, above all, chiefly for silver.[85] There, Chinese silks, brocades and porcelain brought by junks mainly from Fujian, but also Canton and Macao, together with, for example, Indian cottons and various other products from the larger Indian Ocean world, were shipped to Acapulco and on to other Spanish markets in the Americas by galleons which returned to Manila with silver ingots and gold, Spanish coins and European manufactures. This "silver run" is described in numerous Chinese sources.[86] Thus trade led merchants to Japan where "there were no goods but silver",[87] and to Luzon where "the locals paid everything in silver and there was plenty".[88]

The Seventeenth to Eighteenth Centuries: A Copper Era?

During the period under review, China changed from an exporter of money metals to an importer of silver and copper, chiefly from Japan. From the twelfth to seventeenth centuries, Chinese coins remained the principal currency in Japan where, however, local experiments in minting coins, some in gold, started in the sixteenth century. An independent monetary system was introduced in 1601 under the first Tokugawa ruler, Ieyasu, following which gold and copper coins were cast in addition to the standard silver ingot. As a gold, silver and copper producer, Japan was

[84] Kenneth Pomeranz and Roy Bin Wong, 'China and Europe, 1500 to 2000 and Beyond: Was it "Modern?",' http://afe.easia.columbia.edu/chinawh/web/s5/s5_4.html (accessed on March 29, 2015).

[85] Ibid., 154–92; Anthony Reid, *Southeast Asia in the Age of Commerce 1450–1680*, vol. 2 (New Haven, Yale University Press, 1993) 22–3.

[86] "The wide nine-rail state avenues in Nanjing were often encroached on by bazaars", see Xie Zhaozhi 謝肇制, *Wu zazu* 五雜組, 3.23a, in Jinhui, zi 子, fasc. 37; "Peasants in Guangdong put down their hoes and got on boats for overseas trade", see Qu Dajun 屈大均, *Guangdong xinyu* 廣東新語, 14.1a-2a, in Xuxiu, fasc. 73.

[87] *Tianxia junguo libing shu*, Fujian, 100. Much of the silver that entered China behaved more like a commodity than "a disembodied form of money", observes Richard von Glahn in his *Fountain of Fortune*, 244.

[88] Su Chengze 孫承澤, *Chunming menyu lu* 春明夢餘錄, 42.41a-b, in Siku quanshu, fasc. 868.

extremely attractive for the Chinese, and Japanese rulers were continually preoccupied with controlling the outflow of metals. The early Tokugawa rulers pursued an expansion of centrally supervised maritime trade,[89] but at the same time they attempted to control the outflow of gold, silver and copper. Gold ore, for example, was exported either through Korea via Tsushima to China, by Portuguese and Dutch merchants via Macao or through the China trade via the Ryūkyūs.[90] On the other hand, strictly maintaining money metals within the country was obviously not a desired path to go by local bureaucrats. Strict control and export limitations should, therefore, also be considered a problem of procurement of the highly demanded copper, as Bettina Gramlich-Oka suggests.[91] In the early seventeenth century, the Japanese permitted Chinese and Dutch traders to exchange silk for silver at Nagasaki.[92] However, they exported such amounts from 1648, that in 1668 Tokugawa rulers prohibited silver exports. This caused enormous protest from foreign, especially Chinese, merchants. The Dutch East India Company (VOC) interestingly also saw an opportunity to make profits with Japanese gold coins, so-called *koban* 小判, one of few examples of gold as a locally circulating currency in East Asia.

In 1671, possibly due to pressure from Chinese traders, the Japanese authorities permitted silver exports to recommence. However, the *shōgunate* restricted the number of Chinese merchants permitted to trade and introduced middlemen to control the exportation of silver and gold. But because Japan did not possess many other goods to sustain the desired

[89] Robert L. Innes, *The Door Ajar: Japan's Foreign Trade in the Seventeenth Century*. PhD dissertation. University of Michigan, 1980; Ronald P. Toby, *State and Diplomacy in Early Modern Japan: Asia in the Development of the Tokugawa Bakufu* (Princeton, Princeton University Press, 1984).

[90] Hamashita Takeshi, *China, East Asia and the Global Economy. Regional and Historical Perspectives* [Critical Asian Scholarship, Asia's transformations], Linda Grove and Mark Selden, eds. (London, New York, Routledge, 2008) 51.

[91] Cf. Bettina Gramlich-Oka, 'Shogunal Administration of Copper in the Mid-Tokugawa Period (1670–1720),' in *Metals, Monies, and Markets in Early Modern Societies: East Asian and Global Perspectives*, Thomas Hirzel, Nanny Kim, eds. (Berlin, LitVerlag, 2008) 65–105, 95, 98; Bunka, vol. 17. The *shōgunate*, for example, began to purchase a proportion of copper directly from the mines and sent it to the refiners in Ōsaka.

[92] John E. Wills, 'China's Farther Shores: Continuities and Changes in the Destination Ports of China's Maritime Trade, 1680–1690,' in *Emporia, Commodities and Entrepreneurs in Asian Maritime Trade, c. 1400–1750*, Roderich Ptak and Dietmar Rothermund, eds. (Stuttgart, Franz Steiner Verlag, 1991) 53–77, 73.

volume of imports at previous levels, the relatively unrestricted outflow of gold and silver continued. In the late 1600s, the *shōgunate* became more directly involved in Nagasaki's export trade and opened a new office, the *Nagasaki kaisho* 長崎會所 (Nagasaki Accounting House) or, as the Dutch called it, the Geldkamer, to supervise foreign trade.[93]

From that time, copper played an increasingly important role in Sino-Japanese trade. This was because expanding local markets in China required a reliable currency in circulation for retail marketing. Rising population and growing local markets in general required increasing quantities of such an equivalent of value in small denominations, paying for commodities of low value. Consequently, Qing rulers promoted copper coinage. Before 1684 when the Qing maritime trade ban was lifted, to a large extent old coinage and copper utensils provided the copper for new coins. However, until 1715 "copper" (*tong* 銅) was loosely defined, referring to raw copper of different qualities as well as copper alloys (lead and zinc),[94] and private melting and minting constituted a big problem for the official authorities.[95] In 1699, increased demand for copper led the Kangxi Emperor to grant a monopoly over the copper trade to a select group of merchants.[96] This resulted in a dramatic increase in the import of Japanese copper from 536,700 (327,875) catties (1 catty = ca. 0.6 kg) in 1681 to 3,021,850 (3,283,925) catties the following year.[97] Chinese imports of

[93] Bettina Gramlich-Oka, 'Shogunal Administration of Copper,' 82.

[94] Helen Dunstan, 'Safely Duping with the Devil: The Qing State and its Merchant Suppliers of Copper,' *Late Imperial China* 13:2 (1992) 42–81, here 44 and 47.

[95] Cheng Wing-cheong (Zheng Yongchang) 鄭永昌, 'Mingmo Qingchu de yingui qianjian xianxiang yu xiangguan zhengzhi jingji sixiang 明末清初的銀貴錢賤現象與相關政治經濟思想,' Taiwan Shifan daxue lishi yanjiu yuan zhuankan 台灣師範大學歷史研究院專刊, no. 24 (1994) 65 (MA thesis 1993); Hans-Ulrich Vogel, 'Chinese Central Monetary Policy, 1644–1800,' Late Imperial China 8:2 (1987) 1–52.

[96] For the Sino-Japanese copper trade see also my 'Brokers and "Guild" (*huiguan* 會館) Organizations in the Sino-Japanese Copper Trade during the Qing Dynasties,' in 明清時期江南市場經濟的空間、制度與網絡 *The Market Economy of the Lower Yangzi Delta in Late Imperial China: Space, Institutions and Networks*, Billy So Kee Long et al., eds. (London, Routledge, 2011), 278–99; and 'Brokers and 'Guild' (*huiguan* 會館) Organizations in China's Maritime Trade with her Eastern Neighbours during the Ming and Qing Dynasties,' *Crossroads—Studies on the History of Exchange Relations in the East Asian World* 1/2 (2010) 99–150.

[97] Liu Hsü-feng (Liu Xufeng) 劉序楓, 'Qing Kangxi~Qianlong nianjian yangtong de jinkou yu liutong wenti' 清代康熙乾隆年間洋銅的進口與流通問題, in Zhongguo haiyang fazhanshi lunwenji 中國海洋發展史論文集, vol. 7, j. shang., T'ang Hsi-yung (Tang Xiyong) 湯熙勇, ed. (Taibei, Nankang, 1999) 93–144, 138–9, 140–1 (3b). (3); Liu Xufeng,

copper from Japan continued to rise during the 1680s and 1690s and stimulated interest in Japan in opening new copper mines.[98]

Interestingly, the Chinese government even used silver from imperial reserves to buy copper from Japan:

> In Kangxi 35 (1696), [the Emperor] drew 200,000 [taels] of silver from the treasury and gave it to merchants to manage the purchase of red copper (*hongtong* 红銅), as well as Japanese lead to assist in casting. After his reign, Japanese copper was frequently used to assist in the casting of Chinese (*Zhongtu* 中土) coins. Silver from the treasury was issued to enable official merchants (*guanshang* 官商) to establish an office (or authority, *ju* 局) to prepare ships for their overseas journey from the port of Zhapu 乍浦.[99]

This clearly attests to the importance of copper as a raw material for the casting of coins in China's growing economy. The decrease in copper imports from the 1730s also stimulated renewed investment in domestic copper mining, especially in Yunnan 雲南.[100] Indeed, by 1738, the central mints in China had become independent of Japanese copper, which, however, continued to be in great demand in the rest of Asia, especially South Asia. From 1710 onwards, for example, approximately one million Dutch pounds of Japanese copper were annually sold in Asia, 90 per cent of it in South Asia, by the Dutch VOC.[101]

"Qingdai de Zhapu gang yu ZhongRi maoyi" 清代的乍浦港與中日貿易, in *Zhongguo haiyang fazhanshi lunwenji* 中國海羊發展史論文集, vol. 5, Chang Pin-ts'un 張彬村, Liu Shih-chi 劉石吉, eds. (Taibei, Zhongyang yanjiuyuan, 1993) 187–244, 219–21. The figures in brackets are taken from Chinese sources.

[98] Shimada Ryuto, *The Intra Asian Trade In Japanese Copper by the Dutch East India Company During the Eighteenth Century* [TANAP] (Leiden, E. J. Brill, 2006).

[99] *Zhapu xuzhi* 乍浦續志, compiled and edited by Xu He 許河, *Xiangzhen zhi zhuanji* 鄉鎮志專輯 [Zhongguo difangzhi jicheng 中國地方志集成] (Shanghai, Shanghai shudian, 1992) 1.5a–b (484).

[100] Various studies have been written on this subject. Cf. amongst others Yan Zhongping 嚴中平 *Qingdai Yunnan tongzheng kao* 清代雲南銅政考 (Beijing: Zhonghua shuju, 1957); Quan Hansheng 全漢昇, 'Qingdai Yunnan tongkuang gongye' 清代雲南銅礦工業, *Xianggang Zhongwen daxue Zhongguo wenhua yanjiusuo xuebao* 香港中文大學中國文化研究所學報 7:1 (1974) 155–82; Hans Ulrich Vogel, 'Chinese Central Monetary Policy, 1644–1800.'

[101] Shimada Ryuto, *The Intra Asian Trade in Japanese Copper*, 142–3.

Conclusion

China was a major *primum mobile* of East Asia's currency flows. Its qualitative role, however, changed over the centuries. From antiquity, bronze coins served as the standard currency in China. During the Qin dynasty, the government cast the "*banliang*" 半兩 coin, weighing half a *liang* or 12 *zhu* 銖 (= 7.8 g) as part of its programme to standardize China's currency and weights and measures. In 119 BCE, the Han emperor Wudi 漢武帝 (r. 140–187 BCE) issued the so-called Wuzhu 五銖 coins, weighing 5 *zhu* (or roughly 3.25 g). These coins, which remained the Chinese standard currency until Tang times, have been found in archaeological sites throughout East Asia, especially in Korea and Japan.

The Tang dynasty witnessed a steady growth in long-distance maritime trade. As this trade was initially largely dominated by Iranian and Arab merchants, Iranian and Arab gold and silver coins appeared in China where particularly Chinese silver ingots served as "international currencies", that is they were accepted as supra-regional measures of value and means of payment.

During the mid- to late Tang and Song eras, when China emerged as the economic motor of the entire East and Southeast Asian region, Chinese bronze coins and silver ingots were possibly the predominant currencies in Southeast and East Asian waters. For China, the sharp upswing in maritime trade was marked by a continuous outflow of bronze coins and silver that continued throughout the Yuan period, when the Mongol rulers, partly in reaction to the lack of money metals, initiated a countrywide issue of paper money which they also tried to oblige their trading partners to use. However, oversupply and lack of convertibility caused by the continuing lack of money metals in state coffers, eventually resulted in token currency being abandoned and a restoration of bronze coins and silver as standard currencies.

Consequently, over the *longue-durée*, official attempts to maintain a monetary system based on paper notes failed. In the second half of the sixteenth century, the influx of silver that coincided with the advent of European trade in the region, led to the restoration of silver as the major international currency in the wider Southeast and East Asian world. This in turn stimulated Japanese investment in its silver deposits with the result that during the sixteenth and seventeenth centuries Japan, rather than the New Wold, constituted China's major source of silver.[102] Many economic

[102] For details see Richard von Glahn, *Fountain of Fortune*, 113 *et seq.*

historians have subsequently described China as the world's greatest silver sink[103]—a situation that changed only due to the opium trade in the early nineteenth century. As early as the late sixteenth century an estimated 7.5 per cent of the silver mined in Potosí was shipped to China.[104] In this context, some scholars have recently argued that it was the immense Chinese demand for silver that motivated Spanish merchants to increase local production in Latin America.[105] This is certainly not incorrect, but it is important to note that without the demand for and resale of Chinese and Asian goods in Latin America and Europe, this trade would not even have existed. Consequently, it still was the Spanish and European demand for Chinese and Asian products that directed all the silver into China and not, vice versa, the Chinese demand for silver that directed Chinese goods to Latin America.

At the same time, expanding domestic exchange in China required a standard currency and equivalent of value for daily use, leading again to increased circulation of copper coins. Thus, during the late seventeenth and the eighteenth centuries, imports of Japanese copper—in which European traders were also involved—became more significant. In summary, during the early modern era, Japan and the New World became the chief sources of money metals for China and the East Asian world.

[103] Cf. for example, Dennis O. Flynn and Arturo Gíraldez, 'Born with a 'Silver Spoon': The Origins of World Trade in 1571,' *Journal of World History* 6:2 (1995) 201–21; also in *Metals and Monies in an Emerging Global Economy*, Dennis O. Flynn and Gíraldez, Arturo, eds. (Aldershot, Variorum Books, 1997); 'Asia is the center of the world economy at this time and China, a 'sink' for silver. (The British eventually found a way to reverse this trade pattern with the introduction of opium in the 1800s),' *Asia for Educators, Key Points of Developments in East Asia, 1450–1750 China: The Ming (1368–1644) and the Qing (1644–1912)*, http://afe.easia.columbia.edu/main_pop/kpct/kp_ming.htm (accessed December 14, 2015).

[104] Lin Man-houng, 'The Shift from East Asia to the World,' 85.

[105] See, for example, the argumentation of Dennis O. Flynn or of Charles P. Kindleberger, *Spenders and Hoarders, The World Distribution of Spanish American Silver, 1550–1750* (Singapore, Institute of Southeast Asian Studies, 1989).

CHAPTER 3

Indian Kingdoms 1200–1500 and the Maritime Trade in Monetary Commodities

John S. Deyell

The economies of the Indian subcontinent (serving the largest population on the shores of the Indian Ocean) have historically exerted a dominant influence on the trade in monetary commodities across that ocean basin. Indeed, some "world system" theorists have assigned it a central role in bullion movement in the greater world economy in pre-modern, and even pre-colonial, times.[1] This study will examine that role in the period between 1200 and 1500 CE, which in Indian history is a convenient block of time with fuzzy edges but a robust identity. On land, this period begins with the arrival of Central Asians who brought a highly centralized and ideological model of state formation to North India, just prior to the devastation of their homeland by the Mongol onslaught. At sea, it begins with

[1] Janet Abu-Lughod, *Before European Hegemony: The World System A.D. 1250–1350* (New York, Oxford University Press, 1989). Andre Gunder Frank, *Re-orient: Global Economy in the Asian Age* (Berkeley, University of California Press, 1998).

J. S. Deyell (✉)
Kanata, ON, Canada

S. Serels, G. Campbell (eds.), *Currencies of the Indian Ocean World*, Palgrave Series in Indian Ocean World Studies,
https://doi.org/10.1007/978-3-030-20973-5_3

the demise of Chola maritime supremacy and the arrival of Chinese traders at India's southern ports. On land, it ends with the dissolution of the Bahmanid Sultanate of the Deccan and the arrival of the Mughals on India's northern frontiers. At sea, it ends with the arrival of the Portuguese on India's western coastline. Finally, from the point of view of monetary studies, 1500 is almost a century before the first appearance in India of New World silver.

The secondary literature on this period is less extensive than that on the post-1500 period because there is a better historical record for the latter period, which includes the span of the Mughal Empire, its diplomatic and commercial links with Safavid Iran, Ottoman Turkey, Ming/Qing China, as well as the maritime trading enterprises of the Europeans in the Indian Ocean. It is also a simple fact that the quantity of historical documentation for this later period far outweighs the meagre sources for the earlier. Nonetheless, there are a number of scholarly works on the links between India and other trading nations of the Indian Ocean littoral prior to 1500.[2] However, very few researchers have considered the role of Indian monetary systems in forging and maintaining these links. Perhaps the most noteworthy is the work of Najaf Haider, who elegantly situated North and West Indian monetary systems within the sphere of the trade in coinage and bullion encompassing Africa, Europe, the Levant, the Red Sea and the Persian Gulf.[3] His work is especially noteworthy for linking larger economic

[2] Simon Digby, 'The Maritime Trade of India (c. 1200–1500),' in *The Cambridge Economic History of India, Vol 1, c. 1200–1750*, Tapan Raychauduri and Irfan Habib, eds. (Cambridge, Cambridge University Press, 1982) 125–59; K.N. Chaudhuri, 'The Rise of Islam and the Pattern of Pre-Emporia Trade,' in *Trade and Civilisation in the Indian Ocean: An Economic History from the Rise of Islam to 1750* (Cambridge, Cambridge University Press, 2005) 34–62; Michael Pearson, 'Muslims in the Indian Ocean,' in *The Indian Ocean* (London, Routledge, 2010) 62–112; André Wink, 'Islam, Trade and the Coastal Societies of the Indian Ocean,' in *Al-Hind: The Making of the Indo-Islamic World. Vol. III, Indo-Islamic Society, 14th–15th Centuries* (Leiden, Brill, 2004) 170–243; Ranabir Chakravarti, 'Merchants, Merchandise and Merchantmen in the Western Seaboard of India (c. 500 BCE—1500 CE)' in *The World of Indian Ocean Commerce 1500–1800*, Om Prakash, ed. (New Delhi, Pearson, 2011) 53–171; Philippe Beaujard, *Les Mondes de l'océan Indien, tome II. L'ocean Indien, au coeur des globalisations de l'ancien monde (7e-15e siècles)* (Paris. Armand Colin, 2012); Edward A. Alpers, *The Indian Ocean in World History* (New York, Oxford, 2014) 40–68; Ranabir Chakravarti, *India and the Indian Ocean—Issues in Trade and Politics (up to c. 1500 CE)* (Mumbai, Maritime History Society, 2014).

[3] Najaf Haider, 'International Trade in Precious Metals and Monetary Systems of Medieval India: 1200–1500,' *Proceedings of the Indian History Congress*, 59th Session (Patiala, 1998) 237–54. Parts of this were integrated into his more recent article: Najaf Haider, 'The Network of Monetary Exchange in the Indian Ocean Trade, 1200–1700,' in *Cross Currents*

trends, usually discussed in terms of Europe and the Levant, with Indian history. His Indian perspective however is more or less limited to the monetary systems of the coastal Gujarat Sultanate and the inland Delhi Sultanate. As a result, he virtually ignores eastern and southern India. As Wink and others have recently shown, the fullest understanding of the oceanic system requires consideration of most, if not all, of India's regional polities.[4] This study will build on this earlier work by expanding consideration to the monetary systems of most of India's coastal and interior regions, in the context of events and developments in both the east and the west of the Indian Ocean World.

Prior to the industrial era, trade in the Indian Ocean relied on wind power and ocean currents that were subject to the annual cycle of the monsoon. Sitting squarely between the Levant and China, the Indian subcontinent dominated the central Indian Ocean. Within these relatively fixed geographic and climatic parameters, the pattern of trade in the Indian Ocean changed considerably over time. These changes were not so much in the principal products that were traded but rather in the trade routes and the merchants who undertook the trading.[5] In the ninth century, Arab merchants sailed all the way to China and established a considerable presence in Chinese ports. The merchant Sulaiman, who visited "Canfu" (the port of Xifu, the present Hangzhou) before 851 CE noted that "Arabs" had frequented the port even prior to the birth of Islam in 622 CE. A mosque had been built in the city and Muslims were allowed to dispense their own justice.[6] In the eleventh century, the Chola rulers of southern India managed to establish control over the centre of this oceanic

and Community Networks: The History of the Indian Ocean World, Himanshu Prabha Ray and Edward A. Alpers, eds. (New Delhi, Oxford University Press, 2007) 181–205.

[4] André Wink, *Al-Hind: The Making of the Indo-Islamic World. Vol. II, The Slave Kings and the Islamic Conquest 11th–13th Centuries* (Leiden, Brill, 1997) 265–93. More recently, see Ranabir Chakravarti, 'The Pull Towards the Coast: Politics and Polity in India (ca. 600–1300 CE),' *Proceedings of the Indian History Congress*, 72nd Session, (Patiala, 2011) 22–42.

[5] Sen notes that 'From the eighth century onwards, the maritime routes between India and China … became more popular than the overland routes.' He attributes this to disturbances in Central Asia, improvements in shipbuilding techniques and navigational understanding. Tansen Sen, *Buddhism, Diplomacy and Trade: The Realignment of Sino-Indian Relations 600–1400* (Delhi, Manohar, 2003) 176.

[6] Eusebius Renaudot (tr.) *Ancient accounts of India and China* (London, Harding, 1733) 7. A more recent translation is Gabriel Ferrand (tr.), *Voyage du marchand arabe Sulaymân en Inde et en Chine, rédigé en 851, suivi de remarques par Abû Zayd Hasan (vers 916)* (Paris, Brossard, 1922) 38.

axis. Their naval might supported their commercial guilds from the Maldives in the west to the Malay Peninsula as well as Sumatra and Java in the east.[7] By the thirteenth century, the Chinese merchants were trading as far as India's Malabar Coast, where Arab merchants made their purchases for onward shipment to the Red Sea.[8] So more or less, in the period 1200–1500, there were in effect two different trading spheres in the Indian Ocean: one operating from east Africa, the Red Sea and the Persian Gulf to India's west coast ports, and the other operating from China, Java/Sumatra and Pegu to India's east coast ports, Bengal, Sri Lanka and India's southern tip (see Map 3.1).[9]

Early memoirs of traders from both west and east, to the extent they survive, recount the need to wait in Indian ports after the completion of business transactions for the return of favourable winds. Over time, traders found it expedient to simply settle in foreign ports and make the best use of this seasonal "down-time".[10] Prior to the twelfth century, permanent Arab communities were established in both Gujarat (the Bohras) and in northern Malabar (the Mapillas).[11] Both communities survive to the present day. In addition, Arabic-speaking Jewish traders based in Fustat (Cairo)

[7] Hermann Kulke, K. Kesavapany and Vijay Sakhuja, *Nagapattinam to Suvarnadwipa: Reflections on the Chola Naval Expeditions to Southeast Asia* (Delhi, Manohar, 2010); Kenneth Hall, *Networks of Trade, Polity and Societal Integration in Chola-Era South India, c. 875–1400* (New Delhi, Primus, 2014).

[8] Sen notes, 'the aggressive policies of the Yuan court … (1260–1294) facilitated the creation of Chinese maritime networks to southern Asia, consisting of intertwined private trade, governmental and shipping segments. Consequently, for the first time in the history of India-China relations, court officials, traders and ships from China made recurrent trips to the coastal regions of India.' Tansen Sen, 'The Formation of Chinese Maritime Networks to Southern Asia, 1200–1450,' *Journal of the Economic and Social History of the Orient* 49:4 (2006) 422.

[9] 'From the twelfth century or slightly later we have three segments: The Arabian Sea, the Bay of Bengal and the South China Sea. Chinese and Indians went to Melaka, Persians and Arabs only to India.' Pearson, 88.

[10] 'Since merchants and shippers often had to wait many months for the monsoon winds to shift before resuming their sailing, foreign merchants tended to settle in semi-permanent communities. Ethnically these enclaves were quite diverse, consisting of Gujaratis, Bengalis, Malays, Chinese, Persians and Arabs, though most tended to share a common religious identity as Muslims.' Richard M. Eaton, 'Multiple Lenses: Differing Perspectives of Fifteenth-Century Calicut,' *Essays on Islam and Indian History* (New Delhi, Oxford, 2001) 79.

[11] Genevieve Bouchon and Denys Lombard, 'The Indian Ocean in the Fifteenth Century,' in *India and the Indian Ocean, 1500–1800*, Ashin Das Gupta and Michael N. Pearson, eds. (Calcutta, Oxford University Press, 1987) 62–4.

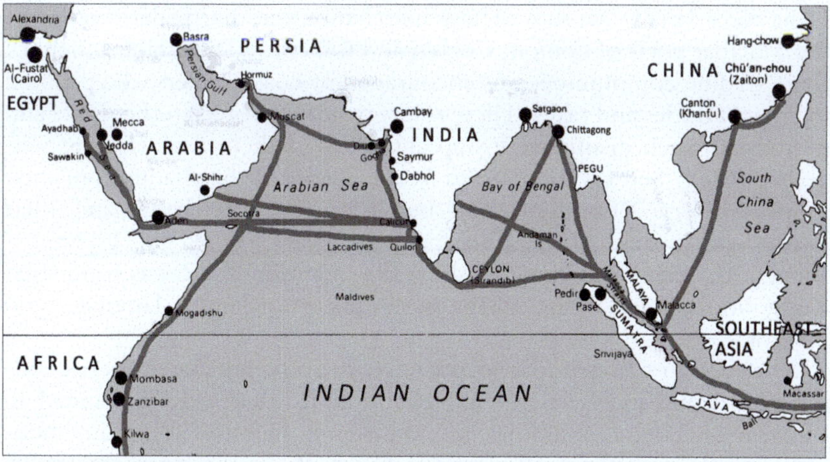

Map 3.1 Maritime trade patterns in the Indian Ocean 1200–1500. (Overlay by the author; underlay simplified from K. N. Chaudhuri, *Trade and Civilisation in the Indian Ocean: An Economic History from the Rise of Islam to 1750* (Cambridge, Cambridge University Press, 1985) *Map 7*, 38. See also Frank, *Map. 2.4*, 86, or more recently, Philippe Beaujard, "The Indian Ocean in Eurasian and African World-Systems before the Sixteenth Century", *Journal of World History* 16:4 (2005) 427–9.)

and Aden established themselves in the Malabar coastal ports late in the first millennium, and had well-established trade links by the dawn of the thirteenth century.[12] Remnants of this community, even its synagogue, survived in Kochi (Cochin) until recently. Similarly, from the Sasanian period onwards, Christians from Iraq and Socotra became active in the trade between the Persian Gulf and southern India. Marco Polo observed the following upon visiting Quilon in about 1292: "The people are idolaters [Hindus], but there are also some Christians and some Jews."[13] Indeed, Polo travelled on a Chinese junk, which made landfall on the Malabar Coast because Chinese traders had extended their range from Southeast Asia into southern India.[14] Chinese merchants active in southern

[12] Shelomoh Dov Goitein and M.A. Friedman, 'Letters and Documents on the India Trade in Medieval Times—A Preview,' in *India Traders of the Middle Ages: Documents from the Cairo Geniza* (Leiden, Brill, 2008) 3–25.

[13] Henry Yule (tr., ed.), *The Book of Ser Marco Polo the Venetian, Concerning the Kingdoms and Marvels of the East*, Vol. II (London, Murray, 1871) 312.

[14] Yule, *The Book of Ser Marco Polo*, 312.

India were largely Muslim. These merchants were particularly active in the Malabar ports of Quilon, Cochin and Calicut.[15] The establishment of these trading communities was encouraged by coastal rulers who profited from port duties and taxes. These rulers typically protected the rights and customs of each distinctive group and allowed them a measure of self-governance.[16] Settlers often acted as the agents of merchants from their home country. Communication between these merchants and their agents was through written instruction transmitted by ship captains.[17] Indeed, the Geniza documents show that maritime trade was conducted along lines of trust: the strongest bonds were family, language and religion.[18]

The foreign merchant networks active in India purchased local goods for export and imported foreign commodities that were demanded in India. Monetary commodities are consistently mentioned in contemporary accounts as important imported goods. While there was reasonably consistent demand overall, it is also clear that there were considerable variations in the nature of this demand depending on time and place (see Map 3.2). The following sections chart this important "demand differential" along its geographic and temporal axes.

Delhi

Prior to 1200, the money of the Chauhan kingdom around Delhi was the "bull and horseman" *dilliwal*, a 4g coin of about half silver, half copper. To the west, in the Punjab, the rump Ghaznavid kingdom relied on a highly debased billon *jital*, which was mostly copper in composition. To

[15] In about 1342, the traveller Ibn Battuta noted, 'We stayed in the port of Calicut in which there were then thirteen ships of China. … The China Sea is navigated only by the Chinese ships' Mahdi Husain (tr.), *The Rehla of Ibn Battuta* (Baroda, Oriental Institute, 1976) 191.

[16] 'Consequently, by the middle of the fourteenth century, a new phenomenon characterized by the shifting of the headquarters of rulers from inland agrarian regions to maritime centres of exchange started appearing in Kerala in the attempt to carve out independent states with the gains accruing from trade.' Pius Malekandathil, *Maritime India: Trade, Religion and Polity in the Indian Ocean* (Delhi, Primus, 2010) 85.

[17] Goitein and Friedman, 'Letters and Documents on the India Trade in Medieval Times—A Preview,' 9.

[18] Goitein and Friedman, 'Letters and Documents on the India Trade in Medieval Times—A Preview,' 13–14.

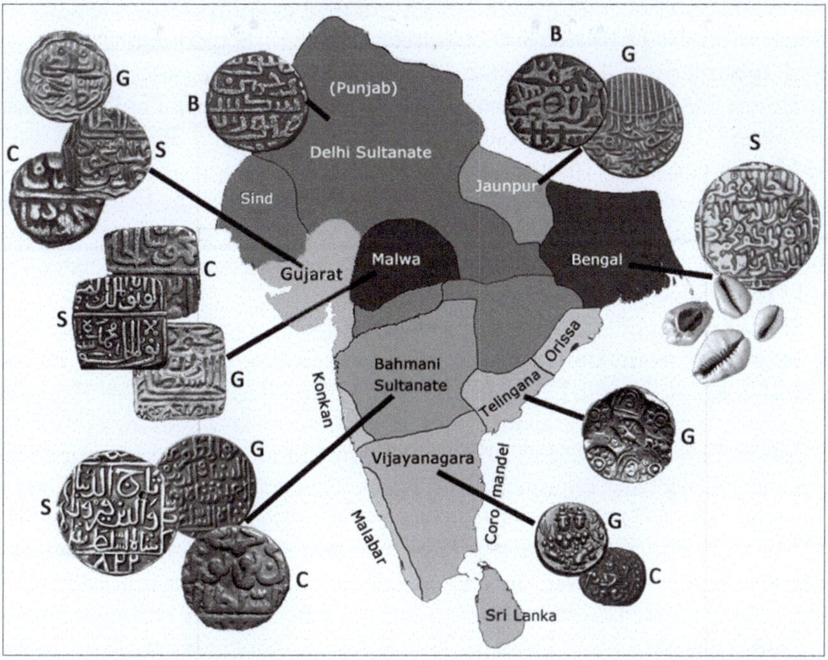

Map 3.2 Major Indian political divisions and their currencies in the fifteenth century (Map by the author, based on information in Joseph E. Schwartzberg, *A Historical Atlas of South Asia* (Chicago, University of Chicago, 1978), and using the format of C. Colin Davies, *An Historical Atlas of the Indian Peninsula* (Madras, Oxford University Press, 1959) 37.). Key: G—gold; S—silver; B—billon (silver/copper alloy); C—copper

the east, the Gahadavala kingdom relied on putatively gold *dinaras* of an equal alloy of gold, silver and copper.[19]

On the establishment of the Delhi Sultanate in 1192, the scattered regional coinage systems of incorporated Hindu kingdoms were initially continued. However, by the 1220s, the indigenous coinage systems had all been replaced with a trimetallic currency system that related in form to the Islamic norm of the Omayyad and Abbasid caliphs, but was based on Indian metrology. Gold *tankas* of ca. 11g, silver *tankas* of the same weight,

[19] John S. Deyell, *Living Without Silver: The Monetary History of Early Medieval North India* (Delhi, Oxford University Press, 1999) 67–192.

billon (silver/copper alloy) *jitals* of 4g and copper coins of 4g or less, were issued from ca. 1210 to 1399.[20] Shireen Moosvi has recorded the recovered specimens of Delhi Sultanate coins published in various museum catalogues and in treasure trove hoard reports from Uttar Pradesh.[21] For the period 1210–1388, she tallied 271 gold, 2995 silver, 3667 billon and 6441 copper coins.[22] In other words, the ratio of coinage composition was 1 gold to 11 silver, to 14 billon to 24 copper.[23] If we assume that, on average, the billon was half silver and half copper, then the ratio of coinage metals used by the Delhi Sultanate in that period was approximately 1 gold to 20 silver to 30 copper.

Initially, the Ghurid rulers of landlocked Delhi relied on overland supplies of silver from Afghan mines, which were subsequently destroyed by Genghis Khan around 1220. In the immediate aftermath of the Mongol invasions, the Delhi Sultanate maintained its monetary system, as well as supported its cavalry and elephant corps, by plundering and levying tribute from subject and conquered kingdoms. Especially from 1295 to 1334, the expansion of Delhi's power into the peninsula was accompanied by the "dethesaurization" of massive amounts of gold and silver, much of which was re-coined.[24] However, once the entire subcontinent was subordinated, access to imported currencies and raw metal became key to maintaining the monetary systems.[25] From 1335 onwards, and increasingly from 1399

[20] Deyell, *Living Without Silver*, 193–232.

[21] Shireen Moosvi, 'Numismatic Evidence and the Economic History of the Delhi Sultanate,' *Proceedings of the Indian History Congress*, 50th Session, Gorakhpur (1991) 208–15.

[22] Moosvi, 'Numismatic Evidence and the Economic History of the Delhi Sultanate,' Table 1, 208 and Table II, 210.

[23] This is an approximation since it ignores the fact that coins of different metals were often of different individual weights.

[24] The assay master of the Delhi mint in 1318 recorded the precious metal content of almost 200 coin types from all over India that had been melted before fashioning into current coin. Thakkura Pheru, *Dravya Parīkshā*, Muni Jinavijaya, ed. (Jodhpur, 1961).

[25] However, not all types of trade produced a net import of currencies. It is possible that the overland trade, which was dominated by the import of horses from Central Asia, was a drain on precious metal reserves, while the seaborne trade produced a net gain. However, Jackson mentions that in the early fourteenth century, the Delhi Sultans maintained a customs point on the Mongol frontier to tax the horse trade. Certainly the import taxes on Central Asian horses must have been substantial. It is also likely that the horse traders did not travel back to their homelands empty-handed, but carried high-value items to sell. See: Peter Jackson, *The Delhi Sultanate, a Political and Military History* (Cambridge, Cambridge University Press, 1999) 232.

onwards, Delhi progressively lost control of the coastal regions to newly independent regional sultanates. As a result, the money of Delhi was radically altered in ways that reflected both the reduced status of the kingdom and the loss of overseas bullion flows. Gold coins became scarcer and all but vanished for a number of decades; silver coins disappeared; 9g "black *tankas*" of heavily debased billon became the workhorse of the economy, along with an equal number of large copper coins.

Similarly, the currencies in circulation in the eastern tracts of the Delhi Sultanate altered when the region became the independent Jaunpur Sultanate in 1393. This new Sultanate was equally constrained in its supply of bullion. As a result, the state mint issued only small issues of gold coins. Instead, it made considerable issues of 9g black *tankas*, as well as copper coins of the same size, from 1402 until 1479.[26]

Gujarat

In 1200 Gujarat was an independent kingdom ruled by kings of the Chaulukya or Solanki dynasty. The region remained under the rule of this dynasty through to the start of the fourteenth century. During these two centuries, Gujarat was northern India's main coastal interface with the Persian Gulf and Oman, just as Calicut was with the Red Sea and Yemen. As early as the eleventh through the thirteenth century, the Hindu rulers of Gujarat granted extensive privileges to Persian traders within their kingdom.[27] Around 1292, Marco Polo noted that the "Kingdom of Cambaet" (which he differentiated from the "Kingdom of Gozerat") imported considerable quantities of foreign precious metals.[28] Nonetheless, the country relied on a single coin type—a silver *dramma* that lacked any inscriptions. The coins have been attributed to a community of merchants in Bhillamala in southern Rajasthan/northern Gujarat. Though these merchants minted the coins for their own commercial purposes, the coins subsequently became the dominant currency in Gujarat. By the thirteenth century the

[26] Both Delhi and Jaunpur monetary systems are discussed in John S. Deyell, 'Precious Metals, Debasement and Cowrie Shells in the Medieval Indian Monetary Systems (ca. 1200–1575),' in *Money in the Pre-industrial World: Bullion, Debasements and Coin Substitutes*, John H. Munro, ed. (London, Pickering & Chatto, 2012) 163–82.

[27] An inscription of 1264 records the endowment of a mosque by a Persian trader enjoying strong local protection. Ranabir Chakravarti, 'Nakhuda Nuruddin Firuz at Somanatha: AD 1264' in *Trade and Traders in Early Indian Society* (Delhi, Manohar, 2007) 220–42.

[28] Yule, *The Book of Ser Marco Polo*, 332.

Bhillamala *dramma* was the sole coin type of Chalukyan Gujarat; gold and copper were evidently not produced. Nine recovered hoards yielded 3763 specimens.[29] Further north in Rajasthan, a hoard comprising almost 100,000 such *drammas* has been recovered.[30] These coins also circulated well into the northern Konkan and the interior of Maharashtra, despite the fact that these territories were under different political jurisdictions.[31]

The Gujarati currency system experienced two radical shifts over the course of the thirteenth and fourteenth centuries. First, the *dramma* was radically debased. Though the *dramma* had maintained its silver fineness for centuries prior to 1200, its purity declined precipitously during the course of the thirteenth century.[32] This would suggest that Gujarat relied on both maritime and overland trade for its silver imports. However, the early Delhi Sultanate blocked access to the Panjshir silver mines of Afghanistan. After these were destroyed by the Mongol invasions, the Bhillamala *dramma* was debased until it effectively became a copper coin. In 1299, Delhi conquered Gujarat. The new rulers subsequently displaced the indigenous monometallic coinage system with Delhi's trimetallic system of gold, silver, billon and copper coins. For the better part of the next century, Gujarati ports played a crucial role in the flow of precious metals into Delhi.[33]

Even after Gujarat regained its independence in 1399, the Gujarat Sultanate's coinage system remained trimetallic. Though there is no evidence that the region suffered from a paucity of gold or silver, the unit weight of the coinage was reduced to provide a more convenient value for the markets.[34] By this time, overland imports of precious metals had dried

[29] Hoards 22, 34, 35, 47, 73, 75, 86, 91 and 98 in P.L. Gupta *Coin Hoards from Gujarat State* (Varanasi, Numismatic Society of India, 1969).

[30] Prem Lata Pokharna, 'A Huge Hoard of Gadhaiya Coins from Kasindra,' *Journal of the Numismatic Society of India* 66 (1984) 51–2.

[31] Ranabir Chakravarti, 'Monarchs, Merchants and a Matha in Northern Konkan (c. 900–1053 AD),' *Indian Economic and Social History Review* 27:2 (1990) 189–208.

[32] Metallurgical tables in K.K. Maheshwari, *Imitations in Continuity: Tracking the Silver Coinage of Early Medieval India* (Mumbai, IIRNS Publications, 2010) 88–9.

[33] Gujarat imported silver from Ilkhanid Persia, gold *dinars* from Egypt and Rasulid silver coins from Yemen. Haider has highlighted this flow of coins by reviewing the 'Broach hoard' of 448 gold coins and 1,200 silver coins, imported into Gujarat as bullion sometime after 1382. Haider, 'International Trade in Precious Metals and Monetary Systems of Medieval India: 1200–1500,' 240–2.

[34] Except silver from 1400 to 1450: see the section titled 'Synchronicity of Bullion Supply and Demand,' later in this paper.

up and maritime trade was the sole source. The same was true of the neighbouring Malwa Sultanate, closely linked with the Gujarati economy. Nonetheless, P. L. Gupta's analysis of coin hoards indicates that copper was the dominant coinage, circulating at a ratio of approximately 13 copper coins for every 4 silver coins or 1 gold coin.[35]

The Deccan, the Bahmanids and Vijayanagara

Prior to the fourteenth century, the major polities of the Deccan were the Yadava kingdom of Devagiri and the Kakatiya kingdom of Warangal. The Yadavas issued 4g gold coins in substantial numbers. These were supplemented by tiny 1g silver coins. Their principal port was Thana (near modern Mumbai), which had been seized from its Silahara rulers in the mid-thirteenth century. In 1292, Marco Polo observed that this well-trafficked port primarily exported leather and cotton goods and imported horses, gold, silver and copper.[36] Yadava gold coins have been found in hoards in Telingana, which was ruled by the Kakatiyas of Warangal who issued their own 4g gold coins during the thirteenth century.[37] In the second half of the thirteenth century, the Yadavas conquered Gopakapattana (modern-day Goa). Rather than replace the local system with their own, the new Yadava rulers maintained the earlier Gopakapattana currency system, which was based on small gold coins and even smaller silver coins.[38] Further south, the Hoysala Kingdom issued 4g gold coins throughout the twelfth century. However, it is uncertain if the practice continued into the thirteenth century.[39]

During the first third of the fourteenth century, the Delhi Sultanate conquered the Deccan and reconfigured the local currency systems. In 1311, it extended its rule over the Yadava Kingdom and, thereafter, the new ruler's currencies began circulating in the region. In the early 1320s, the government mint in the fort of Deogir (Devagiri) began striking 11g

[35] Hoards 4, 11, 12, 14, 39, 40, 41, 42, 61, 72, 99, 102, 104, 108, 116, 120, 121 and 125 in Gupta *op. cit.*

[36] Yule, *The Book of Ser Marco Polo*, 330.

[37] 'Find Spots of the Coins,' in R. Subrahmanyam, *A Catalogue of Yadava Coins in the Andhra Pradesh State Museum, Hyderabad* (Hyderabad, Government of Andhra Pradesh, 1965) 23.

[38] P.L. Gupta, *Coins* (New Delhi, National Book Trust, 1969) 76.

[39] Gupta, *Coins*, 425.

silver *tankas*.[40] In 1323, the Delhi Sultanate conquered the Kakatiya kingdom. Just as it was doing in the former Yadava realm, the Sultanate began striking 11g silver *tankas* at Mulk-i-Tilang (Telingana) for circulation in the newly conquered territory.[41]

After becoming independent from Delhi in 1347, the Bahmanid Sultanate maintained the imperial trimetallic coinage. The Sultanate issued a large variety of gold, silver and copper coins to meet the demands of the land revenue system, the requirements for military pay and the needs of internal trade. Phillip Wagoner's analysis of 120 hoards of Bahmanid coins recovered showed the dominance of copper in this system. Copper coins circulated in a ratio of 2400 copper to 1 gold to 20 silver.[42] Only a small fraction of the metal in these coins was locally sourced. Some gold was mined in the Deccan goldfields, which had been worked since ancient times.[43] Similarly, copper was mined in the Deccan and in the Singhbhum copper belt further north-east in Jharkhand.[44] Nonetheless, the majority of the metal was imported by sea. All of the silver was imported via west coast ports, most likely from the Persian Gulf, ultimately from Persia, itself a silver coin-based economy.[45] In addition, there is evidence that copper was a major import item. In the eleventh century, Jewish merchants regularly sent copper ingots to Kerala.[46] Copper was also imported from China.[47] Later, the European companies imported significant quantities of copper to their Indian factories in the Konkan and Malabar.[48]

[40] H. Nelson Wright, *The Coinage and Metrology of the Sultans of Delhi* (Delhi, Oxford University Press, 1936), 113; S. Goron and J.P. Goenka, *The Coins of the Indian Sultanates* (New Delhi, Munshiram Manoharlal, 2001), 47.

[41] Wright, *The Coinage and Metrology of the Sultans of Delhi*, 113. Goron and Goenka, *The Coins of the Indian Sultanates*, 48.

[42] Private correspondence, July 2013, updated March 2015. Among other sources, he consulted *Indian Archaeology—A Review* (1953–1954 through 2000–2001), and D. Raja Reddy, 'Hyderabad Museum Collection of Treasure Trove Coins of Bahmani, Vijayanagara, and Yadava Dynasties,' *Journal of the Numismatic Society of India* 71 (2009) 105–14.

[43] Deyell, *Living Without Silver*, 249–50.

[44] Deyell, *Living Without Silver*, 252.

[45] Haider, 'International Trade in Precious Metals and Monetary Systems of Medieval India: 1200–1500,' 188.

[46] Goitein and Friedman, 'Letters and Documents on the India Trade in Medieval Times—A Preview,' 19.

[47] "The ships that come from the east bring copper in ballast": Yule, *The Book of Ser Marco Polo*, 324.

[48] Chaudhuri, *Trade and Civilisation in the Indian Ocean*, 90.

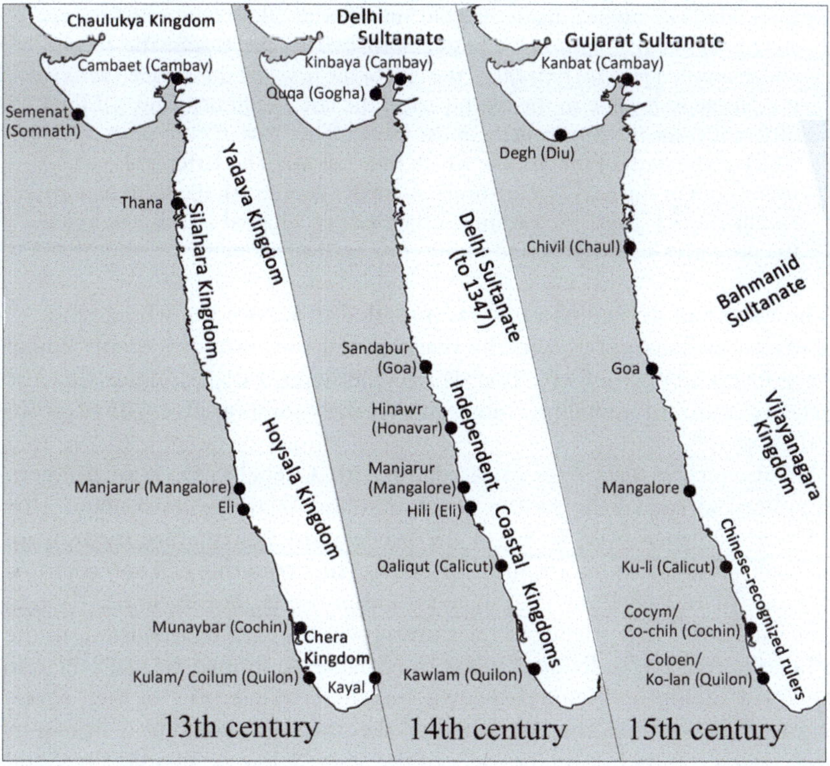

Map 3.3 Ports of note and political changes on India's western coast 1200–1500 (Spellings of place names are as given in the original sources, as transcribed or transliterated. "Modern" place names in parenthesis are those most frequently used in the current historical literature, which usually reflect pre-Independence usage.)

In 1336, Vijayanagara, which was on the Bahmanids' southern border (see Map 3.3), gained independence from Delhi. Though this region was Hindu, the structure of its government was essentially that of the neighbouring sultanates. Vijayanagara had the renowned Kolar goldfields, as well as its own internal sources of copper. Nonetheless, copper and gold, as well as silver, was imported via maritime trade. The government used both imported and domestic metals to mint mainly small 3.3g gold coins called *pagodas* or *huns* and tiny copper coins. Nonetheless, there was a wide variety of other coins struck. The Persian ambassador of Shah Rukh described the Vijayanagara's monetary system as based on:

three kinds of money, made of gold mixed with alloy; one called *varaha* weighs about one *mithkal*, equivalent to two *dinars kopeki*; the second, which is called *pertab* [*pratap*], is the half of the first; the third, called *fanam*, is equivalent in value to the tenth part of the last-mentioned coin. Of these different coins the *fanam* is the most useful. They cast in pure silver a coin which is the sixth of the *fanam*, which they call *tar*. This latter is also a very useful coin in currency [circulation]. A copper coin worth the third of a *tar*, is called *djitel* [*jital*]. According to the practice adopted in this empire, all the provinces at a fixed period, bring their gold to the mint.[49]

The variety of denominations was intended to service the whole range of transactions encountered in the markets and the revenue system. Phillip Wagoner's analysis of 162 hoards of Vijayanagara coins reveals that the relative ratio of metallic coins was roughly 800 gold to 1 silver to 20 copper.[50]

Wagoner has also demonstrated through a detailed study of the geographical spread of the various Bahmanid and Vijayanagara coinages that the latter's small gold *hun* was the predominant circulating medium of virtually the whole peninsula.[51] However, this coin did not spread to all regions of India where Vijayanagara had interests. For example, though Vijayanagara had a privileged relationship with the ports of Malabar in the fifteenth century, individual rulers in Malabar continued to issue operate their own mints and issue their own currencies as a symbol of their sovereignty.[52] In contrast, the Bahmanid gold coinage struggled to maintain its influence even within the borders of the state.[53] The Bahmanid silver and copper coinage had a much larger circulation. Bahmanid copper coins circulated throughout the Deccan and eventually served as the prototype of the renowned copper *dam* of the Mughal Empire.[54]

49 'Narrative of the journey of Abd-er-Razzak,' in *India in the Fifteenth Century, Being a Collection of Narratives of Voyages to India*, R.H. Major, ed. (London, Hakluyt Society, 1992 reprint of 1858 original) 26.

50 Private communication, 20 July 2013. Also see Phillip B. Wagoner, 'Money Use in the Deccan, c. 1350–1687: The Role of Vijayanagara *Hons* in the Bahmani Currency System,' *The Indian Economic and Social History Review* 51:4 (2014) 457–80.

51 Wagoner, 'Money Use in the Deccan, c. 1350–1687,' 469 and 478–9.

52 Ma Huan, 130 and 136.

53 Wagoner, 'Money Use in the Deccan, c. 1350–1687,' 468 and 478–9.

54 John S. Deyell, 'Monetary and Financial Webs: The Regional and International Influence of Pre-modern Bengali Coinage,' in *Pelagic Passageways: The Northern Bay of Bengal Before Colonialism*, Rila Mukherjee, ed. (Delhi, Primus, 2011) 300.

Malabar Coast

It was mentioned above, that trade with Malabar from both the Persian Gulf and the Red Sea was well established by the thirteenth century. In this period as well, we have the first documentation of Chinese traders frequenting this coast. Sen, quoting the *Yuan Shi*, mentions a Yuan diplomatic mission to Malabar in 1281. He notes, "This source indicates that ships from Quanzhou were making direct voyages to the South Asian coast".[55] Slightly later in the fourteenth century, the relationship of the many ports was described by the Moroccan traveller Ibn Battuta thusly:

> In the country of al-Malaybur [Malabar] there are twelve infidel [Hindu] rulers—some being so powerful as to possess an army of fifty thousand men and some being weak, their troop amounting to three thousand men. There is absolutely no dissension amongst them.[56]

It is noticeable on Map 3.3 that the port which seemed to prosper throughout the period of this study was Calicut. Ibn Battuta mentioned:

> We travelled to the city of Calicut, one of the chief harbours of the country of Malabar where people from China, Jawa [Sumatra], Saylan [Ceylon], Mahal [Maldives], Yemen and Fars come, and here gather merchants from all quarters of the globe. And the harbour of Calicut is one of the largest in the world.
>
> We stayed in the port of Calicut in which there were then thirteen ships of China. … The China Sea is navigated only by the Chinese ships.[57]

About 1445, the Ikhanid ambassador Abdur Razzaq Samarqandi described this port:

> Calicut is a perfectly secure harbour, which like that of Ormuz, brings together merchants from every city and from every country; in it are to be found abundance of precious articles brought thither from Maritime countries, and especially from Abyssinia, Zirbad, and Zanguebar [Zanzibar]; from time to time ships arrive there from the shores of the House of God

[55] Tansen Sen, 'The Formation of Chinese Maritime Networks to Southern Asia, 1200–1450,' *Journal of the Economic and Social History of the Orient* 49:4 (2006) 424–5, 429–30.

[56] Husain, *The Rehla of Ibn Battuta*, 183.

[57] Husain, *The Rehla of Ibn Battuta*, 188–9.

> [i.e. from Jeddah, the port of Mecca] and other parts of the Hedjaz. … When a sale is effected, they levy a duty on the goods of one-fortieth part [2.5%].[58]
>
> Although the Sameri [Zamorin] is not subject to the laws of Bidjanagar [Vijayanagara], he nevertheless pays him respect, and stands extremely in fear of him.[59]

In the previous section above, it was mentioned that Vijayanagara had a privileged relationship with the ports of Malabar. By the fifteenth century these were by and large independent. A potent symbol of sovereignty exercised by individual rulers was the operation of a mint and the issue of local money, which was noted by the Chinese. Ma Huan, who accompanied admiral Zheng He's flotilla in the first half of the century, carefully noted the monetary particulars of the three cities the Chinese most frequented:

> The country of little Ko-lan [Quilon]: … The king uses gold to cast coins; each coin weighs one *fen* on our official steelyard; in general use.[60]
>
> The country of Ko-chih [Cochin]: "The king uses gold of ninety percent [fineness] to cast coins for current use; they are called fa-nan [*fanam*]; each weighs *one* fen one *li* on our official steelyard. They also use silver to make coins; … and each four *li* on our official steelyard; they are called ta-erh [*tara*]. Each one gold coin is exchanged for fifteen silver coins; for petty transactions in the market-streets they use these coins.[61]
>
> The country of Ku-li [Calicut]: "If a treasure-ship goes there. … The king uses gold of sixty percent [fineness] to cast a coin for current use; it is named a pa-nan [*fanam*] … it weighs one *fen* on our official steelyard. He also makes a coin of silver; it is named ta-erh [*tara*]; each coin weighs about three *li*; this coin is used for petty transactions.[62]

It is clear from the travellers' testimonies that the source of the precious metals for these coastal currencies was the seaborne trade itself.[63]

[58] 'Narrative of the journey of Abd-er-Razzak,' 13–14.
[59] 'Narrative of the journey of Abd-er-Razzak,' 19.
[60] Ma Huan, 130.
[61] Ma Huan, 136.
[62] Ma Huan, 141.
[63] Phillip Wagoner reminds us that currency is not to be confused with revenue, which even in coastal states might be largely derived from taxes on agriculture: Phillip B. Wagoner, '"Lord of the Eastern and Western Oceans": Unguents, Politics and the Indian Ocean Trade in Medieval South India,' in *From Local to Global: Papers in Asian History and Culture*, Vol. I, Kamal Sheel, Charles Willemen and Kenneth Zysk, eds. (Delhi, Buddhist World Press, 2017) 311.

East Coast and Bengal

India's east coast and Bengal present somewhat different pictures because of the prominent role played by cowry shells in local monetary systems (see Map 3.4). Cowries were imported into this region from the Maldives by private merchants who were also engaged in the export of rice. The trade of rice for cowries was profitable in both directions and thrived

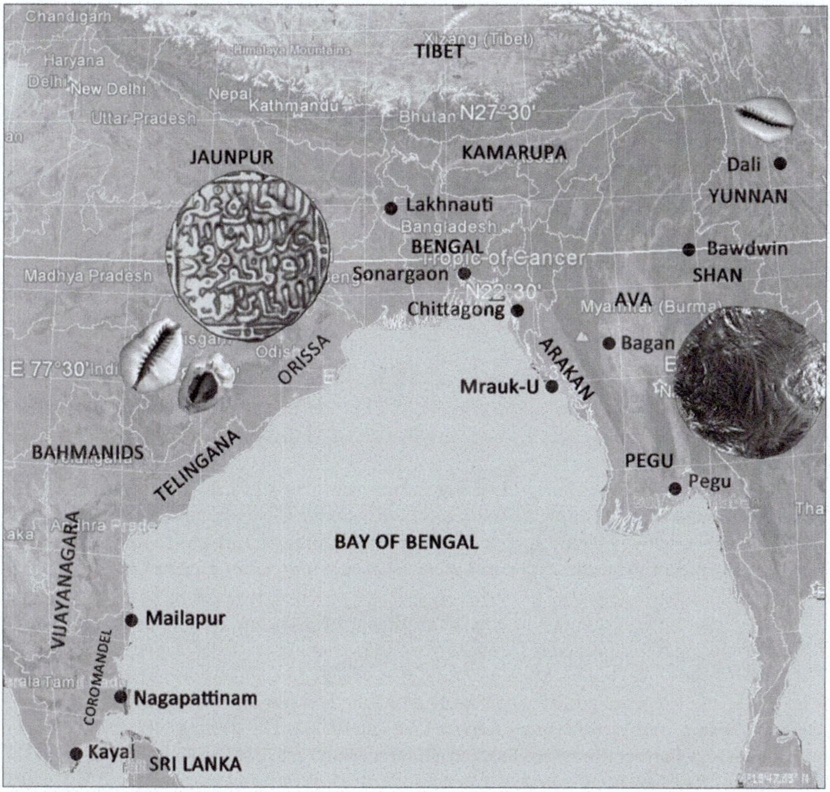

Map 3.4 Bay of Bengal ports, major currencies and sources of precious metals, 1200–1500 (Overlay by the author; underlay by Google Maps under their "fair use" policy.)

throughout the period of study.[64] The local use of cowries continued despite regular contact with regions that used metallic coins. Though the Vijayanagara Kingdom and the Bahmanid Sultanate routinely intervened in the internal dynamics of the local principalities and small states along the Coromandel Coast up to Orissa, the coinage system of Western India did not spread eastward. In Orissa, the monetary system was based primarily on cowries, supplemented by sporadic local issues of gold coins. In fact, Orissa's reliance on cowries lasted well into the 1820s.[65] Similarly, cowries circulated in Bengal. Until the thirteenth century, Bengal's monetary system utilized a notional money of account for most official transactions, with cowries fulfilling the role of tangible medium, as and when required.[66] Following the establishment of the Bengal Sultanate in 1342, a silver coin was introduced to complement the cowry in circulation. Bengal maintained maritime links with Arakan and Pegu in Burma and Melaka on the Malay Peninsula which enabled it to maintain a relatively constant supply of silver bullion from inland sources in Yunnan and upper Burma via Pegu and Arakan.[67] This silver was not imported in the form of coinage, since contemporary Bagan relied on a money of account, the *klyap*, settled in

[64] Ibn Battuta who visited the Maldives Islands after 1342 CE, noted 'All transactions take place in this country by means of the cowrie. … They are sold to the inhabitants of Bengal for rice, because the cowries are also current in Bengal.' Husain, *The Rehla of Ibn Battuta*, 201.

[65] Deyell, *Living without Silver*, 74, citing J. Heimann, 'Small Change and Ballast: Cowry Trade and Usage as an Example of India Ocean Economic History,' *South Asia* 3:1 (1980) 57; H.U. Vogel, 'Cowry Trade and its Role in the Economy of Yunnan: From the Ninth to the Mid-Seventeenth Century,' *Journal of the Economic and Social History of the Orient* 36 (1993) 342.

[66] This section relies on data and analysis in Richard M. Eaton, *The Rise of Islam and the Bengal Frontier 1204–1760* (New Delhi, Oxford University Press, 1994); Syed Ejaz Hussain, *The Bengal Sultanate: Politics, Economy and Coins, AD 1205–1576* (Delhi, Manohar, 2003); John S. Deyell, 'Cowries and Coins: The Dual Monetary System of the Bengal Sultanate,' *Indian Economic and Social History Review* 47:1 (2010) 63–106.

[67] Pranab K. Chattopadhyay, 'In Search of Silver: Southeast Asian Sources for the Coinage of Bengal' in *Kalhar—Studies in Art, Iconography, Architecture and Archaeology of India and Bangladesh*, Gouriswar Bhattacharya et al., eds. (New Delhi, Kaveri Books, 2007) 296–305. John S. Deyell, 'The China Connection: Problems of Silver Supply in Medieval Bengal,' in *Precious Metals in the Later Medieval and Early Modern Worlds*, John F. Richards, ed. (Durham, Carolina Academic Press, 1983) 207–27; Deyell, 'Cowries and Coins: The Dual Monetary System of the Bengal Sultanate,' 88–91; Bin Yang, 'The Bay of Bengal Connections to Yunnan,' in *Pelagic Passageways*, 317–42.

silver ingots or other commodities.[68] Nonetheless, it took another century and a half before the silver coin had displaced the cowry as the major form of circulating medium.[69] However, the evolution of Bengal's monetary system was not a smooth one. The supply of silver varied over time. Yunnan's mines experienced periods of strong production as well as periods of relative decline between the thirteenth and sixteenth centuries.[70] In addition, the demand for silver in China constantly shifted and impacted the availability of Yunnan silver for Bengali importers.[71]

The Supply and Demand of Precious Metals in India

Though detailing temporal cycles of precious metal supplies is beyond the scope of this chapter, the differential impact of the "bullion famine" of the first half of the fifteenth century is quite illuminating. Haider pointed out that the acute shortage of silver in European countries noted by Spufford, Day, Munro and others for the period prior to 1460 was concurrent with a monetary silver shortage in Gujarat and Delhi.[72] In fact, the phenomenon was more widespread. Studies of coin quantities in the numismatic trade, rather than in institutional collections, show that there was little silver coinage in Jaunpur, the Bahmanid kingdom and Malwa in the first half of the fifteenth century. The only region that issued large quantities of silver during this period was Bengal.[73] Atwell has linked this "bullion famine" to the early Ming Dynasty's encouragement of silver remittances.[74]

[68] Kenneth Hall, 'Coinage Trade and Economy in Early South India and its Southeast Asian Neighbours,' *Indian Economic and Social History Review* 36:4 (1999) 449–50.

[69] Ma Huan, 159.

[70] For example, von Glahn notes a collapse of silver production prior to the 1430s: Richard von Glahn, *Fountain of Fortune: Money and Monetary Policy in China, 1000–1700* (London, University of California, 1996) 83, 113. Later the mines must have recovered; Bin Yang notes a doubling of silver mining taxes between 1458 and 1460: Bin Yang, *Between Wind and Clouds: The Making of Yunnan (Second Century BCE to Twentieth Century CE)* (New York, Columbia University Press, 2009) 195.

[71] Richard Von Glahn, 'Monies of Account and Monetary Transition in China, Twelfth to Fourteenth Centuries,' *Journal of the Economic and Social History of the Orient* 53 (2010) 463–505.

[72] Haider, 'International Trade in Precious Metals and Monetary Systems of Medieval India: 1200–1500,' 244–6.

[73] Goron and Goenka, *The Coins of the Indian Sultanates*, relevant geographic chapters.

[74] William S. Atwell, 'Time, Money and the Weather: Ming China and the "Great Depression" of the Mid-Fifteenth Century,' *The Journal of Asian Studies* 61:1 (2002) 87.

Table 3.1 Relative demand for monetary commodities in the Indian kingdoms, 1200–1500

Kingdom (location)	*Gold*	*Silver*	*Copper*
Delhi Sultanate (Inland, North)	1	20	30
Bengal Sultanate (Eastern Coast)	1	30	0
Gujarat Sultanate (Western Coast)	1	4	13
Bahmanid Sultanate (Inland, Central)	1	20	2400
Vijayanagara Kingdom (Inland, South)	800	1	20

This suggests that supplies of silver, and potentially other precious metals, throughout most of India were linked to developments in Europe and China well before the discovery of New World silver. Bengal was not similarly linked because it was able to depend on receiving supplies from Yunnan and Burma throughout the first half of the fifteenth century.

The particular experience of Bengal during the "bullion famine" highlights the importance of regional and local perspectives in analysing the movement of precious metals, in particular, and goods, in general, within the greater Indian Ocean World. The demand for monetary commodities in India was shaped by the internal logic and dynamics of each of the subcontinent's multiple monetary systems. In turn, the structure of each of these systems was oriented towards domestic concerns. This created a large amount of variability (see Table 3.1). Silver was by far the dominant precious metal in the north of India and the Deccan. Gold was mined in southern India and therefore occupied a prominent role in this region's monetary systems both before and during the period of our study. Local sources could not meet the level of demand and gold was frequently imported. Nonetheless, foreign gold coins did not circulate as money in Indian kingdoms. Rather, gold was imported to be melted down and restruck. Copper was in great demand all along India's west coast because it was the basis of low-value coinage in the Delhi, Gujarat and Bahmanid Sultanates. In contrast, in Bengal there was no demand at all for copper for monetary purposes prior to 1538 because cowries served the function that copper coins otherwise would have.

It is noticeable that the emphasis by modern "world system" proponents on the global silver bullion trade is reflected in the persistent demand of many Indian states for this coinage metal, prior to 1500. However, it is equally important to note the strong demand in some regional states for copper, which was only partially satisfied by indigenous sources. We remarked earlier that copper formed a consistent item of import for foreign merchants who could source it in their home ports. This dual demand for silver and copper set the pattern for the succeeding "early modern" period, when Indian coinage systems developed a voracious appetite for both metals.

CHAPTER 4

What East Africans Got for Their Ivory and Slaves: The Nature, Working and Circulation of Commodity Currencies in Nineteenth-Century East Africa

Karin Pallaver

The concurrent circulation of metal coins and commodity currencies characterized the history of the Swahili world over the long term. The first coins were minted on the Swahili coast in the eighth century and became

---

I am playing here on the title of an article by Stanley Alpern called "What Africans got for their Slaves", that provides a detailed, but yet not analytical, list of goods used in West Africa to buy slaves. By using the term "got", I do not imply passivity on the parts of consumers. Rather, as scholars—see, among others, J. Prestholdt, *Domesticating the World. African Consumerism and the Genealogies of Globalization* (Berkley, University of California Press, 2008)—have stressed in recent years, Africans in fact demanded products, which European and American merchants were forced to supply; see S. Alpern, "What Africans Got for their Slaves: A Master List of European Trade Goods", *History in Africa* 22 (1995) 5–43.

K. Pallaver (✉)
Department of History and Cultures, University of Bologna, Bologna, Italy

S. Serels, G. Campbell (eds.), *Currencies of the Indian Ocean World*, Palgrave Series in Indian Ocean World Studies,
https://doi.org/10.1007/978-3-030-20973-5_4

part of an articulated monetary system in which commodity currencies, including cloth, beads, axes and grains, circulated. These currencies were in use in pre-colonial Swahili towns and were traded for centuries between the interior and the coast.[1] During the nineteenth century, however, the East African regions became connected to the coast and the global market in an unprecedented way. The huge increase in the export of ivory to satisfy the growing demand of the Western middle class and of slaves for Zanzibar and coastal plantations resulted in an intensified "commodification" of the local economies through the import of new goods.[2] This created a new link to the international economy that had profound implications for the patterns of local economic change. As trade was widespread and involved multilateral relations, goods were not easily interchangeable, and forms of currency were needed to facilitate market transactions.[3] From the intersection of formerly distinct economic orders, imported commodities started to be invested with new exchange value and emerged as currencies. In East Africa, glass beads, cowrie shells, imported cloth and metal wires crystallized into a monetary form.

With reference to West Africa, Paul Lovejoy points out that virtually all pre-colonial economies required the use of circulating mediums of exchange and units of account.[4] However, as David Richardson has pointed out, the discussion on these currency objects has been "usually restricted to a cursory listing of certain well-known trade goods without a serious analysis of what this means".[5] This has resulted into a limited

[1] K. Pallaver, 'Currencies of the Swahili World,' in *The Swahili World*, S. Wynne-Jones and A. La Violette, eds. (London and New York, Routledge, 2018) 447–57; S. Wynne-Jones and J. Fleisher, 'Coins and other Currencies on the Swahili Coast,' in *The Archaeology of Money*, C. Haselkgrove and S. Krmnicek, eds. (Leicester, Leicester University Press, 2016) 115–36.

[2] J. Glassman, *Feasts and Riot. Revelry, Rebellion, and Popular Consciousness on the Swahili Coast, 1856–1888* (Portsmouth, Heinemann, 1995) 36.

[3] A. G. Hopkins, *An Economic History of West Africa* (London, Longman, 1973) 67.

[4] P. Lovejoy, 'Interregional Monetary Flows in the Precolonial Trade of Nigeria,' *Journal of African History* 15 (1974) 563.

[5] D. Richardson, 'West African Consumer Patterns and their Influence on the Eighteenth-Century English Slave Trade,' in *Uncommon Markets: Essays in the Economic History of the Atlantic World*, H.A. Gemery and J.S. Hogendorn, eds. (London, Academic Press, 1979) 304. This is connected to what Philip Curtin defined as the "gewgaw myth", see P.D. Curtin, *Economic Change in Pre-colonial Africa: Senegambia in the Era of the Slave Trade* (Madison, University of Wisconsin Press, 1975). With specific reference to beads, there is another myth that it is worth mentioning here, that could be dubbed "the ornament myth", that is, the idea that the huge amounts of beads imported to Africa were mainly used to produce ornaments. For an example, see S. Alpern, 'What Africans got for their Slaves.'

understanding of the actual use that African societies made of these imported commodities, and particularly of the values that these goods acquired when they entered African economic circles, in relation to local and regional systems of value.

While the history of pre-colonial West African currencies has received much scholarly attention,[6] the history of East African currencies remains largely unexplored.[7] Yet, explaining the emergence and development of East African monetary systems, both on a regional level and in terms of their connection to the wider Indian Ocean world, will further the understanding of both economies into the evolving world system. As Thomas Hakansson has recently argued, the development of the ivory trade and the connected circulation of imported currencies in East Africa promoted exchange and wealth accumulation in ways that ultimately favoured the development of pastoralist economies and agricultural production. Commodity currencies were incorporated into the value systems of African political economies and had consequences on regional processes of labour and resource exploitation, as well as on craft production.[8] Drawing methodological and theoretical inspiration from the literature on West African currencies, this paper uses accounts of nineteenth-century travellers, missionaries and traders, as well as early colonial records, to analyse (1) the connection between the use of currency and the nature of East African economies and markets and (2) the growth of economic culture and practice among the population.[9]

[6] See, among others, J. Hogendorn and M. Johnson, *The Shell Money of the Slave Trade* (New York, Cambridge University Press, 1986); J. Guyer, *Marginal Gains. Monetary Transactions in Atlantic Africa* (Chicago, University of Chicago Press, 2004); B. Naanen, 'Economy Within an Economy: The Manilla Currency, Exchange Rate Instability and Social Conditions in South-Eastern Nigeria 1900–48,' *Journal of African History* 34 (1993) 425–46; W.I. Ofonogoro, 'From Traditional to British Currency in Southern Nigeria: Analysis of a Currency Revolution, 1880–1948,' *Journal of Economic History* 39:3 (1979) 623–54.

[7] Very little research has been done on the monetary history of East Africa, especially for the pre-colonial period. There are, however, some works on the colonial period, among which R. Maxon, 'The Kenya Currency Crisis, 1919–21 and the Imperial Dilemma,' *Journal of Imperial and Commonwealth History* 17 (1989) 323–48; W. Mwangi, 'Of Coins and Conquest: The East African Currency Board, the Rupee Crisis and the Problem of Colonialism in the East African Protectorate,' *Comparative Studies in Society and History* 4:4 (2001) 763–87.

[8] N.T. Hakansson, 'Socio-ecological Consequences of the Ivory Trade,' in *Ecology and Power: Struggles over Land and Material Resources in the Past, Present and Future*, A. Hornborg, B. Clark and K. Hermele, eds. (New York, Routledge, 2014), 124.

[9] On the problems connected to the historical research on pre-colonial currencies, see J. Guyer, 'Introduction: The Currency Interface and Its Dynamics,' in *Money Matters.*

Geographically, the paper covers the region corresponding to present-day Tanzania, Kenya and Uganda, that is the region that in the nineteenth century became the Zanzibar commercial hinterland.[10] Adopting a regional, rather than a "national" perspective, is particularly appropriate given the circulating nature of currencies. Such a perspective allows for an examination of how currency areas expanded in the nineteenth century and of how changes in currency systems related to other alterations in political and market institutions. The vastness of the area analysed and the different institutions and environments involved necessarily require a series of generalizations.

This chapter argues that the monetary systems of nineteenth-century East Africa were integrated through the external demand for ivory and slaves, the use of imported currencies and a shared value system based on cattle. At the same time, it shows how the co-existence of regional and imported currencies both created opportunities for traders who operated across currency zones and led to craft specialization. Finally, this chapter contends that the adoption of imported currencies throughout the Zanzibar commercial hinterland facilitated transactions where indigenous and external economies intersected.

The Gold, Silver and Copper of East Africa: Commodity Currencies Along and Around the Caravan Roads

The nineteenth-century expansion of the international demand for ivory changed the terms of East African participation in the international economy. In East Africa, trade contacts between the interior and the coast had existed before, but commercial exchanges were generally from hand to hand, and did not involve the organization of caravans to and from the coast. The demand for ivory to produce luxury items for the Western growing middle class, together with the demand for slaves for coastal plantations, set off a process of integration of the regions of the interior into the commercial empire of Zanzibar. Coastal traders penetrated the interior with the backing of the Omani state, which supported their commercial enterprises, and

Instability, Values and Social Payments in the Modern History of West African Communities, J. Guyer, ed. (Portsmouth, Heinemann, 1995) 35.

[10] From the point of view of currency circulation also some areas of Eastern Congo and Southern Sudan will be occasionally included.

Indian financers on the coast, who provided long-term credit facilities. This trade was given a further impetus from the extremely favourable terms of trade that African commodities, particularly ivory, enjoyed throughout the nineteenth century.[11] At the same time, a growing awareness of the increasing value of ivory led enterprising African businessmen in the interior to participate to its commercialization. In so doing, these businessmen assumed the increased risks associated with a longer journey to the coast.[12] As the century progressed, a steady increase in the price of ivory expanded the area of operations of Swahili, Arab and African traders.[13] Export trade dynamics were controlled from the Tanzanian coast, but interior communities, formed by both African and (a limited number of) coastal traders, facilitated the commercialization of ivory and slaves. On the coast, the Maria Theresa Thaler and the Indian copper pice, which served as the small-denomination coin, were the currencies used at the interface between international and coastal trade circuits. From the 1860s, the Indian rupee gradually replaced the thaler, which however remained in use as a unit of account. None of these coins had any monetary value in the interior, though they were occasionally prized as ornaments.[14]

The arrival of new imported commodities in the regions of the interior preceded long-distance caravans by over 50 years.[15] We do not know exactly when and why cloth, glass beads, cowries, iron and brass wires began to mediate commercial exchanges between coastal and African traders. What is evident is that, starting from the first decades of the century, and increasingly from the 1840s to 1850s, these imported goods became the accepted medium of exchange over a huge area extending from the coast to beyond Lakes Victoria and Tanganyika.

[11] A. Sheriff, *Slaves, Spices and Ivory in Zanzibar: Integration of an east African Commercial Empire into the World Economy, 1770–1783* (London, James Currey, 1987) 156.

[12] C.F. Holmes, 'Zanzibari Influence at the Southern End of Lake Victoria: The Lake Route,' *African Historical Studies* 4:3 (1971) 479.

[13] On ivory prices, see Sheriff, *Slaves, Spices and Ivory in Zanzibar*, Appendix B, 250–56.

[14] The obvious exceptions were the populations living in the northern parts of the commercial empire (in the areas bordering with present-day Somalia and Ethiopia), which continued to use Maria Theresa Thalers well into the colonial period, especially in cattle trade. On pice used as ornament see C.J. Sissons, *Economic Prosperity in Ugogo, East Africa, 1860–1890*. PhD Thesis, University of Toronto (1984) 38–9; F.J. Jackson, *Early Days in East Africa* (London, E. Arnold, 1930).

[15] J. Tosh, 'The Northern Interlacustrine Region,' in *Pre-colonial African Trade: Essays on Trade in Eastern and Central Africa*, R. Gray and D. Birmingham, eds. (London, Oxford University Press, 1970) 109.

Cloth played the most important role in commercial transactions throughout the Zanzibar hinterland. In the eighteenth century, textiles imported from Kutch, India, dominated the East African market. However, by the mid-1830s, American cloth was rivalling Indian cloth, overcoming it by the late 1840s. The increasing local preference for this unbleached cloth, locally called *merikani* or *merekani*, was undoubtedly a function of its material characteristics. American cloth was thicker, more durable and of a general superior quality than British, Indian or locally made cloth. At the same time, the American traders based in Zanzibar who traded in ivory, hides and copal helped to bridge the local demand with the expanding production capabilities of the Massachusetts cotton factories.[16] Although American merchants came to dominate textile imports, Indian traders were able to continue to sell their own cottons because of the outsized demand of the rapidly expanding East African market.[17] When the outbreak of the American civil war interrupted the exports of cloth to East Africa, Indian-made, unbleached cotton cloth replaced the no-longer-available American variety.[18]

In the East African region, imported cloth was used to buy export goods like ivory, slaves and hides, and to pay tribute along the caravan roads. For traders cloth became the common means for accumulating and storing wealth and for chiefs it represented an invaluable asset. A wealthy chief distributed cloth to his/her followers as a way to secure loyalty and political support.[19] In nineteenth-century East Africa, cloth became a mark of high status and wealth. It was also used to pay porters' wages.[20]

The use of cloth as currency in nineteenth-century East Africa has not yet been studied, but its role as a standard unit of currency is clearly depicted by travellers and missionaries. Richard Burton reported that the standard unit of currency in the interior was a *shuka* of cloth, or about two yards. In the second half of the century the lowest standard unit of cloth

[16] Prestholdt, *Domesticating the World*, 72.

[17] C.S. Nicholls, *The Swahili Coast: Politics, Diplomacy and Trade* (London, Allen and Unwin, 1971) 348.

[18] Prestholdt, *Domesticating the World*, 77.

[19] F.P. Nolan, *Christianity in Unyamwezi 1878–1928*. PhD Thesis, University of Cambridge (1977) 27.

[20] M.J. Hay, 'Changes in Clothing and Struggles over Identity in Colonial Western Kenya,' in *Fashioning Africa. Power and the Politics of Dress*, J. Alleman, ed. (Bloomington, Indiana University Press, 2004) 67. On porters' wages, see S. Rockel, *Carriers of Culture. Labor on the Road in Nineteenth-Century East Africa* (Portsmouth, Heinemann, 2006).

currency was increased from two to four yards and by 1870 the standard unit had increased to the *doti*, four yards.[21] This increase in the unit of currency was determined by the divergence between the price of ivory and that of *merikani* at the coast. As Abdul Sheriff shows, the juxtaposition of the price curve of ivory and of *merikani* shows a divergence of about 9 per cent per year between 1830s and 1850s.[22] In the second half of the nineteenth century, the *doti merikani* became the standard unit of currency in relation to which export commodities were measured. The *doti merikani* became a convenient accounting device that continued to be in use well into the early colonial period.[23] The use of cloth as a currency was so widespread in the early colonial period that a British administrator in Uganda complained of having to store such large quantities of cloth to be paid out as wages to indigenous government employees that government stations were "looking like draper's shops".[24]

In some areas of the Zanzibar commercial hinterland, metal wires (*masango*) were used as an alternative to cloth. Brass wire was generally in demand in the interlacustrine region and in parts of present-day Kenya and Uganda.[25] In Unyoro, *masango* was used to buy slaves. The Kamba of Machakos used brass wire as a high-denomination currency to buy goats and bullocks and used glass beads as small change.[26] The Turkana, on the north-western border of Kenya, also employed brass wire as currency. The Kavirondo from the Mount Elgon area, who showed no interest in imported cloth, came to use beads, metal wires and cowries as currencies

[21] Owing to transport costs, the value of cloth increased going inland and therefore the standard units of currency changed: The *doti merikani* measured 4 yards on the coast, three and half in Tabora and 3 in Ujiji; see J. Becker, *La Vie en Afrique ou trois ans dans l'Afrique Centrale*, Vol. 1 (Paris, J. Lebègue, 1881) 465; E. Hore, *Eleven Years in Central Africa* (London, Stanford, 1892) 71.

[22] Sheriff, *Slaves, Spices and Ivory in Zanzibar*, 434.

[23] For similar standard units of currency in West Africa, see Curtin, *Economic Change in Pre-colonial Africa*, 249.

[24] Hardinge [quoting a private letter from Colvile] to Kimberley, Zanzibar, 28/7/1894, FO 107/2, The National Archives, London [hereafter NA].

[25] Tosh, 'The Northern Interlacustrine Region,' 115; R.F. Burton, *The Lake Regions of Central Africa*, Vol. 1 (Santa Barbara, The Narrative Press, 2001 reprint of the 1860 edition) 138.

[26] J. Ainsworth, 'Report on the District,' Machakos, 1/1/1894, FO 2/73, NA; Jackson, *Early Days in East Africa*, 175; G.N. Uzoigwe, 'Pre-colonial Markets in Bunyoro-Kitara,' *Comparative Studies in Society and History* 14 (1972) 447.

as a result of their trade relations with Buganda.[27] Metal wires were on sale in the main markets along the caravan roads and were then used as currency in other regions. In Tabora, for example, metal wires were converted into *kitindi*, or coil bracelets, that were then used in the ivory and slave trade in Ujiji, on Lake Tanganyika.[28]

Though cloth and metal wire served as high-denomination currencies, glass beads and cowries served as their small-denomination counterparts. They were used in small market transactions, and to buy food for porters and slaves along the caravan roads.[29] Glass beads were very likely among the first imported commodities introduced at the beginning of the nineteenth century into the interior, where they were used to buy ivory and slaves. But with the growing number of caravans travelling inland and the increase in ivory prices, cloth, with its higher value, replaced beads as a means to buy export goods.[30] Beads then became the most widespread means to buy food during caravan journeys; they were sometimes even given to porters as *posho* (daily food rations) in alternative to sorghum or rice.[31] Stanley calculated the amount of beads needed to pay his porters, and in 1875 wrote:

> Just outside the door of my hut are about two dozen of my men, squatted in a circle and stringing beads. A necklace of beads is each man's daily sum wherewith to buy food. I have now a little over 160 men. Imagine 160 necklaces given for food each day for the last three months; in the aggregate the sum amounts to 14,400 necklaces; in a year it will amount to 58,400.[32]

Strands of glass beads were measured in standard scales of value: the *bitil* (from the tip of the index finger to the wrist), the *khete* (from the elbow to the thumb and back, 1 *khete* corresponding to 4 *bitil*) and the *fundo*

[27] Johnston 'Report on Uganda,' Entebbe, 27/4/1900, FO 2/298, NA.

[28] R.F. Burton, 'The Lake Regions of Central Equatorial Africa,' *Journal of the Royal Geographical Society* 29:139 (1859) 428.

[29] On the use of cowries to buy food for slaves, see R. Beachey, *The Slave Trade of Eastern Africa* (London, Rex Collings, 1976) 191.

[30] K. Pallaver, 'From Venice to East Africa: History, Uses and Meanings of Glass Beads,' in *Luxury in Global Perspective: Commodities and Practices, c. 1600–2000*, K. Hofmeester and B.S. Grewe, eds. (Cambridge, Cambridge University Press, 2016).

[31] C. Hobley, *Kenya. From Chartered Company to Crown Colony. Thirty Years of Exploration and Administration in British East Africa*, 2nd edition (London, Frank Cass, 1929) 246.

[32] N.R. Bennett (ed.), *Stanley's Despatches to the New York Herald 1871–1872, 1874–1877* (Boston, Boston University Press, 1970), 457.

(10 *khete*). Similarly to the *shuka* of cloth, the *bitil* largely disappears from the sources in the 1860s, and is replaced by the *khete*, a higher unit of value. This was due to the increasing value of export commodities and the decreasing purchasing power of beads. According to Burton:

> The price of provisions in Unyamwezi has increased inordinately since the Arabs have settled in the land. Formerly a slave-boy could be purchased for five fundo, or fifty strings of beads: the same article would now fetch three hundred. A fundo of cheap white porcelain-beads would procure a milk cow; and a goat or ten hens its equivalent, was to be bought for one khete.[33]

There were different colours and sizes of beads in circulation and their variable value was, according to many contemporary observers, with a function of their fashionableness. Père Léon Livinhac of the White Fathers wrote that as exchange goods, glass beads were second in importance only to cloth, but were far more subject to the "caprice" of the people he met along the road.[34] Joseph Thomson made the same point when he wrote:

> In one year a tribe goes mad for a particular bead; but the trader having supplied himself with the fashionable article, according to latest news, might, if his journey was long, arrive to find a fashion changed and his stock just so unmarketable rubbish.[35]

Nonetheless, as I have discussed elsewhere, the limited flexibility of the demand should be attributed more to the fact that these items were used as currency and as a measurement of value rather than to the "fastidious tastes of African women", as Henry Morton Stanley put it, or their "caprice".[36]

Cowries similarly were used as a small-denomination currency. In fact, they shared many functions and characteristics with beads. They were both durable, impossible to counterfeit, and, owing to their size and shape, easy to handle. They had a very low unit value that made them

[33] R.F. Burton, *The Lake Regions of Central Africa*, 292.

[34] Pére Livinhac, S. Marie près de Roubaga, 9/9/1879, White Fathers Archive, Rome [hereafter WF] C 11–12.

[35] J. Thomson, *To the Central Lakes and Back: The Narrative of the Royal Geographical Society's East Central African Expedition, 1878–80*, Vol. 1 (London, Sampson Low, 1881) 353.

[36] K. Pallaver, '"A Recognized Currency in Beads": Glass Beads as Money in 19th-Century East Africa: The Central Caravan Road,' in *Money in Africa*, C. Eagleton, H. Fuller and J. Perkins, eds. (London, British Museum Research Publications, 2009) 20–9.

particularly suitable to be used as currency in regions where incomes and prices were very low. Cowries were both employed to buy food in the local markets and various sources refer to items sold at the price of one cowry or one bead. Both could also be strung into strands to form larger currency denominations.[37] However, cowries did not circulate as widely. In fact, they were mainly used as a currency in the kingdom of Buganda and neighbouring regions.[38] Cowries reached Buganda during the reign of Semakookiro (c. 1800–1812), became popular by the mid-nineteenth century under *kabaka* Ssuna II (1830–1857) and started to be used as a recognized means of exchange under *kabaka* Mutesa I (1857–1884).[39] Trade with the Congo basin region could have made Ganda people familiar with cowries coming from the West coast and could have favoured the quick adoption of shell money when traders from Zanzibar first introduced cowries from the coast.[40] Cowries were plentiful and easily obtainable along the coast and in Zanzibar, but could not be directly accessed by Ganda traders, who did not generally visit the coast.[41]

In nineteenth-century Buganda, cowries circulated alongside *merikani* cloth. In the 1880s trade between coastal and Baganda traders was based on two currencies: "an arms' length of calico and a string of 100 cowries".[42] In Buganda, cowries (*simbi*) were in fact bored and put on strings of one hundred shells, called *kiasa*. This could be easily divided into halves of 50 each, and again into five parts of 10 each, the smallest division being five

[37] F. Bontnick (ed.), *L'Autobiographie de Hamed ben Mohammed el Murjebi Tippo Tip (ca. 1840–1905)* (Bruxelles, Académie Royale des Sciences d'Outre-Mer, 1974); J. Jorgensen, *Uganda: A Modern History* (London, Croom Helm, 1981) 68.

[38] On this see K. Pallaver, '"The African Native has no Pocket": Monetary Practices and Currency Transitions in early Colonial Uganda,' *International Journal of African Historical Studies* 48:3 (2015) 471–99.

[39] These are the dates of reign according to Henri Médard, as reported in H.E. Hanson, *Landed Obligations. The Practice of Power in Buganda* (Portsmouth, Heinemann, 2003) XVII–XVIII.

[40] V.L. Cameron, *Across Africa* (Daldy, Isbister, 1877) 176; G.A. Schweinfurth et al. (eds.), *Emin Pasha in Central Africa, Being a Collection of his Letters and Journals* (London, Philip, 1888) 114. According to Burton, cowries were collected in the various places along the coast between Ras Hafun and Mozambique. This trade was in the hands of Muslim hucksters; see Burton, 'The Lake Regions of Central Equatorial Africa,' 448.

[41] Some expeditions to the coast are reported, but it was not a direct and systematic connection; see R. Reid, *Political Power in Precolonial Buganda: Economy, Society and Warfare in the Nineteenth Century* (Oxford, James Currey, 2002) 159.

[42] Berkeley to Foreign Office, Port Alice, 21/4/1896, FO/2/112, NA.

shells.[43] This made cowries particularly suitable to buy goods of very small value, like foodstuffs. From 1882 cowries were used in the markets of the capital of Buganda[44] and were circulating in the neighbouring regions, where "The people have become accustomed to this money, by which, except in a few cases of direct barter *all trade* is transacted".[45]

Intermediary and Complementary Currencies[46]

The existence of different currency areas created the demand for intermediary currencies. This was particularly important in market towns, such as Tabora and Ujiji, where long-distance trade routes originating from the coast and interregional and regional trade routes intersected. Like the introduction of currencies, the development of market centres was essential for the expansion of trade. Commercial towns were established along the most important caravan roads because traders needed places to store their goods, supply their caravans and obtain fresh groups of porters. There were daily markets in these towns where ivory, slaves and other products were for sale. Every caravan going into the interior from the coast, or travelling the opposite direction, had to stop in these markets in order to obtain supplies and this created the need for intermediary currencies. In these towns, in fact, coastal and African traders met and negotiated the price of ivory and slaves, as well as other African goods, and purchased food supplies for their caravans. The traders operating in these markets came from different regions and, therefore, needed a common currency to settle their commercial exchanges.[47] As a result, these towns became unified economic units that favoured the adoption of a single commercial currency[48] that could

[43] Schweinfurth et al., *Emin Pasha in Central Africa*, 81.

[44] H. Médard, *Le Royaume du Buganda au XIXe siècle: mutations politiques et religieuses dans un ancien état d'Afrique* (Paris, Khartala, 2007) 133.

[45] Schweinfurth et al. (1888), 114; the evidence is mine.

[46] Akinobu Kuroda introduced the concept of complementarity among currencies. Given that markets in history were many layered, and each layer had its interface open to others, currencies were exchangeable, but not always substitutive. See A. Kuroda, 'What is Complementarity among Monies? An Introductory Note,' *Financial History Review* 15:1 (2008) 7–15.

[47] Curtin, *Economic Change in Pre-colonial Africa*, 238; Guyer, *Marginal Gains*, 70.

[48] R. Austen, 'Patterns of Development in Nineteenth-Century East Africa,' *Journal of African History* 4:3 (1971) 654.

serve as a commonly accepted means of exchange at these "interfaces",[49] where different market layers and types of currencies were put in relation to one another. Glass beads were able to serve this function.

Various historical sources confirm that in Tabora, the main connecting point of the caravan roads in the central hinterland, there was a recognized currency in beads. Captain Stairs, stopping at the market of Tabora, found that food was set out in small quantities equivalent to a string of beads. He was able to buy foodstuffs with one string, and with 30 strings he could get a hoe or a dozen eggs. Larger quantities of beads could be exchanged for cloth, which, in turn, could be used to buy higher value goods.[50] The first evidence of a market currency in beads comes from Msene, Western Unyamwezi, where in 1858 Burton found that black and white glass beads called *sofi* were locally used as currency.[51] *Sofi* beads were also the currency in use in the market of Ujiji on Lake Tanganyika, at least from the 1870s onwards. The missionary Edward C. Hore reported that:

> Here for the first time we find a regular currency or money in use by the natives; it consists of strings of blue and white cylindrical beads, each string containing 20 beads. Bunches of 10 strings are called "fundo". From 9 to 11 fundo are given in exchange for 4 yards [one *doti*] of good heavy American calico; the value varying daily, according to the quantity of cloth in the market.[52]

According to Stanley, "one piece is called *Masaro*, and is the lowest piece of currency that will purchase *anything*".[53] This was a later development compared to Msene, where *sofi* were already in use in 1858.[54] When

[49] Guyer introduced the concept of "interface", a point of meeting where difference was maintained, albeit on changing terms; see Guyer, 'Introduction,' 8.

[50] A. Dodgshun, *Journal. From London to Ujiji, 1877–79*, 20/1/1879, Central Africa, Box 1, Council for World Mission, London, SOAS; M.A. Quiggin, *A Survey of Primitive Money* (New York, Barnes & Noble, 1970) 102.

[51] Burton, 'The Lake Regions of Central Equatorial Africa,' 189.

[52] E.C. Hore, 'On the Twelve Tribes of Lake Tanganyika,' *Journal of the Anthropological Institute of Great Britain and Ireland* 12:9 (1883) 2–21.

[53] H.M. Stanley, *Through the Dark Continent* (London, Sampson Low, Marston, Searle and Rivington, 1878), 4; the evidence is mine.

[54] Coastal traders were established in Msene, whereas Omani traders were settled in Tabora. The fact that the first evidence on the use of a currency in beads comes from Msene, suggests that coastal traders introduced *sofi* beads as currency in the local market; see Burton, 'The Lake Regions of Central Equatorial Africa,' 188; H. Leonard, *Notes sur Tabora*, manuscript, WF.

Burton visited Ujiji the same year, he did not mention the use of beads as a recognized currency; various beads, and also *sofi*, were in demand at the time, but no standard currency was in use in the market. Neither the chronology nor the exact nature of this major change is known, but what is clear is that from the 1870s a currency in beads was in use also in the market of Ujiji.[55] According to Beverly Brown, this shift marked the transition from a small-scale, multicentric economy to a market-oriented economy.[56] In the market of Ujiji, moneychangers exchanged different kinds of beads into *sofi* as well as into cloth, in this way facilitating market transactions.[57] According to Verney Lovett Cameron, writing in September 1874:

> A curious currency is in vogue here, everything being priced in beads called sofi, something in appearance like small pieces of broken pipe-stem. At the commencement of the market, men with wallets full of these beads deal them out in exchange for others to people desirous of making purchases; and when the mart is closed, they receive them again from the market-people and make a profit on both transactions, after the manner usual among money-changers.[58]

In 1895, the British officer Charles Hobley decided to establish a food market in Mumia in order to facilitate the supply of food to the Eldama Ravine government station. People were induced to come to the market to sell their produce "and all the trading had to be done through the medium of beads as currency".[59]

Despite their importance in trade, the value of beads, as well as cowries, was determined in relation to cloth.[60] In Ujiji, the rate of exchange for beads was based on a cloth standard and was set each morning. This

[55] B. Brown, 'Muslim Influence in the Lake Tanganyika Region,' *African Historical Studies* 4:3 (1971) 621.

[56] B. Brown, *Ujiji: History of a Lakeside Town*, PhD Thesis, University of Boston (1973) 72.

[57] H.M. Stanley, *How I Found Livingstone* (Vercelli, White Star, 2006 reprint of the 1872 edition) 421.

[58] Cameron, *Across Africa*, 176.

[59] Hobley *Kenya*, 90–1.

[60] Cloth, in fact, circulated in association with glass beads *or* cowries. I have found very few references in the sources to the concurrent circulation of beads and cowries. One of these is the explorer Jerome Becker, who describes a market in Bunyoro, where: "Every morning after sunrise, men might be heard crying their wares throughout the camp—such as Tobacco, tobacco; two packets for either beads or simbis [cowries]! Milk to sell for beads or salt! Salt to exchange for lance heads"; quoted in Tosh, 'The Northern Interlacustrine Region,' 117.

offered to moneychangers a profitable daily business, as market prices were supplemented with service charges for any buyer not dealing in *sofi*.[61] In Buganda, the relation of cowries to cloth and the control of the *kabaka* on the imports of cloth, favoured the stability in the value of shells. The available evidence suggests, even when taking into consideration the complexity of the currency system and the fluctuating rates of exchange of international currencies in use on the coast, that the cowry in Buganda had a stable value before colonial rule.[62] From the end of the eighteenth century, the import, distribution and possession of cloth in Buganda was regulated by the *kabaka*.[63] Coastal traders could only sell cloth to the *kabaka* and his representatives. Trading cloth outside the capital was prohibited. On the other hand, cowries were generally allowed to circulate without similar restrictions.[64] According to Reid, the control of the *kabaka* over trade should not be exaggerated. Nonetheless, this control may have influenced the value of the cowry in so far as the limitations on trading cloth may have limited the circulation of the latter in the capital and markets under tight royal control.[65] The connection between the value of cloth and cowries is clearly depicted in the sources of the early colonial period, when the British administration had to introduce cowries and cloth in Uganda in order to pay troops and local staff. James MacDonald, Acting Commissioner of the Uganda Protectorate, noted that

> [O]wing to the large cloth payments due to the Government establishments in Uganda, and the hopeful signs of development of private trade, we may reasonably expect a much larger quantity of cloth introduced into Uganda during 1894–95 than in the past. This will further appreciate the value of shells unless we introduce sufficient from the coast to neutralize it, or at all events to ration our men properly [...]. At the end of last year 300 shells were equivalent to one Rupee: while shells have now appreciated to a value of 200 shells to one Rupee.[66]

[61] Stanley, *How I Found Livingstone*, 421.

[62] Pallaver, 'The African Native has no Pocket.'

[63] Reid, *Political Power in Precolonial Buganda*, 151–8.

[64] The one exception to this occurred in 1882 when *kabaka* Mutesa attempted to limit the import of cowries in order to favour the import of cloth and firearms. However, these regulations had little real effect and quickly became a dead letter. Médard, *Le Royaume du Buganda au XIXe siècle*, 133.

[65] Reid, *Political Power in Precolonial Buganda*, 158.

[66] MacDonald to Consul General Zanzibar, Port Alice, 21/10/1893, FO 107/18, NA.

In Buganda the circulation of currencies was controlled by the king. On the contrary, beads in use in other areas of the Zanzibar commercial hinterland were a currency adopted by traders to facilitate trade and were controlled by the market itself. These small-denomination currencies were always related to high-denomination currencies, like cloth and metal wires, but were also connected to local and interregional currencies, and worked in a shared concept of value, that is cattle.

The introduction of imported currencies did not lead to the displacement of regional or interregional currencies. Rather, the same economic conditions that led to the introduction of imported currencies also spurred the further use of these pre-existing currencies. The export trade in ivory and slaves caused an increase in the production and interregional trade in local products such as salt, iron hoes and tobacco that were used by caravans as exchange goods.[67] The value of imported currencies such as beads, metal wire and cloth increased proportionally with distance from the coast. The prices between Zanzibar and Tabora increased from two to five times, depending on the period, and increased again from Tabora to Lake Tanganyika or Victoria. There was often a 50–100 per cent difference in costs between Zanzibar and Tabora and the same difference between Tabora and Ujiji.[68] Therefore, merchants travelling with caravans going from inland to the coast did not use beads or cloth as currency. Instead, they bought interregional goods in the markets of the interior, which they then used along the road to purchase food and pay tributes. Burton noted that in Uzaramo, "[t]he P'házi, or chief of the district, demands a certain amount of cloth for free passage from all merchants on their way to the interior; from those returning he takes cattle, jembe, or iron hoes, shokah or hatchets […]".[69]

[67] A. Roberts, 'The Nyamwezi,' in *Tanzania before 1900. Seven Area Histories*, A.D. Roberts, ed. (Nairobi, East African Publishing House for the Historical Association of Tanzani, 1968) 117–50.

[68] W.T. Brown and B. Brown, 'East African Towns: A Shared Growth,' in *A Century of Change in Eastern Africa*, W. Arens, ed. (The Hague, Mouton, 1976) 189–90; according to Burton, between Zanzibar and Unyanyembe the prices increased five times; Burton, 'The Lake Regions of Central Equatorial Africa,' 185; according to Becker, the prices between Zanzibar and Tabora doubled; see Becker, *La Vie en Afrique ou trois ans dans l'Afrique Centrale*, Vol. 1, 466.

[69] Burton, *The Lake Regions*, 87–8 and 149.

Interregional Currencies, Shared Concepts of Value and "Marginal Gains" in the Zanzibar Commercial Hinterland

The circulation of multiple currencies created opportunities for traders who, being well aware of prices and the extent of currency areas, traded across currency zones and borders in order to obtain "marginal gains". As Guyer has shown in relation to West Africa, commercial relations between African and European traders contributed to the formation of a range of scales of value and types of transactions that enabled parties to capture marginal gains above the rates of return that would have prevailed in a single market with a single scale of value.[70] Charles Hobley described the ways in which the Kavirondo traded across currency zones:

> The great object of an Mkavirondo's life is to obtain cattle or failing that sheep and goats and all his trading is but a means to this end. [...] There is a considerable trade between Kavirondo and Usoga which is a good example of the circuitous methods of native trade. An Mkavirondo of Mumia's sells goats, sheep or hoes for brass wire which is the usual medium of exchange for their articles; he then starts off to Usoga with his brass wire where it is in considerable demand and there purchases goats and sheep; the goats and sheep he takes to Samia which is the greatest centre of the native ironworkers and there trades them for hoes which he brings back to Mumia's; in this way he about doubles his capital in a trip. When the hoes have accumulated to a sufficient extent he exchanges them for cattle at the average rate of about 20 for a cow.[71]

Good profits could also be made by exploiting the exchange rates between the coins in use on the coast and the commodity currencies circulating in the interior. Ludwig Krapf reported that traders from Mombasa could obtain great profits trading across currency zones:

> A Mombassian takes for instance a slave girl who he bought at Kiloa ... for 7 or 8 dollars or German crowns and carries her to the Wanika-country, selling her for 2 large and 2 small cows which are worth 18 dollars on the spot-with these he proceeds to the neighboring Wakamba, who bring ivory form

[70] Guyer, *Marginal Gains.*

[71] C. Hobley, 'A general report on Kavirondo', inclosure in Berkeley to Foreign Office, Port Alice, 12/5/1896, FO 2/112, NA.

> the Interior, and buys there a piece of ivory which sells at Mombas [for] 40 or 50 dollars, which sum he then takes and goes or sends to Kiloa at the proper season where he buys another supply of slaves.[72]

As these two examples show, cattle were always involved in these complex trade networks. As Hakansson points out, East Africa was integrated through a common value system based on cattle that were everywhere in demand and acted as the most valued prestige goods in social transactions.[73] For example, monetary transitions in pre-colonial Buganda were facilitated by the existence of a commonly held conceptualization of value derived from cattle. Cattle had both economic and social functions. Cattle were an accepted measure for evaluating wealth, as they served as a unit of account against which the value of prestige goods, like hoes or cloth, was measured. The credit system, which was a well-established feature of Buganda economic and social life, was based on cattle, and credit and wealth were accumulated through their acquisition and reproduction.[74] Though small value goods were valued against cowries, high-value goods were evaluated on the estimated worth of an ordinary cow, whose value remained fairly stable until the 1890s.[75] This created a shared regime of value in which various monetary changes, resulting from the adoption of the most convenient currency from the point of view of availability and transactional value, could be absorbed.[76]

According to Harold Schneider, cattle were convertible into most other things of value, "giving their producers the kind of economic freedom and multiple options we obtain with money, and if grain is not so easily convertible, then it follows that the prudent farmer, when he can, will convert his grain into livestock".[77] Livestock were used as repositories of value, and large payments, like bridewealth payments, were set, at least in part, in

[72] Quoted in J. Lamphear, 'The Kamba and the Northern Mrima Coast,' in *Pre-colonial African Trade*, 90.

[73] Thomas N. Hakansson, 'The Human Ecology of World Systems in East Africa: The Impact of the Ivory Trade,' *Human Ecology* 32 (2004) 574 and 586.

[74] L. Mair, *An African People in the Twentieth Century* (London, Routledge, 1934) 145.

[75] J.A. Rowe, *Revolution in Buganda 1856–1900. Part One: Reign of Mukabya Mutesa 1856–1884*, PhD Thesis, University of Wisconsin (1966) 47. On the value of cattle, see Médard, *Le Royaume du Buganda au XIXe siècle*, 134.

[76] Pallaver, 'The African Native has no Pocket.'

[77] H.K. Schneider, *Livestock and Equality in East Africa. The Economic Basis for Social Structure* (Bloomington, Indiana University Press, 1979) 65 and 102.

cattle.[78] The role of cattle and small domesticated animals in evaluating goods is further confirmed by the use, in some parts of East Africa, of imaginary units of account based on cattle or goats. The Turu, when dealing with problems of inheritance, calculated its total value in terms of cattle, and then partitioned it according to these terms, even though the inheritance was goats or sheep.[79] The Kikuyu had an exchange system based on an abstract goat or sheep, the *mburi*. Louis Leakey reports that:

> In assessing the amount of a fine, the value of a piece of land, or the price of any object of value, the assessment was always made in terms of *mburi*, even though the payment might be made in other things to the value of the number of *mburi* assessed. […] Looked at from another point of view, the nearest approach of the conception of a *mburi* to a unit of currency is shown by the fact that one would not go to another and ask to buy a *mburi*, any more than in our society I would go to someone and ask to buy bank notes. If a man wished to acquire *mburi*, he could do so only by making, manufacturing, growing or in some other way producing something which someone else would want to buy.[80]

Imaginary units of account were developed in order to have reliable anchors against which the value of commodities or other currencies could be ascertained and compared.[81] In order to respond to changes in patterns of trade, standard units of currency, as well as types of currencies in use, changed over time, in this way facilitating market exchanges.

East African Markets, Economic Change and the Development of Currency Areas

The use of imported currencies in East Africa was connected to global processes of industrialization. As a rich field of studies has showed in the last decades, the cultural, economic and social role of commodities cannot

[78] K. Pallaver, 'Paying in Rupees, Paying in Cents. Colonial Currencies, Labour Relations and the Payment of Wages in Kenya (1890–1920),' in *Colonialism, Institutional Change and Shifts in Global Labour Relations*, K. Hofmeester and P. de Zwart, eds. (Amsterdam, University of Amsterdam Press, 2018) 295–325.

[79] H. Schneider, 'Livestock as Food and Money,' in *The Future of Pastoral Peoples*, J.G. Galaty et al., eds. (Ottawa, International Development Research Center, 1981), 213.

[80] L.S.B. Leakey, *The Southern Kikuyu before 1903*, Vol. 1 (London, Academic Press, 1977) 503.

[81] Debin Ma, 'Money and Monetary Systems in China, in the 19th and 20th Century: An Overview,' *Economic History Working Paper*, London School of Economics (2012) 5.

ultimately be divorced from questions of technology, production and trade.[82] Competition, in the case of imported cloth, and innovation, in the case of glass beads, were key component in the organization of their global commodity chains and in the success of these commodities on the East African market.[83] The industrialization process that took place in the Western world in the nineteenth century created the conditions to produce and export great quantities of glass beads and cloth to East Africa, in this way supporting the development and expansion of a unified currency zone.

The decreasing price of commodity currencies on the coast, determined by the mechanization process in the Western world, helped the expansion of trade activities in the interior. According to Burton, the price of cloth and beads on the coast declined by half between 1802 and 1856, and this is confirmed by the data on the price of *merikani* elaborated by Sheriff, who shows a decline by 47 per cent of the cloth price between the early 1830s and 1850s, at an average of 2.5 per annum. At the same time, the price of ivory on the coast increased by about 6 per cent per year.[84]

Given the huge demand for ivory, its price, as well as that of other commodities, increased also in the interior. Between 1870 and 1890, there was an increase in the price of commodities along the central caravan road. In turn, this price increase caused a gradual devaluation of beads.[85] For example, the White Fathers, during their first travel into the interior in 1878 found beads of almost no use until Unyamwezi, except for the payment of some tributes in Ugogo. They paid their porters with cloth until Unyamwezi and with glass beads from Unyamwezi to Lake Victoria.[86] The increasing trade relations and the monetization of the economy caused a

[82] A. Appadurai, 'Introduction: Commodities and the Politics of Value,' in *The Social Life of Things: Commodities in Cultural Perspective*, A. Appadurai, ed. (Cambridge, Cambridge University Press, 1986) 35; G. Gereffi, M. Korzeniewicz and R.P. Korzeniewicz, 'Introduction: Global Commodity Chains,' in *Commodity Chains and Global Capitalism*, G. Gereffi and M. Korzeniewicz, eds. (Westport, Greenwood Press, 1994) 2.

[83] On cloth, see Prestholdt, *Domesticating the World*; on glass beads see K. Pallaver, 'From Venice to East Africa.'

[84] According to Sheriff, the accumulation of capital by Indian merchants was primarily based on the momentous divergence between the price curves of African exports and those of manufactured imports, which constituted a dynamic force for commercial expansion; Sheriff, *Slaves, Spices and Ivory in Zanzibar*, 103–4; A. Sheriff, 'Ivory and Commercial Expansion in East Africa in the Nineteenth Century,' in *Figuring African Trade*, 434.

[85] Sissons, *Economic Prosperity in Ugogo, East Africa, 1860–1890.*

[86] Rapport du Père Guillet, 8/10/1881, WF C 20-62.

gradual abandonment of glass beads in the areas that were firstly monetized. In the 1850s many varieties of glass beads were in demand along the caravan roads, but their increased circulation and decreasing value led to the dismiss of the biggest part of them as currency—even if they continued to be widely used as ornaments—and to the adoption of *sofi* beads in the markets and of a limited, generally standardized, variety of beads in other areas. For example, in the region of Ugogo, between the coast and Unyamwezi, the value of glass beads declined so dramatically that, in the 1870s, they were replaced by tobacco as the commonly accepted small-denomination currency.[87]

Building a map of the circulation of pre-colonial currencies in East Africa has a lot of potential for the reconstruction of the scale and dimensions of the expansion of coastal and regional trading activities. There were, for instance, places where imported currencies were not known at all, which testifies to the local absence of commercial contacts with the coastal economy. Along the new road opened in 1894 in the East Africa Protectorate, there were "populous districts" where *merikani* was completely unknown.[88] In 1896, Hobley reported that in the region of Mount Elgon, North of Lake Victoria, local people did not have a word to say cloth or beads: "[...] unlike all other natives I have met with, they were entirely unacquainted with cloth or beads, and have no word in their language to express the same; cowries were seen and these we were informed were imported from Unyoro being passed on through the intermediate tribes."[89]

There were some areas where only beads were used as currency, like among the Bari People, in the West Nile region and the Bukedi in North-east Uganda.[90] These were areas situated on the fringe of the commercial hinterland of Zanzibar that did not export high-valued commodities, as the absence of cloth confirms. At the same time, however, the presence of beads confirms the existence of trading activities with neighbouring areas. The extent of cowry circulation is a clear indication of the scale of Baganda trading activities and their connection with Zanzibar. The Banyoro, for instance, did not have direct contacts with coastal traders, because the

[87] Sissons, *Economic Prosperity in Ugogo, East Africa, 1860–1890*, 55–6.

[88] Gray Dawes and Co. to Under Secretary of State for Foreign Affairs, 8/8/1894, FO 107/65, NA.

[89] Hobley to Foreign Office, Mumias, 5/2/1896, FO 2/112, NA.

[90] Johnston to Salisbury, Entebbe, 18/4/1900, FO 2/298, NA; Sadler to Foreigno Office, Entebbe, 14/8/1902, FO 2/956, NA.

Kabaka impeded it. But they obtained coastal goods from the Baganda, to whom they sold ivory in exchange for cloth, beads and metal wires.[91] Cowries were in use also in Toro, Ankole and Busoga as a consequence of commercial relations with Buganda, as well as of the extension of Ganda political power.[92]

The monetary systems of nineteenth-century East Africa were much more integrated than it is generally assumed. The expansion of the ivory trade in the nineteenth century went hand in hand with the development of a relatively stable culture of commensuration and calculation over the growth of commoditization.[93]

Conclusion

The currencies that were imported into pre-colonial East Africa all shared a number of characteristics. First, they were imported along extensive networks of supply that automatically created a physical limit on money imports.[94] All imported currencies were, in fact, carried by human porters, as no other form of transport was available before the building of colonial railways in the early twentieth century. This limited the amount of currency that could be introduced into the interior. Second, imported currencies were also almost impossible to counterfeit or substitute. When the British colonized Uganda and Kenya, they made several attempts to introduce British-made cloth as a replacement for *merikani*, to no avail.[95] Third, these currencies were never re-exported, as they were currencies only for trading with Africans.[96] Finally, these currencies spread as a result of market forces. With the exception of cowries in Uganda, they were not imposed by centralized political authorities. Their circulation grew with

[91] Hobley to Foreign Office, Mumias, 5/2/1896, FO 2/112, NA.

[92] Sadler to Foreign Office, Entebbe, 14/8/1902, FO 2/956, NA.

[93] Guyer, *Marginal Gains*, 53.

[94] J.S. Hogendorn and H.A. Gemery, 'Continuity in West African Monetary History? An Outline of Monetary Development,' *African Economic History* 17 (1988) 127–46.

[95] British-made *merikani* shrunk and became flimsy when washed. It was considered of bad quality and therefore refused by the African staff in government employment, like the Sudanese troops; see Jackson, *Early Days in East Africa*; Colvile to Foreign Office, 2/4/1895, FO 107/65, NA; Crown Agents to Foreign Office, 4/9/1899, FO 2/235, NA.

[96] Joseph Inikori, 'Africa and the Globalization Process: Western Africa, 1450–1850,' *Journal of Global History*. 2:1 (2007) 84; P.D. Curtin, 'Africa and the Wider Monetary World 1350–1850,' in *Precious Metals in the Late Medieval and Early Modern Worlds*, J.F. Richards, ed. (Durham, Carolina Academic Press, 1983) 233.

the expansion of exports. Incontrollable waves of pre-colonial currencies were absorbed within African societies through market exchanges.[97]

The regional economies based on the exchange of foodstuffs, livestock, iron and salt that connected different people and ecological zones, were integrated through the external demand for ivory, slaves, copal and hides and linked to the trade circuits of the Indian Ocean.[98] By exploiting the variations in exchange rates that followed a spatial continuum, traders could optimize returns in trade goods that were in turn invested in cattle or other goods.[99] The co-existence of regional and imported currencies created opportunities for African traders to trade across currency zones and obtain marginal gains where different currency circuits overlapped. African and coastal traders operated to connect the various interfaces at place. The introduction and gradual adoption of imported commodities as currency over such a vast area facilitated commercial transactions.[100] And the use of standard measures of value made commodity currencies more manageable both as a unit of account and as a standard of value.

The arrival of coastal traders and of new goods in the interior produced significant economic changes: markets were enlarged, old trade routes extended and flows of goods increased.[101] The introduction and adoption of imported currencies facilitated commercial exchanges. Gradually, these currencies came to be used at the most important commercial nodes of intersection of the Zanzibar hinterland, like Tabora, Ujiji and the capital of Buganda. Coastal traders and Indian financers accumulated huge quantities of merchant capital, thanks to the price divergence between imported commodities and African exports. This enlarged the scale of trade, extended the frontiers of the Zanzibar commercial empire and increased the use of commodity currencies in the heart of Africa.[102]

[97] Hogendorn and Johnson, *The Shell Money of the Slave Trade.*

[98] Mwangi, 'Of Coins and Conquest,' 782.

[99] Hakansson, 'The Human Ecology of World Systems in East Africa,' 574.

[100] Mwangi, 'Of Coins and Conquest,' 782–3.

[101] Brown, *Ujiji*, 51.

[102] Sheriff, *Slaves, Spices and Ivory in Zanzibar*, 109.

CHAPTER 5

Currency and Currency Problems in Imperial Madagascar, 1820–1895

Gwyn Campbell

This chapter examines the role of currency in Madagascar in the period 1750–1895. This era was characterized by the rise of Imerina, a formerly landlocked kingdom in the central highlands of Madagascar, to the pre-eminent political power in the island, and by its attempts from the 1820s to ward off European colonial ambitions through an ambitious programme of modernisation that included attempted industrialisation through import substitution, the development of cash crops, notably coffee, sugar, vanilla and cocoa, the export of animal and forest products, notably oxen and hides, rubber, wax and hardwoods, and the exploitation of extensive gold fields. In Merina-controlled regions of Madagascar, namely the central and eastern regions of the island, foreign coinage dominated commercial transactions, although counterfeiting and disruptions to trade caused major problems that remained unresolved up to the French conquest of the island in 1895. This chapter demonstrates that currency issues formed a core reason for the failure of indigenous authorities to retain independence.

G. Campbell (✉)
Indian Ocean World Centre, McGill University, Montreal, QC, Canada

S. Serels, G. Campbell (eds.), *Currencies of the Indian Ocean World*, Palgrave Series in Indian Ocean World Studies,
https://doi.org/10.1007/978-3-030-20973-5_5

Traditional Trade and Currency

Swahili traders probably introduced coinage into northwest Madagascar from the tenth century, and from the 1500s, Swahili-imported currencies were supplemented by European coinage. Nonetheless, it took until the early seventeenth century for the use of imported coinage to reach Imerina, a small landlocked but commercially vibrant kingdom in the central highlands of Madagascar. By 1650 Imerina lubricated much long-distance trade in the interior of Madagascar and foreign money, notably the Spanish *de plata* silver piastre, became common currency in the island's main commercial centres.

However, the main boost to the foreign trade of Madagascar, and thus to the influx of coinage, was the rise of the Mascarene plantation economy from the time of Mahé de La Bourdonnais (1699–1753), governor from 1735 to 1746. On the Mascarenes, the specialization in cash crop production, and the creation of a dockyard and communications network, resulted in a spectacular rise in demand for imported provisions and labour for which Madagascar was the closest supplier. This promoted monetisation, notably in the centre and north-east of Madagascar, respectively the greatest source of slaves, and provisions.[1] Indeed, King Andriambelomasina (r. *c*.1730–1770) established a short-lived mint in Imerina that printed *tavaiky* coins. By the late eighteenth century, due to the volume of coin imported to pay for the slaves and provisions required by the burgeoning plantation economy on the Mascarenes, coins became the predominant currency in the foreign trade of north-eastern and possibly also north-western Madagascar.[2] Certainly on the north-east coast the strong bargaining position of the Malagasy allowed them to insist on payment from European traders in coin, much to the chagrin of Mascarene traders: "It is well know that the purchase of slaves in … Madagascar [necessitates] the export from Bourbon [Réunion] of a very large quantity of coins that

[1] Huguette Ly Tio Fane-Pineo: *Île de France, 1715–1746*. Tome I, *L'émergence de Port Louis* (Moka, Mahatma Gandhi Institute, 1993); Auguste Toussaint, *History of Mauritius* (London, Macmillan, 1977).

[2] Morice, 'Plan of Operation for the Trade of the Coast of East Africa' (n.d.) and *idem*, 'Plan for a Trading Centre on the East Coast of Africa' (Île de France, 24 Sep. 1777)—in *The French at Kilwa Island*, G.S.P. Freeman-Grenville, ed. (Oxford, Clarendon Press, 1965) 190, 196; Gwyn Campbell, *The Role of the London Missionary Society in the Rise of the Merina Empire, 1810–1861*. PhD, University of Wales, Swansea (1985) 32–129; *idem*, 'Madagascar and the Slave Trade, 1810–1895,' *Journal of African History* 22:2 (1981) 203–27.

flows there [to Madagascar]; which explains the penury of cash in our island."[3] Some Malagasy recipients of imported coinage hoarded it, or transformed it directly into jewellery, while most used it to engage in further trade. As a result, $96,000 or an estimated 80 per cent of east coast foreign trade earnings were used to pay Swahili traders for imported textiles and muskets. Indian traders subsequently sent most gold and silver coinage to India.[4]

Nevertheless, by 1810, coins, alongside gunpowder and cloth, constituted one of the main forms of domestic Malagasy currency, as is confirmed by the steady inflation of prices in the island. Gunpowder, cloth and coins formed a distinct category in that they could be subdivided to represent the value of the smallest purchase and were generally accepted in payment for goods, taxes and fines throughout the island. However, slaves, cattle, iron bars, muskets, flints, cartridges, knives, scissors, razors, mirrors, coral and other beads, earrings, thimbles, seeds and salt all enjoyed occasional use as currencies, notably outside the main centres of foreign trade (Table 5.1).[5]

[3] Lebel to M. le Baron Milius, St. Leu, 20 Oct. 1819, FM (Fonds ministériels) SG (Série géographique) REU//515-5990, Archives d'Outre-Mer, Aix-en-Provence.

[4] Hastie, 'Diary' (1817) 157, 188 CO 167/34, National Archives, Kew (henceforth NAK); *idem*, 'Diary' (1824–1825), CO 167/78, NAK; Samuel Copland, *A History of Madagascar* (London, Burton and Smith, 1822) 12–18; Samuel Oliver, *Madagascar. An Historical and Descriptive Account of the Island and Its Former Dependencies*, Vol. 2 (London, Macmillan, 1886) 16–17; Alfred & Guillaume Grandidier, Histoire *Physique, Naturelle et Politique de* Madagascar 4. *Ethnographie de Madagascar* Tome 4.1 (Paris, Imprimérie Nationale, 1908) 106, 160, 162, 171 and (1928) 260, 302–3, 322–3, 327, 332; Alfred Horn, *The Waters of Africa* (London, Jonathan Cape, 1929) 97; Nicolas Mayeur, 'Voyage dans le nord de Madagascar' (1775) 86, British Library (henceforth BL), Add.18128; *idem*, 'Voyage au pays d'ancove, par le pays d'ancaye autrement dit des Baizangouzangoux' (1785) 227, BL Add.18128; Anon, 'Mémoire historique et politique sur l'Isle de Madagascar' (1790) 55, BL Add.18126; Dumaine, 'Voyage à la côte de l'ouest, autrement dite pays des Séclaves' (1793) 294–7, BL Add.18128; Chapelier, 'lettres adressées au citoyen préfet de l'ile de France, de décembre 1803 en mai 1805,' *Bulletin de l'Académie Malgache* (hereafter *BAM*) 4 (1905–1906) 34.

[5] Le Sage, 'Mission to Madagascar' (1816) 99, CO 167/34, NAK; Raombana, *Histoires* (1853) 19, 24, Académie Malgache, Tsimbazaza, Antananarivo; Oliver, *Madagascar*, Vol. 2, 205, 209; Lars Dahle, 'The influence of Arabs on the Malagasy Language,' *Antananarivo Annual and Madagascar Magazine* (hereafter *AAMM*) 2 (1876) 84, 105–13; P. Taix, 'Extrait du diaire de Tamatave' (14 janvier 1885) in *idem*, 'Tamatave: Notes historiques' (1908), Archives historiques de la Vice-Province Société de Jésus de Madagascar, Antananarivo; J.S. Chauvicourt, 'Les premières monnaies de Madagascar,' *Bulletin de Madagascar* 261 (1968) 146–52; Grandidier, *Histoire* (1908) 268; E.A. Alpers, 'The French

Table 5.1 Currencies, 1800

Easily divisible	*Not easily divisible*	*Non-divisible*
Cloth	Iron bars	Slaves
Coinage (NE & centre)	Muskets	Cattle: little illness (capital; bank; sacred—not eaten except ancestral ritual)
Gunpowder	Flints	
Salt	Cartridges	
Beads	Knives	
Seeds	Scissors	
	Razors	
	Mirrors	
	Earrings	
	Thimbles	

The Rise of Imperial Madagascar

The British conquest of the French Mascarenes in 1810 and retention of Mauritius at the 1814 Treaty of Paris altered the situation in Madagascar considerably. The Franco-British dispute severely disrupted commercial exchange in the region, and curtailed revenue for the Merina regime. Foreign trade resumed from 1815, but coastal entities, notably the Boina Sakalava to the northwest and the Betsimisaraka and Betanimena to the east, placed major obstacles in the path of Merina communications with the main ports of Majunga and Tamatave. The influx of foreign currency was curtailed as export earnings fell from approximately $200,000 in 1810 and $22,500 in 1817 to a low of $1500 by 1820. The decline in export earnings was reflected in the fall in average individual slave prices on the Merina market from $45 in 1817 to only $3 in 1820.[6] This in large part

Slave Trade,' *Historical Association of Tanzania paper* 3 (1967) 87, 101–4; Lars Sundström, *The Exchange Economy of Pre-Colonial tropical Africa* (New York, St. Martin's Press, 1974) 96–8; Micheline Rasoamiaramanana, *Aspects économiques et sociaux de la vie à Majunga entre 1862 et 1881*. thèse, Université de Madagascar (1973) 55; Campbell, 'Role of the London Missionary Society,' 66–7.

[6]Chapelier, 'Lettres en mission à Madagascar de décembre 1803 en mai 1805,' ed. M. Jully, *Bulletin de l'Académie Malgache* (1904) 34; Chazal, 'Notes' (1816) 24, British Library (henceforth BL) Add.18135; Chardenoux, 'Journal' (1816) 163; N. Leminier, 'Notes sur une excursion faite dans l'intérieur de l'Île de Madagascar en 1825,' *BdM* 292 (1970) 797; Hastie, 'Diary' (1817) 137, 147, 157, 164, 170, 177, 188–9, 197, 211; *idem*, 'Diary' (1820) 489, CO 167/50, NAK; Raombana, *Histoires*, 21, 67, 82, 93–4; Raombana,

explains why Radama I, King of Imerina (r. 1810–1828), eagerly accepted the Britanno-Merina Treaty of 1820 in which he was recognized as sovereign of the entire island, guaranteed the military assistance and arms needed to substantiate that claim and, in return for a ban on slave exports, was provided by the British with an annual compensation of $20,000 in goods and cash ($1000 in gold and $1000 in silver coins).[7]

By 1822, cash crop plantations and workshops (manufacturing furniture, clothes and leather goods) had been established in Imerina and with them so had the promise of export alternatives to slaves and an associated strong positive balance of trade and plentiful money supply. Moreover, by 1825, Merina garrisons had been established in all major east coast ports, and in Majunga, the predominant west coast port. In these ports, Merina officials imposed duties on foreign trade of 10 per cent ad valorem, except for the British who, by treaty, paid 5 per cent (Map 5.1).[8]

Nevertheless, by 1825, it was obvious to the Merina crown that the Britanno-Merina Treaty had failed to fulfil its promise. There were multiple reasons for this. First, non-British foreign trade transferred to areas independent of Merina rule where duties were cheaper, slaves were available and all commodities could be purchased by barter. Thus the proportion of Réunionnais ships trading in non-Merina ports increased from 42 per cent in 1819 to 61 per cent by 1823.[9] Second, the Merina failed to develop alternative exports to slaves such as silk cloth and, quintessentially, European cash crops such as wheat and oats. Third, Radama I embarked

'Texts,' 13; William Ellis, *History of Madagascar*, Vol. 2 (London, Fisher, 1838) 16, 198; G.-S. Chapus et G. Mondain, 'Un chapitre inconnu. Des rapports de Maurice et de Madagascar,' *Bulletin de l'Académie Malgache* 30 (1951–1952) 117; François Callet, *Histoire des Rois* (Tananarive, Éditions de la Librairie de Madagascar, 1974) 441–2, 658, 120; Prud'homme, 'Contribution à l'histoire de l'Imerina,' in 'Notes d'histoire malgache,' *BAM* 14 (1931); G.-S. Chapus, 'le soin du bien-être du peuple sous le règne d'Andrianampoinimerina,' *BAM* 30 (1951–1952) 1; Jean Valette, *Études sur le règne de Radama Ier* (Tananarive, Imprimérie Nationale, 1962) 19; Oliver, *Madagascar*, Vol. I, 221–2, 227–9, 252–3; *idem*, 'General Hall and the Export Slave Trade from Madagascar. A Statement and a Vindication,' *AAMM* 12 (1888) 678; Grandidier, *Histoire* (1908) 113, 233, 235, 249–52, 268 and (1928) 113, 235, 268, 297, 335; Campbell, 'Madagascar and the Slave Trade,' 206, 208.

[7] Gwyn Campbell, 'The Adoption of Autarky in Imperial Madagascar, 1820–1835,' *Journal of African History* 28:3 (1987) 398–9.

[8] Gwyn Campbell, *An Economic History of Imperial Madagascar, 1750–1895: The Rise and Fall of an Island Empire* (Cambridge, Cambridge University Press, 2005) 70.

[9] Campbell, *An Economic History of Imperial Madagascar*, 70–1.

Map 5.1 The Southwest Indian Ocean in the nineteenth century (drawn up by the Indian Ocean World Centre, McGill University)

on a campaign of imperial expansion, the positive returns on which were less than had been expected. Though the crown was entitled to about 25 per cent of all booty seized during military campaigns, the senior army officers who led campaigns devastated conquered provinces. They preferred plundering and laying waste much fertile territory to seizing provincial assets that they would have to hand over to the crown.[10] Consequently,

[10] Duhaut-Cilly, 'Notices sur le royaume d'Emirne, sur la capitale de Tananarivou et sur le gouvernement de Rhadama,' in Jean Valette, 'Deux documents français sur Madagascar en 1825; les rapports Duhaut-Cilly et Frère,' *BAM* 16:1–2 (1968) 237.

these campaigns failed to boost royal coffers with booty and additional tax revenue. Instead, military campaigns of imperial expeditions, because they required the crown to pay for armaments and other military equipment, emptied the Merina treasury of money. As Mauritian trader Louis Blancard explained:

> As his Majesty Radama, having subjugated almost all Madagascar, has been obliged to greatly expand his army and to maintain it continually on a war footing, this has incurred a growth in expenditure which has forced him to increase his revenues.[11]

Moreover, the crown received insufficient compensation from the British for the slave export ban. After the slave export ban, Merina royal revenue slumped dramatically, from $32,927 in 1821 to $22,360 in 1822. By 1824 it had increased to $50,000, but still fell far short of crown requirements.[12] Robert Farquhar, Governor of Mauritius (1810–1823), promised an annual compensation valued at $20,000. From 1820 to 1826, Radama I received $18,000 in cash, in addition to military and other goods. Total compensation amounted to $104,853 worth of species and goods, $35,147 short of that promised. Had the slave export ban not been imposed, royal revenue, raised mostly in cash from taxes on slave exports for the period 1820–1826, would probably have totalled between $198,310 and $204,680.[13] No Merina slave dealer other than the king received compensation for loss of slave export earnings, which over the period 1820–1826 would probably have totalled about $2.5 million. Following the signing of the treaty, Radama I promised the Merina elite compensation for the slave export ban. However, the royal treasury lacked the funds to pay these claims and thus erstwhile elite slave traders determined to reap immediate benefits from imperial expansion within the island, albeit at the crown's expense (Table 5.2).

[11] Louis Blancard to Governor of Mauritius, in Chapus & Mondain, 'Un chapitre inconnu,' 117; see also Duhaut-Cilly, 'Notice sur le royaume d'Emirne,' 238–9.

[12] Campbell, 'Role of the London Missionary Society,' 172–7; Duhaut-Cilly, 'Notices sur le royaume d'Emirne,' 238–9.

[13] Farquhar to Earl Bathurst, Port Louis, 29 July 1822, CO.167/63 and Idem, 'Minute' on Madagascar (Port Louis, August 1822), CO 167/63—NAK; 'Expenses Incurred by the Government on Mauritius on Account of Madagascar,' *House of Commons Parliamentary Papers* 26 (1828) 72–82; Campbell, 'Madagascar and the Slave Trade,' 206, 208.

Table 5.2 Financial compensation for the Merina Ban on slave exports, 1820–1826[a]

Currency	*1820*	*1821*	*1822*	*1823*	*1824*	*1825*	*1826*
Gold Mohurs	750						
$ Spanish	1250		4000	2000		4000	
$ Currency		5851	37,000	9070	6430	12,785	
£ Sterling							3667
Total equivalent in $ Spanish at current exchange rates	8000	3433	26,932	9490	5841	15,762	15,717

[a]Calculations based on data from "expenses incurred" (1828) 72–82; Hastie, "Diary" (1817) 493

In addition, the treaty failed to compensate Radama I for the profit that would have accrued from the export of royal slaves, estimated at a minimum of $1,049,580 for the period 1820–1826. It further failed to compensate him for the decreased value of the royal monopoly on gunpowder imports. Previous to the treaty, Radama I had imported gunpowder in exchange for exported slaves. The domestic retail value of the gunpowder that would have been obtained in exchange for potential royal slave exports from 1820 to 1826 amounted to at least $10 million (although in reality most of the powder would have been stockpiled in imperial arsenals). Under treaty compensation, Radama I received a maximum of $1760 worth of gunpowder up to 1823. Thereafter, he was obliged to pay for additional gunpowder imports in cash.[14] Furthermore, over the same period (1820–1826), Merina slave dealers other than the king lost an estimated $2.5 million in earnings due to the slave export ban. Thus the prohibition on slave exports reduced incomes, the money supply, demand for imports and, as commerce stagnated, the general trade duty revenue collected by the Merina crown levied at a rate of 20 per cent of declared Merina trader profits, $4 per slave sold and 2 per cent of the price of goods purchased from Indian and Swahili merchants.[15] As LMS missionary John Canham stated in 1824:

[14] Hastie, 'Diary' (1817) 188; *idem*, 'Diary' (1820) 472.

[15] Jones and Griffiths to LMS, Antananarivo, 2 June 1824, LMS, Madagascar Incoming Letters, B2.F1.JA, CWM Archives, SOAS; Hastie, 'Diary' (1817) 143, 148, 188; *idem*, 'Diary' (1820), 484, 493, 496; *idem*, 'Diary' (1822), CO 167/63, NAK; Hastie to Barry, Antananarivo, 22 April 1824, CO.167/78, pt.I, 43, NAK; Nicolas Mayeur, 'Voyage au pays d'ancove, autrement dit des hovas ou Amboilamba dans l'intérieur des terres, Isle de Madagascar' (1777) 177–80, BL Add.18128; Duhaut-Cilly, 'Notice sur le royaume d'Emirne,' 238–9; Alfred Grandidier, 'Property among the Malagasy' (trans. James Sibree), *AAMM* 22 (1898) 228, 230.

> The fact is there is no money in the country, nor any channel to bring it. I am often told by the people that when they sold slaves they had plenty of money, but since the slave trade ceased they are become impoverished.[16]

As a result, in 1825–1826, Radama I and his successor Ranavalona I (r.1828–1861) rejected the free trade clauses of the British treaty and adopted autarkic policies aimed at increasing the influx of cash, and promoting economic development through import substitution. Economic progress and higher government revenue would be achieved through the erection of high tariffs, and the regulation of industry and commerce through state monopolies. From 1826 to 1834, customs duties were generally raised from 5 to between 20 and 25 per cent *ad valorem*. Though they were lowered to 5 per cent in 1834, in 1842 they were doubled to 10 per cent. To ensure compliance with the new duties, foreign commerce was restricted to 12 ports.[17] Moreover, from 1824 to 1837, the Merina crown entered into monopolistic foreign trade contracts with about 5 Mascarene individuals or syndicates, and into industrial contracts with about 20 European or Mauritian artisans.[18]

Radama I also ended experiments with wage labour for Merina subjects, and reduced cash payments to foreigners working for the crown. Under the new system, in lieu of full wages, all foreign artisans were provided with housing, servants and food through *fanompoana*, or unremunerated forced labour for the state. They were additionally granted a proportion of the goods they produced. For the crown, this reduced most artisan wages to an annual minimum of $900 from 1826 to 1828, although exceptionally valued craftsmen earned far more: In 1833, for instance, Jean Laborde (1805–1878), who orchestrated a mini-industrial revolution in Imerina, signed a two-year contract for $4500.[19] Further, the

[16] Canham to Burder, Ifenoarivo, 5 Nov. 1824, LMS, Madagascar Incoming Letters, B2.F1.JD, CWM Archives, SOAS; see also Campbell, 'Role of the London Missionary Society,' 171–88.

[17] Campbell, 'Role of the London Missionary Society,' 189–91, 206, 319; G.M. Razi, 'Sources d'histoire malgache aux Etats-Unis, 1792–1882,' Communication présentée le 6 septembre au Colloque des Historiens et Juristes lors du 75ème anniversaire de l'Académie malgache (6 septembre 1977) 13.

[18] Campbell, Campbell, 'Role of the London Missionary Society,' 171–215, 235–70, 293–324.

[19] Campbell, 'Role of the London Missionary Society,' 245, 259, 262.

crown defrayed any necessary European wage and associated "industrial" costs through extraordinary taxation. In 1837, two levies were imposed. The first, $1.00 on every slave owned, was earmarked for the $31,800 owed to Napoléon de Lastelle (1802–1856) for imported European muskets. The second, an additional poll tax of $0.25, raised $70,000. This prompted a further extraordinary levy which yielded the $100,000 required to finance the construction by Laborde of the Mantasoa (Isoatsimanampiovana) cannon foundry in 1837–1839. These additional taxes obliged many subjects to borrow at exorbitant interest rates from, or sell cattle to, members of the court whose monopoly of cattle exports enabled them to dictate a sale price of $0.071 a bullock, which they resold to foreign merchants on the coast for $15.[20]

From the 1820s to 1850s, Madagascar experienced an acute shortage in the money supply due to the universal application of *fanompoana* within Merina domains, the expense of military campaigns against domestic (continual until 1853) and foreign (1828–1831, 1845) enemies, severe disruptions of foreign trade (notably from 1829 to 1831, 1845 to 1853) high levels of arms imports because local arms production proved insufficient. However, these trends were reversed from 1861 to 1875 when there was a marked influx of foreign currency as a result of relative commercial prosperity brought about by the liberalization of foreign trade, a dramatic growth of exports and the absence of war. In Toamasina in 1866, it was noted that "all trading is done exclusively in cash",[21] while on the plateau the surge in foreign trade from 1870 to 1875 induced a "great influx of coins".[22] Available commercial statistics, backed by narrative sources, indicate that the Merina Empire maintained a positive balance of trade for almost a decade from 1865. A particularly large influx of specie in 1872 raised commodity prices and wages. Moreover, increased trade increased the number of porters—the only significant group of salaried workers—who considerably boosted specie circulation and widened the concept of a cash economy within Madagascar.[23]

[20] Oliver, *Madagascar*, Vol. 2, 196.

[21] Finkelmeier to Seward, Tamatave, 1 Oct. 1866, Despatches of United States Consuls in Tamatave, 1853–1906, United States National Archives, Washington, DC (hereafter *USNA*).

[22] Report of the Building Sub-Committee, Imerina District Committee Letterbook (1875–97) 38–49, Archives of the Fiangonana Jesosy Kristy aty Madagascar, Antananarivo (hereafter *FJKM*).

[23] Gwyn Campbell, 'Labour and the Transport Problem in Imperial Madagascar, 1810–1895,' *Journal of African History* 21:3 (1980) 355.

Nevertheless, the surplus on visible commodity trade steadily diminished from 1870 and, by 1876, had evaporated. War from 1883 to 1885 and the imposition by the French of a $2 million war indemnity in 1885 accentuated the problem, and prompted the Merina regime, for the first time, to start exploiting the island's considerable gold deposits. To do so, they applied *fanompoana* in gold-bearing regions on a hitherto unprecedented scale, and to women and children as well as men. However, foreign traders immediately established a large black market for gold which they chose to ship out in preference to coins. Indeed, an estimated 50 per cent of all gold (measured in Malagasy ounces, represented by the weight of a Mexican dollar—approximately 0.958 of a troy ounce)[24] was produced illegally. This indicates that, had the royal monopoly been effective, imperial gold deposits might have enabled the Merina court to meet their financial commitments. Tight supervision of alluvial workings, which often spread for miles along a multitude of minor creeks and were illicitly exploited even by foreigners, was impossible. Detection of smuggled ore also proved difficult. Most gold was ground to dust and sealed in the hollow of bamboo, used as porters' shoulder poles and in the manufacture of cases and *filanzana* (palanquin). Consequently, unlike specie, gold transport in Madagascar was secure: An American agent reported in March 1893 that there had been no known losses of gold in transit between Antananarivo and Toamasina.[25] As early as 1884, it was noted:

> gold-dust is now becoming more and more plentiful in Madagascar, and there is not a foreigner in Antananarivo but will tell you that the Malagasy are daily bringing it in to him for sale. Some bring in as much as 2000 dollars worth at a time.[26]

In the northwest, large-scale smuggling caused the court to declare it a capital offence. "Gold" spies were employed in the main commercial centres and, from 1890, all Malagasy entering Indian or European shops in Majunga were searched. It was commented of the neighbouring "gold" town of Maevatanana:

[24] Raymond Decary, 'L'ancien régime de l'or à Madagascar,' *BAM* 40 (1962) 83–96; *Madagascar Times* (3 Sep. 1884) 328; Gwyn Campbell, 'Gold Mining and the French Takeover of Madagascar, 1883–1914,' *African Economic History* 17 (1988) 99–126.

[25] Ryder to Ropes Emmerton & Co, Tamatave, 27 March 1893, B46.F1 (Jan-July 1893)—Emmerton & Co., and Arnold, Hines & Co., Partner and Agency Records (hereafter *REC/CR-MZL*).

[26] *Madagascar Times* (3 Sep. 1884).

> People working steal the gold, sell it, and, if caught, their heads are cut off and stuck on poles. It is reported that there are dozens of heads of gold-stealers and so-called robbers stuck up like this at Maevatanarivo [Maevatanana]. … Lately I have heard that a young girl of twelve or thirteen years, along with a young man, were caught with a small quantity of gold on them at Maeratanarivo [Maevatanana] and their heads were sawn off by a spear-head, taking hours over it.[27]

One consequence of the inadequate money supply was that the use of coinage was largely restricted to the main Merina-controlled commercial centres. In the areas of Madagascar that remained independent of Merina control, commodity monies, chiefly cloth, circulated as mediums of exchange until after the French conquest of the island in 1896. Thus a missionary remarked of the Sakalava who dominated the western plains and littoral of Madagascar:

> Money in the shape of coin is of little account among the Sakalava, except for use as personal ornaments; wages, where there are any, are nearly always reckoned in fathoms of cloth, but gunpowder, beads, trinkets, and coloured pocket handkerchiefs, the gaudier the better, are readily accepted for barter. The dollar, i.e. the French five-franc piece, is in use to a small extent, but not the cut-money employed in other parts of Madagascar. The latter is not current at all, but if the piece happen to be triangular in shape the natives accept it in exchange and then drill a hole through the apex, and thus suspend it in the centre of the forehead.[28]

Secondly, the circulating volume of whole coins was insufficient, even in times of relative prosperity, as in the late 1860s, to prevent the morselisation of coins. This had a long tradition for as early as 1785 *mpanakalo-vola*, or moneychangers in the plateau interior were using a cold chisel to cut whole coins into fractions (termed *vakim-bola* or *torotorombola*) of $1.00, $0.50, $0.25, $0.125 and $0.0625, determined by weight measured in rice grains.[29] While appearing to many observers to be peculiarly Malagasy, the system derived from that used by Arab merchants, which was in turn based upon the basic monetary weights used in Europe.

[27] Anon, 'Gold in Madagascar,' in *Anti-slavery Reporter* (March and April 1890) 69–70.

[28] George Herbert Smith, *Among the Menabe; or, Thirteen Months on the West Coast of Madagascar* (London, SPCK, 1896) 35–6; see also ibid., 18–19.

[29] See museum examples in Zoë Crossland, *Ancestral Encounters in Highland Madagascar: Material Signs and Traces of the Dead* (Cambridge, Cambridge University Press, 2014) 105.

Table 5.3 Malagasy dollar subdivisions and rice equivalents[a]

Dollar subdivisions	*Equivalence in rice grains*
1.0000	720
0.5000	360
0.2500	180
0.1250	90
0.0625	45

[a]Callet, *Histoire des Rois*, 918; R. Baron, "Malagasy Terms of Monetary Values", *AAMM* 14 (1890) 191–2

Table 5.4 Malagasy monetary weights expressed in rice grains

Name	*Value ($)*	*Equivalent in moist grains*	*Equivalent in dry grains*
Voamena	0.0416666	30	40
Ilavoamena	0.0208333	15	20
Eranambatry	0.0138888	10	13
Varifitoventy	0.0097216	7	10
Varienimbenty	0.0083328	6	8
Varidimiventy	0.0069440	5	7
Variefabenty	0.0555555	4	5
Variteloventy	0.0041664	3	4
Variroaventy	0.0027776	2	3
Variraiventy	0.0013888	1	1.5

Callet, *Histoire des Rois*, 918; Baron, "Malagasy Terms", 191–2

Moneychangers retailed cut coinage in local markets where they received a commission (*sandamparantsa*) of $0.042–$0.125 for every dollar changed, depending on the supply of whole to cut dollars—a ratio that could change daily.[30] As whole and cut coins were weighed to determine their value, both parties to a transaction possessed a pair iron or brass scales (*mizana*) (Tables 5.3 and 5.4).

Though widespread, the system of cut coinage caused considerable problems. First, the small standard scales that were commonly used to evaluate coins were accurate for coins weighing up to 54 g but not for those that weighed more than that.[31] In addition, false weights and loaded

[30]Oliver, *Madagascar*, Vol.2, 206; Callet, *Histoire des Rois*, 919; *Madagascar Times* (7 April 1888); Campbell, 'Role of the London Missionary Society,' 69.

[31]The use of scales, which were probably introduced by the Arabs, spread at the same rate as the use of money—Gunpowder and piastres were generally the only commodities to be measured on scales—see Callet, *Histoire des Rois*, 71; Dahle, 'Influence of Arabs,' 85; Oliver, *Madagascar*, Vol. 2, 210.

scales were commonly used even though the Merina court had by 1810 legislated the use of five iron weights possessing fixed equivalent weights in *ariary* or dollars and in fractions thereof (27 g, 13.5 g, 6.75 g, 3.375 g and 2.25 g).[32] The procedure for weighing was open to further manipulation because it was based on the weight of rice. Though the traditional system was based on weight of moist grains of de-husked rice, from the 1820s the Merina utilised a dual rice-grain weight system using both moist and dry rice grains. Moneychangers profited from this dual system by employing the heavier moist grains when making purchases, and when selling, using the lighter dry grains. This enabled them to represent $0.749 in cut money as the equivalent of a dollar. With his commission added, a moneychanger could expect to make, at a time of rising demand for cut money, approximately $0.375 on every dollar changed.[33] Additionally, weighing of money inevitably delayed commercial exchange because it gave rise to disputes. Both parties carefully weighed the money on their respective scales, often using fraudulent weights and producing disparate results that would have to be renegotiated. Thus transactions involving money could well take longer than barter exchange. For instance, in the early 1890s, Louis Catat estimated that it could take 30 minutes at market to conclude the purchase of a single chicken.[34]

Third, Madagascar, which did not mint its own coinage, accepted a variety of foreign coins. In the early 1800s, Spanish and Mexican piastres of the Hispanic Union comprised the bulk of coins in circulation in the island. From the 1820s, these were joined by Mexican dollars shipped in quantity to Africa from European financial centres, notably London, Amsterdam, and the Iberian and Italian ports. The main coins in circulation were the Spanish *colonne* piastre, and silver dollars; some of the latter bore the images of Charles II and IV, and Ferdinand VII—introduced in 1732 and 1772 respectively (and equivalent in 1780 to 5.6 French francs)—but most common was the Maria Theresa dollar which was first minted in 1751, the year of Maria Theresa's coronation as empress of

[32] The term *ariary*, used for, derives from the Arabic *ar-riyal* or *ar-rial*, which in turn comes from the Spanish *real*—27g was also the weight of the Venetian ounce, which constituted the basis of the Venetian *denier*—Dahle, 'Influence of Arabs,' 84–5; Baron, 'Malagasy Terms,' 192; Campbell, 'Role of the London Missionary Society,' 65.

[33] Callet, *Histoire des Rois*, 918; Baron, 'Malagasy Terms,' 191–2.

[34] Louis Catat, *Voyage à Madagascar, 1889–90* (Paris, Hachette, 1895) 14.

Austria. The Maria Theresa dollar gained such popularity in the east, where European silver and gold commanded a significant premium that annual production of the coin rose from 583,750 in 1751 to 5,091,055 in 1765. When the empress died in 1780, the Austrian government continued to mint coins carrying her effigy, and these soon constituted the standard currency of the western Indian Ocean. Thus on the east African coast, the imperial Austrian dollar circulated from as early as 1754. The Venetian sequin was also accepted there, but was less important.[35] However, in the 1850s the Mexican dollar, which until then was used on Mauritius for servicing the Madagascar trade, was displaced by the French five-franc piece. By 1855, this piece had gained widespread acceptance in Madagascar where it soon became the dominant coin.[36] In addition, the rupee, a standard currency on Mauritius from 1876, also entered east and northwest Madagascar, and by 1890 had gained widespread acceptance on the coast south of Majunga.[37]

Mayeur noted of Imerina in the late eighteenth century, "Provided it is made of silver, each and every minted coin is acceptable to them".[38] All foreign coins were initially accepted as *ariary*, or the equivalent of the Hispanic dollar. This posed problems both because of the different silver content of the various coins, and the use of cut coins which Malagasy silver smiths frequently adulterated with iron, tin and copper (Table 5.5).[39]

Currency speculation accentuated the situation. Speculation started in the 1860s trade boom when it became apparent that the various coins in

[35] Freeman-Grenville, *French at Kilwa Island*, 25, 52, 118; Richard Pankhurst, *Economic History of Ethiopia, 1800–1935* (Addis Ababa, Haile Sellassie I University Press, 1968) 468; Campbell, 'Role of the London Missionary Society,' 67–8.

[36] Ida Pfieffer, *Voyage à Madagascar* (Paris, Librarie Hachette, 1881) 203–4; Robert Chalmers, *A History of Currency in the British Colonies* (London, H.M. Stationery Office, 1893) 367 fn.

[37] J.O. Ryder to Arnold, Hines & Co., and Ropes, Emmerton & Co., Nossi Bé, 24 Jul 1884, Partner and Agency Records. Madagascar Agencies. Correspondence Sent. Letterbook 1884–1887 (February–May 1884), Essex Institute, Bx.44. F.5; Campbell, 'Role of the London Missionary Society,' 68.

[38] Mayeur, 'Voyage au pays d'ancove' (1777) 176–7.

[39] Mayeur, 'Voyage au pays d'ancove' (1777) 176–7; Milices, 'Mémoire sur les moyens de former pour le Roi dans l'isle de Madagascar un établissement de culture, de commerce, et d'entrepôt général pour l'Europe, l'Asie, et l'Afrique' (1780) 20, BL Add.18136; Legentil, 'Voyage à Madagascar' (1781) 557, *BL*.Add.18126; Jacques Dez, 'Considérations sur les prix pratiqués à Tananarive en 1870,' *BAM* 40 (1962) 42–61; Raymond Decary, 'Moeurs maritimes au XVII siècle,' *BAM* 18 (1935) 37–8; Alpers, 'French Slave Trade,' 87, 101–4; Henri Dubois, *Monographie des Betsileo (Madagascar)* (Paris, Institut d'ethnologie, 1938) 601.

Table 5.5 Malagasy terms for dollars

	Term	*Meaning*
Pre-1800	Behatoka	Large neck
	Amparitra	Stretched out like a corpse
	Ampanga	Crown of fern leaves (i.e. Austrian dollar)
	Helatra	Lightening
	Tokazo	A solitary tree
	Adohalambo	An arch
From c.1820	Tombotsisina	"Growth on the edge" (= indentation on edge of French 5 franc coin)
	Malamakely	"Small smooth one" (Mexican dollar with effigy of Napoleon 1 introduced in 1880s)
	Ngita	Well-twisted cord/woolly hair
	Tanomasoandro	The sun and its rays
	Kelihandrina	Small forehead (a coin depicting man with large head and small face)
	Tsanganolona	"Shape of a person" (a 5 franc coin with 3 standing allegorical figures on its obverse)
	Belaka	"Full faced" (type of dollar)
	Tranompitaratra	A window frame (refers to coin with outline relief of mirror frame in reverse)

Campbell, *Economic History of Imperial Madagascar*, 288

circulation, traditionally all accepted at par, possessed different silver contents. For example, the Maria Theresa dollar contained less silver than the Spanish piastre, and the New Mexican dollar, issued in the 1880s and bearing the image of Napoleon I, contained 8 per cent less silver than the dominant five-franc piece. When gold was worked into the piastre, the latter was considered 12 times more valuable than its silver counterpart, despite the fact that internationally gold was normally accepted as being only 8 times the value of silver.[40] In the 1880s, speculators such as the American firm of *George Ropes* flooded the island with new Mexican coins, which they purchased in bulk in the United States and used to meet customs duties and other obligations in Madagascar. However, from 1886 the French refused indemnity payments from the imperial court in coins

[40] Mayeur, 'Voyage au pays d'ancove' (1777) 176–7; Milices, 'Mémoire' (1780) 20; Legentil, 'Voyage à Madagascar' (1781) 557; Dez, 'Considérations sur les prix'; Decary, 'Moeurs maritimes,' 37–8; Alpers, 'French Slave Trade,' 87, 101–4; Dubois, *Monographie des Betsileo*, 601.

with a silver content less than that of an unsullied five-franc piece.[41] In similar circumstances, in Merina-controlled regions of the west coast in 1879, the imperial government had attempted in vain to ban the rupee, the circulation of which permitted considerable exploitation of exchange rates. Thus in 1889, an American trader complained of his Swahili agent on Nosy Be, a French-controlled island off the northwest coast:

> I am thinking seriously of returning to the old custom of giving Sheik Adam our limits in dollars instead of, as at present, in Rs [rupees] as he buys nearly all our produce in dollars and it creates thus an exchange a/c between ourselves and him in which we are always I believe the losers. On a recent shipment of five francs from Nossi-be of 14000 bought there at 280 per 100 Sheik [*sic*] would only allow 270 making a loss to us of $35 or 2½%.[42]

The Merina court broached the question of currency reform several times. Radama I, like some of his predecessors, entertained the idea of minting a Malagasy coinage with the short-term aim of devaluing the currency to relieve state finances. In 1826, several 13g silver coins were minted, 36 mm. in diameter and embossed with the royal profile. They were intended to pass as *loso*, even though they were 0.5g lighter. However, few such coins entered circulation and the venture crumbled due to a shortage of domestic silver deposits and to autarkic policies that, like state trade monopolies, raised expectations of increased foreign exchange earnings.[43] Thereafter, little was done until the build-up to the Franco-Merina War. Article 160 of the Merina Code of 1881 stipulated that the only coins to be accepted as standard monies at par would be the Mexican and Spanish dollars, the five-franc piece of Subalpine Gaul and Louis XIII, "and any other dollars that are smooth by usage or that have the inscription on the exergue engraved instead of being in relief".[44] Also, some measures were taken to counter adulteration; for instance, between May and September 1884, government officials seized on Merina markets counterfeit coins nominally valued at $52.[45] However, such measures proved woefully inadequate.

[41] Campbell, 'Role of the London Missionary Society,' 68.
[42] Bachelder to Ropes, Emmerton & Co, Mojanga, 23 Jan. 1889, *REC/CR-MZL*.
[43] Chauvicourt, 'premières monnaies,' 150; Valette, Études, 45.
[44] *Madagascar Times* (30 July 1884) 276.
[45] *Madagascar Times* (3 September 1884) 330.

In 1885 and 1888, on the strength of new gold exploitation, the Merina court again considered minting a Malagasy coinage. However, foreign investors, who alone could finance the equipment necessary to fully exploit the gold deposits, were initially deterred by the stringent conditions proposed by the court. Although the court lifted most restrictions by early 1895, domestic insecurity and the renewal of French hostilities that year reinforced the doubts of potential foreign investors.[46]

The attempt in December 1889 by Rainilaiarivony, Merina prime minister from 1864 to 1895, to regulate the currency by imposing a ban on the import of the new Mexican dollar placed George Ropes (1836–1888) and other American agents who had stockpiled the coin in a financially precarious situation. As he held no fund of five-franc pieces, Ropes had to pay his duties in cotton cloth. By the early 1890s, the Mexican coin was again being imported, this time by Abraham Kingdon (1846–1927),[47] for some time the printer in Antananarivo for the Quaker Mission (Friends Foreign Mission Association), who had repeatedly failed to establish a British bank in the island. He introduced such huge quantities of the coin that it was popularly termed *vola Kingdon* ("Kingdon's money") and started to adversely affect the financial standing of the Merina court, which was a major creditor.[48]

In March 1894, in an attempt to remedy the situation, Rainilaiarivony declared that the new Mexican dollar was no longer legal tender, and shortly afterwards extended his ban to the American dollar and French five and ten cent coins. By 20 March 1894, no business was being transacted in the five-franc coin of the Latin Union, while the American dollar could only be exchanged at a loss of 3.5 per cent. In May 1894, the *Tanomasoandro, Ngita, Tsanganolona* and *Tokazo* coins were declared illegal, leaving as valid currency only the *Malamakely, Behatoka* and *Tombotsisina*—thus underlining the dominance of the five-franc piece in the Merina Empire. The effective devaluation of the US dollar hit not only the American but also the Indian mercantile community, which speculated in the different coins, and small

[46] Campbell, 'Gold Mining and the French Takeover.'

[47] In 1897 Kingdon moved to Kenora, Canada where became involved in the Gold Rush—Peter Holden, 'Kingdon—Campaign Medals & Military Service' (23 February 2013). http://www.britishmedals.us/files/Book4_files/KINGDON (accessed July 29, 2018).

[48] Pickersgill to Briggs, Nosibe, 30 May 1882, 'T & F, LMS Local, D & E,' *FJKM*; Campbell to Wharton, 26 April 1890; Campbell to Procter, 23 Aug. 1887 and *idem* to Razafindrazaka, 26 May 1890—*USNA*; Rasoamiaranana, 'Aspects économiques,' 55; *Le courrier de Madagascar* 139 (17 avril 1894).

Malagasy traders and porters. The prohibition on the use of the relatively abundant Mexican *Tanomasoandro* dollar exacerbated the financial plight of all merchants as they found no outlet for their stocks of the proscribed coin.[49] Finally, currency problems, notably adulteration, caused traders to react to the increase of "bad money" by withholding their stocks of *vola madio* (i.e. "good money").[50] This further reduced the money supply; as a result, the internal market shrivelled, credit was withdrawn and trade suffered.[51]

Conclusion

In the traditional economy of Madagascar, commodity currencies, notably cloth, dominated. The growth of foreign trade, from the mid-eighteenth century with the neighbouring European-dominated plantation economies on the Mascarenes, and in the nineteenth century as Madagascar became increasingly drawn into the burgeoning international economy led to imported coinage becoming the accepted medium of exchange in the island's main commercial centres. However, periods of autarkic policy, the cost of military campaigns against domestic and foreign enemies, the almost universal application of *fanompoana*, or unremunerated forced labour, and the inability to efficiently control the exploitation of its significant gold deposits resulted in serious shortages in money supply. This led to continued dominance of commodity monies in most of the island, and in commercial centres in the morselisation of coins, counterfeiting and use of fraudulent weights in valuating coinage. Adulteration of coinage with base metals, a minor problem from 1750 to 1810 due to the high volume of imported coinage and the velocity of its circulation, became a source of growing concern after 1810 as the money supply slumped. Little was done during the years of rigid autarky, or from 1861 to 1875, when a recovery

[49] Wetter to Strobel, 20 March and *idem* to Uhl, 26 May and 7 Sep.1894—*USNA*; *Le courrier de Madagascar* 139 (17 avril 1894) and 150 (5 juillet 1894).

[50] Mayeur, 'Voyage au pays d'ancove' (1785) 227; Anon, 'Mémoire historique,' (1790) 95–6; Dumaine, 'Voyage au pays d'ancaye' (1790) 267; *idem*, 'Voyage à la côte de l'ouest' (1793) 308; Raombana, *Histoires*, 10; Grandidier, *Histoire* (1928) 268, 335; Sundström, *Exchange Economy*, 111, 114, 117–18; Ellis, *History of Madagascar*, Vol. I, 243–7, 254–5; David Griffiths, *Hanes Madagascar* (Machynlleth, R. Jones, 1843) 46; Campbell, 'Role of the London Missionary Society,' 326.

[51] Gwyn Campbell, 'Toamasina (Tamatave) and the Growth of Foreign Trade in Imperial Madagascar, 1862–1895,' in *Figuring African Trade*, Gerhard Liesegang et al., eds. (Berlin, Dietrich Reimer Verlag, 1986) 535.

of trade led to a large increase in the money supply. However, the 1883–1885 war dramatically increased the Merina need for foreign exchange as firms from which it wished to purchase arms were reluctant to accept cut coins and wary of the silver content of uncut coins. In addition, war-time inflation and insecurity encouraged foreign traders to export specie. For instance, the American company, *Ropes, Emmerton* and the Hamburg firm, *O'Swald* shipped from Toamasina in mid-1883 and from June to August 1884 respectively, 20,000 five-franc pieces and 25,000 rupees (a total value of $10,750), and 80,000 five-franc coins.[52] Over time such policies and practices eroded commercial trust and helped push the Merina regime to the verge of bankruptcy in 1894—thus facilitating the French colonial takeover in 1895.

[52] Ropes, Emmerton & Co, to Whitney, Salem, 14 July 1883, ms.103, Ropes, Emmerton & Co. Records (1873–1902), B42.F4; Ropes, Emmerton & Co, to J. Orme Ryder, Salem, 17 July 1884; Dawson to Ropes, Emmerton & Co, and Arnold, Hines & Co, Tamatave, 18 July and 14 Aug. 1884,—*REC/CR-MZL.*

CHAPTER 6

Currency as Commodity, as Symbol of Sovereignty and as Subject of Legal Dispute: Henri Greffülhe and the Coinage of Zanzibar in the Late Nineteenth Century

Catherine Eagleton

Zanzibar in the middle of the nineteenth century was a prosperous and cosmopolitan place, a port growing in wealth and importance, ruled by Sultan Said, who had moved there from Muscat as the wealth of the island increased.[1] The Sultan ruled not only the islands of the Zanzibar archipelago but also the land along the cost of the African mainland. Despite

[1] On the background to the move from Muscat to Zanzibar, see Calvin H Allen, 'The State of Masqat in the Gulf and East Africa, 1785–1829,' *International Journal of Middle East Studies* 14:2 (1982) 117–27. British colonial officials at Zanzibar in the early twentieth century wrote a number of histories of the island: for example, Robert Lyne, *Zanzibar in Contemporary Times A Short History of the Southern East in the Nineteenth Century* (1905); Francis Barrow Pearce, *Zanzibar: The Island Metropolis of Eastern Africa* (London, T Fisher Unwin, 1920); Reginald Coupland, *East Africa and Its Invaders: From the Earliest Times to the Death of Seyyid Said in 1856* (Oxford, Clarendon Press, 1938).

C. Eagleton (✉)
University of St Andrews, St Andrews, Scotland, UK

S. Serels, G. Campbell (eds.), *Currencies of the Indian Ocean World*, Palgrave Series in Indian Ocean World Studies,
https://doi.org/10.1007/978-3-030-20973-5_6

Zanzibar's small size, its position just off the coast enabled it to become a hub for the slave trade, as well as an entrepôt through which produce was traded to and from the mainland.[2] Much of this trade was linked to the monsoon cycles of winds and rains, and merchants from the Horn of Africa, the Gulf and India visited Zanzibar seasonally.[3] European and American merchants were attracted to the island by the potential for trade both there and on the coast. From the 1830s onwards, the Sultan signed a number of treaties encouraging the foundation of European and American businesses and merchant houses in his territory. Most of these treaties, with the exception of that with the United States, allowed trade only on Zanzibar Island; European merchants were not permitted to trade directly on the mainland coast.[4] In addition, a significant community of Indian merchants and moneylenders acted as middlemen. They dominated trade at Zanzibar and with the coast, providing both wholesale goods and credit that enabled business to take place.[5] Although there was limited direct trade between Britain and Zanzibar in the first half of the nineteenth century, there was nonetheless a longstanding relationship between Britain and the Sultans of Muscat and Oman, and later, of Zanzibar. Combined with the interests of merchants from India, this meant that the British officials at Zanzibar had significant influence. This influence increased from the 1860s onwards, despite the ambitions of the French to dominate the western Indian Ocean trade.[6]

[2]The classic work on the economic history of Zanzibar before 1873 is Abdul Sheriff, *Slaves, Spices and Ivory in Zanzibar* (Oxford, James Currey, 1987), and on the role of Indian merchants, see in particular pp. 108–9. Marek Pawelczak, *The State and the Stateless: The Sultanate of Zanzibar and the East African Mainland: Politics, Economy and Society, 1837–1888* (Warsaw, SOWA, 2010) discusses the relationship between Zanzibar Island and the mainland coast of Africa in the nineteenth century.

[3]On the dhow trade and the economy of Zanzibar, see Erik Gilbert, *Dhows & the Colonial Economy of Zanzibar: 1860–1970* (Oxford, James Currey, 2004).

[4]This seems to sometimes have needed reinforcing—for example, in 1872 the Sultan sent a crier around Zanzibar town to issue a proclamation that no British subjects could trade beyond Zanzibar town: India, Mumbai, Maharashtra State Archives, Political 1872, Vol. 203, compilation 1214, 169–82.

[5]Richard Francis Burton, *Zanzibar: The City and the Island*, 2 vols. (Tinsley, 1872) gives a first-hand description of imports and exports in 1860s Zanzibar (Vol. 1, p. 414), and the moneylending business there (Vol. 1, p. 407).

[6]On American merchants at Zanzibar, see, for example, N.R. Bennett, 'Americans in Zanzibar: 1865–1915,' *Tanganyika Notes and Records* 60 (1963) 49–66; Norman Robert Bennett and George E. Brooks, *New England Merchants in Africa: A History Through Documents, 1802 to 1865* (Africana Publication, 1965); N.R. Bennett, 'France and Zanzibar,

Reflecting these global trade connections, there were multiple currencies in use at Zanzibar, including gold and silver coins from around the world, at values that sometimes fluctuated with the changing seasons. The dominant currency was the Maria Theresa Thaler, which served as the unit of account. American gold coins were also used, but changes in the values of gold and silver in the 1870s meant that these gradually fell out of use. The Maria Theresa Thaler also gradually fell out of use in the later nineteenth century, leaving the Indian silver rupee, supplemented by Indian copper pice, as the usual medium of exchange on the island. These coins imported from Bombay were also used in transactions along the coast and had become the standard currency of the entire region by the 1870s and 1880s.[7]

Alongside cash transactions, much business at Zanzibar was based on credit. Caravans going into the interior of East Africa could be supplied with goods that were supplied in advance by merchants, who then shared the profits when the caravan returned to the coast. Written records were sometimes, but not always, made of these credit arrangements, which could amount to very significant sums. There was, however, no requirement for written documentation; Zanzibari legal practices recognized the

1844 to the 1860s [part I],' *The International Journal of African Historical Studies* 6:4 (1973) 602–32. On earlier relations between France and Zanzibar, see Norman R. Bennett, 'France and Zanzibar, 1775–1844,' in *Eastern African History*, ed. Daniel F McCall, Norman R. Bennett, and Jeffrey Butler, eds. (New York, 1969) 148–75. For a personal perspective on the British activity at Zanzibar in the 1860s, see Christopher Palmer Rigby, *General Rigby, Zanzibar, and the Slave Trade: With Journals, Dispatches, etc.* (Allen & Unwin, 1935), particularly extracts from his diary on pp. 100–1, complaining that British merchants were not willing to engage in trade at Zanzibar, and that French, German and American merchants were dominating. The American Consuls, on the other hand, complained about British influence being dominant even in the 1850s, and even that the English government would decide who the next Sultan would be: see, for example, Bennett and Brooks, *New England Merchants in Africa: A History through Documents, 1802 to 1865*, 482. With both Britain and France suspecting that the other was planning to take control of Zanzibar, the two countries agreed in 1862 to preserve the independence of the Sultanate of Zanzibar, on which see A Kieran, 'The Origins of the Zanzibar Guarantee Treaty of 1862,' *Canadian Journal of African Studies* 2:2 (1968) 147–66. The rivalry between the British and French at Zanzibar was so widely known that when children at Zanzibar played games in which two antagonists were needed, they would call themselves the English and the French: see W.E. Malcolm, ed., *England's East African Policy. Articles on the Relations of England to the Sultan of Zanzibar, and on the Negotiations of 1873, etc.* (London, Simpkin, Marshall & Co., 1875) 19.

[7] Pawelczak, *The State and the Stateless*, 61–2 and 75, outlines the currencies in use on the East African coast.

testimony of two witnesses as sufficient proof of a commitment to make it enforceable. Disputes were adjudicated by a *qadi*, or judge, on behalf of the Sultan.[8] Europeans and Americans at Zanzibar came under the jurisdiction of their own consulate, and there were British, French, German, American and Portuguese consular courts on the island. Cases that fell between different jurisdictions were sometimes passed backwards and forwards a number of times until agreement could be reached about who should hear a particular case.[9]

This vision of a cosmopolitan Zanzibar, still presented to tourists visiting the island today with overtones of the 1001 Arabian nights, did not, however, last for many decades. A Zanzibari in 1900 looking back to the year 1875 would have reflected upon a period of dramatic change. In the intervening years the slave trade had been abolished, resulting in decreased profits for both merchants and the Sultan. In addition, American influence had declined and German ambition had disrupted the old rivalry between France and Britain. Further, this three-way European competition for local control had led to the establishment of European land claims and to the establishment of a boundary commission that ultimately excluded the Sultan's input when it limited his territory to a 10 mile-wide strip along the cost.[10] European companies had then secured concessions to trade both on the coastal strip as well as in inland territory.[11] By the time the

[8] Katrin Bromber, *The Jurisdiction of the Sultan of Zanzibar and the Subjects of Foreign Nations* (Würzburg, Ergon, 2001) 32–7.

[9] Ibid., 18–31. Some British Indian legislation was in force for British subjects at Zanzibar: John Molesworth Macpherson and Albert Williams, *British Enactments in Force in Native States*, 2nd ed. (Calcutta, Office of the Superintendent of Government Printing, 1899). However, some Indian merchants would claim to be subjects of the Sultan or of Britain as best suited their purposes at a particular time: Bennett and Brooks, *New England Merchants in Africa: A History Through Documents, 1802 to 1865*, 380.

[10] J. C. Wilkinson, 'The Zanzibar Delimitation Commission 1885–1886,' *Geopolitics and International Boundaries* 1:2 (1996) 130–58, views the boundary commission as a "tool which allowed the Germans, French and British to strip the Sultan of his rights on the mainland and ultimately to deny the Arabs any independent rule in Africa" (on p. 131). Sultan Barghash was furious at the outcome of the Berlin conference, which he saw as having taken from him the most productive part of what he regarded as his possessions—the source of much of the ivory traded at Zanzibar (on p. 134, notes 6 and 7).

[11] H.P. Merritt, 'Bismarck and the German Interest in East Africa, 1884–1885,' *Historical Journal* 21:1 (1978) 97–116, discusses the motivations behind the creation of the German Protectorate, and John S. Galbraith, 'Italy, the British East Africa Company, and the Benadir Coast, 1888–1893,' *Journal of Modern History* 42:4 (1970) 549–63, discusses Italian attempts to set up a concession. On the British East Africa Company, see below. There were

British declared a Protectorate over Zanzibar in 1890, the Sultan had already lost much of his economic and political independence.[12]

In the midst of this turbulent period, the first coinage specifically minted for Zanzibar was issued. This coinage was minted in the name of Sultan Barghash through a concession granted in 1883 to Henri Greffülhe, a French merchant. In the years that followed, the German and British East African concessionary companies also issued new coins for use in their East African territories. Looking at the creation and circulation of these currencies together provides a new perspective on the political and economic change in Zanzibar and in East Africa in the 1880s. The new coins offered their issuers the possibility of profit through seigniorage, which Eric Helleiner has identified as a key motivation for European colonial powers issuing currency.[13] However, it is more difficult to see them in the framework of the European nation-state that is Helleiner's focus, since Zanzibar in this period was not—yet—a British colony. Taking a slightly broader perspective, one of the only unquestioned powers involved in sovereignty is the right to mint and issue currency,[14] so examining the question of who can issue coins, and under what conditions, provides a way of looking at changing ideas of, and claims to, sovereignty at Zanzibar in the 1880s and 1890s.

The images on coins can also offer visible signs of sovereignty, rivalling the significance of a flag.[15] There have been a number of studies that explore the relationship between currency imagery and national identity

at this time a series of treaties between Britain, France and Germany, recognising each other's claims: see Sir Edward Hertslet and Great Britain, *The Map of Africa by Treaty*, 3 vols. (H.M. Stationery Office, 1894) 109–25; Marquess of Salisbury, 'The Anglo-French Agreement,' Hansard (House of Lords, August 11, 1890), http://hansard.millbanksystems.com/lords/1890/aug/11/the-anglo-french-agreement.

[12] One near-contemporary commentator described Sultan Barghash's last years as "embittered by the humiliations imposed upon him" in these years: Pearce, *Zanzibar: The Island Metropolis of Eastern Africa*, 269.

[13] Eric Helleiner, *The Making of National Money: Territorial Currencies in Historical Perspective* (Ithaca, Cornell University Press, 2003) 163 and 177.

[14] Jeffrey Herbst, *States and Power in Africa: Comparative Lessons in Authority and Control* (Princeton University Press, 2000) 201.

[15] This point was made explicitly in the mid-twentieth century, during the period of decolonisation: see Helleiner, *The Making of National Money*, 205, as well as Daniel Hammett and Paul Nugent, *Making Nations, Creating Strangers: States and Citizenship in Africa* (Leiden, Brill, 2007) 248; Emily Gilbert and Erik Helleiner, 'Introduction—Nation-States and Money: Historical Contexts, Interdisciplinary Perspectives,' in *Nation-States and Money: The Past, Present and Future of National Currencies* (London, Routledge, 1999).

or colonial ideals.[16] However, as has been noted in the case of contemporary currency design, this literature often pays insufficient attention to the involvement of non-state organizations, including commercial organizations, in creating images for and subsequently issuing new coins.[17] In the case of Zanzibar, the companies that minted "official" currency had varying degrees of authorization from a competing set of states. In addition, the circulation of "unofficial", merchant-issued currencies was not uncommon. The Zanzibari case, as well as other, similar cases in which non-state actors participated in issuing currencies, challenge conventional understandings of "national identity" and "sovereignty" that have been used in other studies of the history of currencies.

The current case study is particularly instructive because it is a study of failure. The establishment of a British protectorate over Zanzibar in 1890 raised international questions about the status of Greffülhe's coinage concession. The legal claim subsequently brought by Greffülhe revealed details of this event that otherwise may never have been recorded, and the official debates that this court case raised illuminate the conflicting relationship between sovereignty and currency in this period. The parties in the case were a group of European merchants, two imperial companies, and the Sultan of Zanzibar. Europeans at Zanzibar expected their legal disputes to be conducted according to European law.[18] Though Zanzibar was a British Protectorate, the Sultan still retained legislative authority, and as a result the procedure for legal action against the Sultan was not immediately clear.[19] Ultimately, the case went to international arbitration,

[16] To take just a few examples from the colonial period, see Virginia Hewitt, 'A Distant View: Imagery and Imagination in the Paper Currency of the British Empire, 1800–1960,' in *Nation-States and Money*, Gilbert and Helleiner, eds. (1999); Wambui Mwangi, 'The Lion, the Native and the Coffee Plant: Political Imagery and the Ambiguous Art of Currency Design in Colonial Kenya,' *Geopolitics* 7:1 (2002) 31–62, Igor Cusack, 'Tiny Transmitters of Nationalist and Colonial Ideology: The Postage Stamps of Portugal and Its Empire,' *Nations and Nationalism* 11:4 (2005) 591–612; Yair Wallach, 'Creating a Country through Currency and Stamps: State Symbols and Nation-Building in British-Ruled Palestine,' *Nations and Nationalism* 17:1 (2011) 129–47.

[17] Jan Penrose, 'Designing the Nation: Banknotes, Banal Nationalism and Alternative Conceptions of the State,' *Political Geography* 30 (2011) 429–40.

[18] On this and on colonial 'lawfare' more broadly, see Wolfgang J. Mommsen and Jaap de Moor, *European Expansion and Law : The Encounter of European and Indigenous Law in Nineteenth- and Twentieth-Century Africa and Asia* (New York and Oxford, Berg, 1992) 3–5, and the other chapters in the book.

[19] For Zanzibar law in the Protectorate period: Sir Thomas Edward Scrutton (ed.), *The Commercial Laws of the World, Comprising the Mercantile, Bills of Exchange, Bankruptcy and Maritime Laws of Civilised Nations* (London, Sweet & Maxwell Ltd., 1911) 163.

and as a result, this dispute about coinage was at the same time a test of the legal and political boundaries of the new Protectorate and the extent of British and French influence under the new political order.

Coins as Currency and Commodity: Henri Greffülhe and Sultan Barghash

Henri Greffülhe was one of a number of Europeans living and working as a merchant in Zanzibar. He was born in France in 1845 and lived in Lamu for three years before moving to Zanzibar in 1874 to serve as the local agent of Roux, Fraissenet & Co, a commercial house.[20] In Zanzibar, Greffülhe quickly expanded his business endeavours. He engaged in trade in his own name and soon became the agent of a number of additional French Companies, including Rabaud Frères and the *Messageries Maritimes* shipping company.[21] He quickly became recognized for his skill at arranging travel into the interior.[22] In April 1883, he was granted a concession from Sultan Barghash for a 20-year concession to mint coins in the name of the Sultan. The new currency was to circulate alongside the other coins already in circulation in Zanzibar.[23]

Reporting the news of the coinage concession to London, British Consul John Kirk noted that neither he nor the French Consul at Zanzibar were aware in advance of the details of the negotiations. Kirk also noted

[20] Henri Greffülhe, 'Voyage de Lamoo a Zanzibar,' in *Bulletin de la Société de géographie de Marseille* (Marseille, Secrétariat de la Société de géographie, 1878) 209–17. Accessible online at http://gallica.bnf.fr/ark:/12148/cb34349684z/date. Henri Greffülhe's date of birth and other personal details are in France, Paris, Archives Nationales, LH/1195/35, *Award of Legion d'Honneur to Lucien Henri Emile Greffülhe* (1885).

[21] France, Nantes, Archives Diplomatiques, 748 PO/A 151, 22 December 1882, letter from Minister of Foreign Affairs to French Consul. By 1888, Greffülhe's letterhead listed him as agent for companies in France, England, Holland and Belgium: see examples in France, Nantes, Archives Diplomatiques, 748 PO/A 34.

[22] In February 1879, Marseille-based merchant Alfred Rabaud wrote to Henry Morton Stanley, about Stanley's fear of the British Consul Dr John Kirk creating obstacles for him at Zanzibar, and offering the services of Henri Greffülhe: Belgium Tervuren, Royal Museum for Central Africa, Stanley Archives 999. From 1879, Greffülhe was acting as an agent for the Association Internationale de Bruxelles for the exploration of the interior of Africa: France, Archives Diplomatiques, La Courneuve, CCC/Zanzibar/4, letter of March 1879 from French Consul to Minister of Foreign Affairs, and CCC/Zanzibar/5, letter of 6 April 1881 from French Consul to Minister of Foreign Affairs.

[23] The rupee had become the currency of eastern Africa due to a particular set of economic circumstances in the 1860s, on which see Catherine Eagleton, 'When and Why did the Rupee become the Currency of East Africa?' (forthcoming).

his scepticism of the economic footing of this concession; he did not believe it to be possible to mint and import the specified coins, pay the Sultan the required 5 per cent and turn a profit. As a result, Kirk suspected that Greffülhe's ultimate aim was to profit on the importation of copper coin, which "is practically the only money the Sultan has any chance of forcing into operation, this he may do being himself the largest employer of labour on the island".[24] If this was the case, Kirk noted that the Sultan had perhaps been foolish in giving up the profit on the copper coinage. At the time, these coins were imported from the Bombay Mint at a profit of approximately 36,000 rupees per year to the Indian government.[25] Kirk foresaw another problem for the Sultan that could arise from this concession—forcing the use of the new coins would give foreign merchants at Zanzibar "a suspicion that the Sultan may have committed himself to other examples of perhaps a more dangerous nature".[26]

Greffülhe had the coins struck at the Royal Mint in Brussels, one of whose directors was also personally involved as a partner in the coining concession. The copper pice featured a design similar to that of the East India Company pice already in circulation at Zanzibar. The silver and gold coins featured inscriptions giving the name and genealogy of the Sultan.[27] When he saw samples of the new coins, Kirk—himself a coin collector—was unimpressed, describing them as "singularly inartistic and clumsy".[28] However, he also noted that the inscriptions were incorrect—they read "Sultan Said son of Barghash son of Sultan", whereas Barghash's father was Said, and his father (Barghash's grandfather) was called Sultan.

[24] Zanzibar National Archives (henceforth, ZNA) AA 1/48, Zanzibar to Foreign Office, dispatch no 90 of 28 September 1883.

[25] ZNA AA 1/48, Zanzibar to Foreign Office, dispatch no 113 of 19 November 1883.

[26] ZNA AA 1/48, Zanzibar to Foreign Office, dispatch no 90 of 28 September 1883.

[27] Images of the coins could not be included here due to the cost of securing image permissions, but they can be viewed at https://www.britishmuseum.org/research/collection_online/search.aspx. A silver riyal given to the British Museum by John Kirk, and therefore likely to be the example that prompted his comments on the coin's design, is acquisition number 1886,0806.1; one of the copper pice struck at Brussels is acquisition number 1895,0202.7. The punches and matrices used for the coinage are still preserved in the collections of the Royal Belgian Mint: Ministere des Finances, Tresorerie, Monnaie Royale de Belgique, *Catalogue des poincons & matrices du musee de l'hotel des monnaies (prepared by Cabinet des Medailles de la Bibliotheque Royale de Belgique)* (Brussels, Monnaie Royale, 1977) 511, lists 5 obverse and reverse dies and matrices for the riyal, and 4 obverse and 5 reverse dies and matrices for the pice.

[28] ZNA AA 1/48, Zanzibar to Foreign Office, dispatch no 90 of 28 September 1883.

Although he thought the coin would "certainly become in time a great curiosity", Kirk found it hard to understand how Sultan Barghash could have approved the designs.[29] For an Islamic ruler the issuing of coins with their name on was the ultimate sign of sovereignty, and therefore the fact that the names and genealogy on these coins were wrong suggests that Sultan Barghash may have had very little involvement in the process of designing and minting them.

The first shipments of the new coins arrived at Zanzibar in November 1883. However, their subsequent distribution was complicated by the fact that Roux, Fraissenet & Co had failed, leaving behind local debts totalling approximately £100,000.[30] To keep the coins out of the hands of the administrators of the bankrupt company's debts, the shipment was stored with the Sultan.[31] Seeing the coins as a source of bullion and not as currency, the Sultan melted down most of the silver and gold coins to make jewellery and ornaments for his family.[32] His subsequent request that Greffülhe bring more gold coins was declined.

Around the same time, Greffülhe and his associates had identified a flaw in the contract. The omission of the crucial word "copper" in one of its clauses meant that each shipment of copper coin had to be separately agreed upon with the Sultan. Greffülhe offered the Sultan a quarter of the profits in exchange for free rein on the introduction of copper coin, but Sultan Barghash would not agree to a written amendment to the contract. In part, this choice reflected the Sultan's regret at signing the original concession contract—he explained to Kirk that he was worried about the fact that Greffülhe was working with partners in Europe, whom he did not know. The Sultan hoped that Greffülhe could be persuaded to relinquish the concession, however Kirk convinced him that this would be unlikely given the terms of the contract.[33] The stalemate between the Sultan and Greffülhe continued for more than two years. In the meantime, the affairs

[29] ZNA, AA 1/46, Zanzibar to Foreign Office, 10th May 1886, dispatch number 103; and ZNA, AA 1/49, Foreign Office to Zanzibar, dispatch number 224 of 1 July 1886, passing on a letter of thanks from the British Museum, for sending samples of the Zanzibar coins for their collections.

[30] ZNA AA 1/48, Zanzibar to Foreign Office, dispatch no 113 of 19 November 1883.

[31] ZNA AA 1/48, Zanzibar to Foreign Office, dispatch 125 of 5 December 1883.

[32] ZNA AB 14/28, Zanzibar to Foreign Office, memorandum of 20 June 1897: "very few were put into circulation, and ... no more were brought".

[33] ZNA AA 1/48, Zanzibar to Foreign Office, dispatch 125 of 5 December 1883.

of Roux, Fraissenet & Co were settled and it seemed that Greffülhe was preparing to permanently leave Zanzibar.[34]

In June 1885, Sultan Barghash wrote to King Leopold II of Belgium, giving his permission for the striking of $200,000-worth of copper pice.[35] The timing of this letter is important. Three months earlier, Germany announced its claim on part of what Sultan Barghash regarded as his mainland territories. However, the Zanzibar Delimitation Commission had not yet begun to settle the competing territorial claims over the mainland. In fact, Sultan Barghash opens the letter by complains about increasing German and British influence. Though he does not explicitly connect this complaint to the currency concession, this complaint to King Leopold could be interpreted as a sign of the Sultan's frustration with the increasing impositions on his sovereignty (Table 6.1).

Table 6.1 Quantities of coins struck for Zanzibar, from the records of the Belgian Royal Mint

Year of production	*Denomination*	*Number*
1883	1 pice, copper	680,000
	1 riyal, silver	10,000
	5 riyal, gold	2000
1885	1 pice, silver[a]	50,000
1886	1 pice, copper	3,960,000
1887	1 pice, copper	3,520,000
1890	1 pice, copper	2,570,000
1891	1 pice, copper	12,594,000

[a]This entry in the table has to be incorrect—it is presumably a striking of silver riyals, since Greffülhe wrote in 1893 that "we still have of our first coinage of 50,000 silver dollars, 30,000 dollars deposited in Bombay with the Comptoir National d'Escompte" (Zanzibar National Archives, AC/1/9, printed statement on behalf of Henri Greffülhe, 13 January 1893). It is therefore excluded from the total number of pice, calculated here as 23,324,000.

[34] France, Nantes, Archives Diplomatiques, 748 PO/A 177, letters of 26 April 1884 (on the deed of settlement for Roux, Fraissenet & Co affairs) and 8 April 1884 (case for $4000 brought against Greffülhe by a British Indian).

[35] France, Nantes, Archives Diplomatiques, 748 PO/A 141, 25 Chaban 1302/9 June 1885, letter written by Mohamud ben Halem on behalf of Sultan Barghash, to King Leopold II of Belgium.

The coins struck include large numbers of copper pice struck in later years, but using the same dies, and therefore still bearing the date 1881/1299.[36]

Coal and Copper Coins as Commodities: Sultan Barghash and the Birmingham Mint

Following the Sultan's letter to King Leopold, Greffülhe's coins arrived at Zanzibar in May 1886, and the Sultan issued them by paying his servants with the new silver riyals, which in turn could be exchanged at Greffülhe's office for two rupees and six annas each. Despite their official support, merchants at Zanzibar needed additional convincing in order to decide whether and at what valuation they should accept the new coins. The key concern for these merchants was the intrinsic value of the new silver coins.[37] John Kirk therefore sent samples for assay at the Bombay Mint. These tests showed that Greffülhe was exchanging the new silver coins at 4¾ per cent above their intrinsic value. As a result, he was making an 8 per cent loss on every transaction.[38] Kirk was unconcerned about overvalued silver coins driving the rupee from circulation. Rather, he took these results as confirmation of his initial suspicion that the silver coin was being issued at a loss "only to float the new currency" and to secure the anticipated 40 per cent profit on the introduction of the copper coins.[39]

However, there were soon problems that prevented Greffülhe from profiting from the circulation of the copper coins. Greffülhe had been supplying coal to Sultan Barghash under a verbal agreement, but when he asked for an increase in the price, the Sultan became annoyed and declared that if he "would not supply coal, he should not supply copper". The Sultan then approached Smith, Mackenzie & Co, an English company at Zanzibar, to supply both coal and copper coin.[40] The connection here between two commodities—coal and copper—suggests that Sultan Barghash also was motivated by profit and not only by the prerogatives of sovereignty in the decisions he took regarding the copper pice. Smith

[36] Table 6.1 is based on [Didier Vanoverbeek] "Zanzibar" in *Monnaie Info* 28 (2002) 8–9.

[37] ZNA AA 2/42, Zanzibar to Secretary to Bombay Government, dispatch 174 of 11 May 1886.

[38] ZNA AA 2/42, Bombay to Zanzibar code telegram, 20 May 1886, with handwritten notes of calculations added.

[39] ZNA, AA 1/46, Zanzibar to Foreign Office, 10th May 1886, dispatch number 103.

[40] ZNA AC 1/8, John Kirk to Zanzibar, 1 February 1893.

Mackenzie then contracted the Birmingham Mint, a private mint that was independent of, but closely in touch with, the Royal Mint in London.[41] The Birmingham Mint created a new design for the Zanzibar copper pice that was similar, although not identical, to Greffülhe's copper coins because Ralph Heaton, the head of the mint believed them to be "a matter of beauty in design + execution".[42] The new design retained the image of the scales in Greffülhe's design, but now with a simpler inscription of the word "Zanzibar". As a result, there was a continued visual link with the East India Company copper coins that still circulated at Zanzibar. Samples of the new design were sent to the Sultan for approval, but he seemed to be unwilling to give a written authority to strike the coin, claiming in a letter dated 24 October 1887 that it was "not necessary". Instead, he stated that the designs for the coins "pleased us very much" and that he looked forward to receiving the copper pice in due course.[43] Sultan Barghash did not give a clear reason for refusing to give a formal written authority to coin; perhaps he was aware that ordering these coins from Birmingham would violate the exclusive terms of his contract with Greffülhe. More broadly, this episode sheds light on business practises at Zanzibar in the 1880s. At the time, both written contracts and verbal agreements were used and relationships between Zanzibaris and Europeans were governed by a mixture of both types of arrangement. Whatever the Sultan's motivation, the note from him was enough for the Birmingham Mint, who produced and shipped 12 tonnes of copper pice, a total of almost 2 million coins, in 1887.

In October 1887, as the striking of these coins began at Birmingham, the French Consul at Zanzibar (and presumably therefore also Henri Greffülhe) was unaware of the new plans for the provision of copper coin. He wrote a letter to Paris saying only that the Sultan no longer wanted to be bound by the terms of the coining concession, and had shown no interest in receiving further shipments of copper pice from Greffülhe and his

[41] Birmingham City Archives, MS 1623 18.3, copy letterbook, including 14 (letter of 2 January 1883 discussing visit by ambassadors from Madagascar) and 128 (30 November 1883, complaining about machinery standing idle).

[42] Birmingham City Archives, MS 1623 18.3, copy letterbook, 227, 25 January 1886. Images of the copper pice struck at Birmingham can be seen at https://www.britishmuseum.org/research/collection_online/search.aspx—search for acquisition number 1895,0202.9.

[43] Birmingham City Archives, MS 1623 40.4, file "Zanzibar 1887."

partners.[44] There is no record of the Consul's nor of Greffülhe's reaction to the two million copper pice from Birmingham entering circulation. However, it is unlikely that they did not notice the arrival of the three large shipments of coin. Certainly, British officials at Zanzibar were not aware of any objections being made to them entering circulation.[45] It is possible that, given the flaw Greffülhe's concession contract that required him to secure the Sultan's permission for each new shipment of copper coins, Greffülhe could do little about the import of these coins. He may have just resigned himself to a reduction in the total profit he and his partners had hoped to gain from the issue of copper pice.

Coins as Wage Payments and Source of Profit: The Imperial British East Africa Company

This incident was neither the first nor the last time that the partners in Smith, Mackenzie & Co were involved in supplying coins to East Africa. The company had been established at Zanzibar since 1872.[46] By 1877, the company's partners had become sufficiently convinced of the potential for trade on the East African coast that there was talk of both farming the customs of and trading in the Zanzibar mainland territories.[47] One of the company's partners, Scottish businessman and ship owner William Mackinnon, was closely involved in both negotiations to secure a tax farming concession and in schemes to expand trade on the mainland. Mackinnon recognized that securing trading rights on the mainland would allow the company to bypass the Indian merchants that were then supplying exporters with mainland goods.[48] Nonetheless, his aims were broader than this. A draft concession agreement that he presented to the Sultan in December

[44] France, Archives Diplomatiques, La Courneuve, ADC/F/27a/5 (order as 1ADC/595), *Questions monetaires: Zanzibar*, 29 October 1887, French Consul to Direction des Affaires Commerciales. See also France, Nantes, Archives Diplomatiques, 748 PO/A 65*, letter from French Consul to Minister on 29 October 1887.

[45] ZNA AB 14/28, memorandum from Zanzibar to Foreign Office, 20 June 1891.

[46] India, Mumbai, Maharashtra State Archives, Political 1872 Vol. 203, compilation 1101, 19 February 1872, on pp. 183–86.

[47] London, SOAS, PP MS 1/IBEA/1/1C, Grey, Dawes & Co to John Kirk, 9 February 1877. See also *The History of Smith, MacKenzie and Company, Ltd* (London, East Africa, Ltd, 1938) 10–19 and 28–9. The date of the foundation of the company at Zanzibar is given as 1877 on p. 9.

[48] J Forbes Munro, 'Shipping Subsidies and Railway Guarantees: William Mackinnon, Eastern Africa, and the Indian Ocean, 1860–1893,' *Journal of African History* 28:2 (1987)

1877 included the right "to coin and issue money in His Highness's territories … to establish a Bank, or Banks, anywhere in His Highness's territories, with the exclusive privilege of issuing notes".[49] During 1878, however, it became clear that although the concession negotiations had reached a relatively advanced stage, the Sultan was less willing to continue to negotiate, and had become nervous about the implications of some of the proposals.[50] At the same time, Mackinnon had become convinced that he did not have sufficient support from the British government in London. As a result, the negotiations foundered and no mainland concession was established.

Eight years later, the political situation in East Africa was very different, and the Anglo-German agreement had reopened the possibility of mainland concessions for European companies. In 1888 the Imperial British East Africa Company (IBEAC) was incorporated under the directorship of William Mackinnon. The IBEAC, along with the German East Africa Company (GEAC), leased parts of the coastal strip from the Sultan of Zanzibar.[51] In 1888–1889 there was a flurry of correspondence between George Mackenzie, the representative of the IBEAC in Mombasa, and Mackinnon in London, which reveals some of the most pressing concerns of the newly founded company. These concerns included plans for road-clearance and building works. To pay the wages of workers employed on these projects, the two men considered minting coins similar to the Indian and Zanzibari copper pice already in circulation[52] Minting their own coins had the added benefit of the potential for profits from seigniorage. Further, doing so as soon as possible was "desirable" in order "to settle the question of our right to minting".[53] Mackenzie sent samples of the various coins in circulation in East Africa to London and suggested a design for a new copper pice that copied the 1886 pice except with "Mombasa" replacing

209–30. See also John S. Galbraith, *Mackinnon and East Africa 1878–1895: A Study in the "New Imperialism"* (Cambridge, Cambridge University Press, 2008).

[49] London, SOAS, PP MS 1/IBEA/1/58, copy of letter from William Mackinnon to Dr Badger at Zanzibar, December 1877.

[50] Much relevant correspondence is in London, SOAS, PP MS 1/IBEA/1/62 and PP MS 1/IBEA/1/9.

[51] Galbraith (2008) *Mackinnon and East Africa 1878–1895.*

[52] London, SOAS, PP MS 1/IBEA/1/1A, *Mombasa Letters*, letter of 14 November 1888. On currency and wage payments, see Jan Lucassen (ed.), *Wages and Currency: Global Comparisons from Antiquity to the Twentieth Century* (Bern, Peter Lang, 2007).

[53] London, SOAS, PP MS 1/IBEA/1/1A, letter of 23 October 1888.

"Zanzibar" in the inscription.[54] By the end of 1888 a tonne of copper coins had been struck at the Birmingham Mint and shipped to Mombasa, and further orders were placed in 1889. In addition, the IBEAC had silver coins struck in 1889 of the same weight and fineness as the Indian rupee.[55]

For IBEAC in the late 1880s, the issue of coins was initially seen as important in order to facilitate wage payments—so that roads could be cleared and building works undertaken—but it quickly became a question of profit. For both purposes, copper pice were more important than silver rupees, and as seems to have been the case a few years earlier at Zanzibar, the silver IBEAC coins may have been issued in part to secure the higher-profit copper coins as the small change currency of the concession areas. For minting copper coins, the profits were as high as 50 per cent. The company sought to maximize this profit by minting enough coin to gradually replace Indian rupees and pice, and other "foreign" coins in circulation.[56] By April 1890, George Mackenzie proudly reported that in one Somali town, a vendor had specifically asked for Mombasa rupees rather than Indian rupees, describing this as "an indication of how rapidly an innovation extends along even this little frequented coast".[57] It is noteworthy, though, that other than one early reference suggesting that issuing coin could be a way to settle questions about rights that were not made explicit in the concession agreement, there was no link made by IBEAC representatives between the issue of coinage and any claims to sovereignty or to territory. They aimed in the end to be able to replace the Indian and other imported coins, but this was motivated by practicality and by profit, rather than by political or imperial ideals.

[54] Images of these coins can be seen at https://www.britishmuseum.org/research/collection_online/search.aspx—search for acquisition number 1904,0802.1 for the silver rupee, and 1993,1120.24 for the copper pice.

[55] London, SOAS, PP MS 1/IBEA/1/16, letters of 10 May 1889 and 13 May 1889. London, SOAS, PP MS 1/IBEA/1/31, letter of 9 January 1890 on finance and banking details. London, SOAS, PP MS 1/IBEA/1/37, letter of 17 February 1890 regarding the currency order. This proposal initially prompted objections from the Treasury in London. However, the Government of India subsequently reassured the Treasury that the IBEAC coins would not be legal tender in India. ZNA AC 1/2, No 69, 15 April 1891, and copy of memo from the Finance and Commerce Department, Government of India, 15 July 1890.

[56] London, SOAS, PP MS 1/IBEA/1/24, A. Dick (Mombasa) to William Mackinnon: "Notwithstanding the enormous quantities of copper and other coin lately imported there is still a very large field especially if we gradually get rid of the Indian and foreign coin".

[57] ZNA, AC 10/2, letter from George Mackenzie to Colonel Euan-Smith at Zanzibar about navigability of Juba river, ports north of Juba, and the Benadir Coast, 24 April 1890.

Coins as the Subject of Legal Dispute

In 1888, Sultan Barghash died and was succeeded by his brother Khalifa. Almost immediately on becoming Sultan on 26 March, Khalifa lowered the exchange rate of a silver riyal coin from Rs 2 3/8 to Rs 2 1/4. Henri Greffülhe blamed this change on the influence of German company Hansing & Co. and accused their Zanzibar representative of having told the Sultan that the coins' intrinsic value was only Rs 2 1/4. Greffülhe also believed that the British were seeking to undermine his coins so as to ensure that the Indian rupee was the only currency in use at Zanzibar.[58] He believed that his concession agreement was binding on the Sultanate as an institution and, therefore, continued to be in force despite the change in leadership. Sultan Khalifa disagreed and, based on his actions, clearly believed that the concession was a private agreement between Sultan Barghash and Greffülhe.[59]

Though the multiple and overlapping legal jurisdictions at Zanzibar were well understood, it was not clear what could be done about disagreements between the Sultan and a European merchant. In June 1888 the French Consul wrote to Paris explaining that he had no confidence in the Sultan's ability to ignore the vested commercial interests of the local British and German merchant communities and justly resolve this issue. In the consul's view, this dispute could only be settled by a commission of senior officials in the British, French and German finance ministries. The commission of the three European powers at Zanzibar would, Consul Lacan suggested, determine the proper official exchange rate between the riyal and the rupee.[60] For his part, Greffülhe rejected the Consul's suggestion of a commission of European powers, explaining that he doubted the impartiality of such a commission. Further, he stated that the right to strike and issue coin is essentially a royal right, and that submitting this

[58] France, Archives Diplomatiques, La Courneuve, ADC/F/27a/5 (order as ADC/595), *Questions Monétaires: Zanzibar*, 1 June 1888, letter from French Consul at Zanzibar to Direction des Affaires commerciales et Consulaires.

[59] This was not the only contract that Sultan Khalifa denied knowledge of, and he complained that "neither the British nor the Germans had actually produced the treaties each claimed to have concluded with Sultan Barghash": Umar al-Naqar, "Arabic Materials in the Government Archives of Zanzibar," *History in Africa* 5 (1978) 377–82, description of SEC/017 on p. 379.

[60] France, Archives Diplomatiques, La Courneuve, ADC/F/27a/5 (order as ADC/595), *Questions Monétaires: Zanzibar*, 1 June 1888, letter from French Consul at Zanzibar to Direction des Affaires commerciales et Consulaires.

question to anyone other than the Sultan would deprive the Sultan of an attribute of his sovereignty.[61] Nonetheless, Greffülhe claimed that the Sultan's power was "*fictive*" because he could operate only under German and British influence.[62] Ever the businessman, Greffülhe sought profit from the situation. He subsequently wrote to the French Consul that he would raise no objection to the IBEAC coins if either the British government supported his coinage concession at Zanzibar or the GEAC allowed him to transfer his concession to them for a fee.[63] Neither offer was taken up, so the French Consul suggested that Greffülhe should be paid compensation.[64]

In February 1890, Sultan Khalifa died and was succeeded by the third of the brothers, Sultan Ali bin Said. By this time, the IBEAC and GEAC coins had begun to circulate at Zanzibar as well as on the coast. Additionally, French trade at Zanzibar had declined to such an extent that Greffülhe was the only remaining significant French commercial interest, and the coining concession was one of his most important contracts.[65] There was still no legal framework in which Greffülhe could pursue a claim for compensation against the Sultan, but French officials continued to press for a resolution.[66] The disagreement about this coining concession was further complicated by negotiations between the IBEAC and Sultan Ali. The IBEAC was hoping to secure permission to set up a bank that would have the monopoly on issuing paper money in its concessionary areas. The company's directors were not particularly concerned about the coining

[61] France, Archives Diplomatiques, La Courneuve, ADC/F/27a/5 (order as ADC/595), *Questions Monétaires: Zanzibar*, 23 May 1888, letter from Greffülhe to Foreign Ministry, copy forwarded to Zanzibar.

[62] France, Archives Diplomatiques, La Courneuve, ADC/F/27a/5 (order as ADC/595), *Questions Monétaires: Zanzibar*, 22 May 1889, letter from Greffülhe to French Consul.

[63] France, Archives Diplomatiques, La Courneuve, ADC/F/27a/5 (order as ADC/595), *Questions Monétaires: Zanzibar*, 15 May 1889, letter from French Consul at Zanzibar to Direction des Affaires Commerciales et Consulaires, enclosing a copy of a letter just sent to him by Greffülhe.

[64] France, Archives Diplomatiques, La Courneuve, ADC/F/27a/5 (order as ADC/595), *Questions Monetaires: Zanzibar*, undated note by French Consul enclosed with letter of 15 May 1889 to Foreign Minister.

[65] France, Archives Diplomatiques, La Courneuve, ADC/F/27a/5 (order as ADC/595), *Questions Monetaires: Zanzibar*, 15 May 1889, letter from French Consul at Zanzibar to Direction des Affaires Commerciales et Consulaires, enclosing a copy of a letter just sent to him by Greffülhe.

[66] France, Archives Diplomatiques, La Courneuve, ADC/F/27a/5 (order as ADC/595), *Questions Monetaires: Zanzibar*, note of 28 May 1890.

contract between Greffülhe and Sultan Barghash, which they saw as having "only been to a certain extent carried out". They also noted that Greffülhe imported copper pice under a verbal agreement with the Sultan, of which Sultan Ali denied any knowledge.[67] These negotiations reveal that Sultan Ali, like Sultan Khalifa, either did not recognize Greffülhe's concession as still being in force or did not see it as applying to copper pice.[68]

In 1890, Zanzibar became a British Protectorate, following treaties with Germany in July and France in August. Only a month after the Anglo-French agreement had been signed, the French Foreign Minister presented Greffülhe's claim to the British Ambassador in Paris. The Minister explicitly linked the change in the island's political status to the coinage question. He requested that the British government use its influence over the Sultan to arrange a satisfactory solution to this dispute "au moment ou l'Angleterre assume le protectorat de Zanzibar".[69] The French and British governments agreed to settle the matter through binding arbitration. During the proceedings, Kirk, who was then in London, represented the Sultan,[70] and Mr Bertelin, one of Greffülhe's French partners in the coining concession, represented their interests, and Mr Martin, of Martin's Bank in London, acted as arbiter.[71] The arbitration proceedings were designed to settle two claims against the Sultan: firstly for his having failed to protect Greffülhe's interests when part of Zanzibar's mainland territories was ceded to the GEAC; and secondly for his having allowed the IBEAC to put its own money into circulation. No part of the claim was against the two companies for having violated the coining concession by issuing their coins, and no part of the claim related to the coins that had been struck in Birmingham. During the proceedings, Kirk argued that the first claim could be ignored since the

[67] Foreign Office, *Printed Correspondence East Africa* (London, HMSO, 1809), No. 220, 2 December 1890, and No. 261, 9 December 1890.

[68] Nonetheless, IBEAC representatives were cautious enough to insert a clause in the draft agreement for the establishment of a bank at Mombasa, specifying that the Sultan renounced his right to profits from existing coinage contracts, making it his responsibility for these to be "settled and adjusted … with the said contractor": London, SOAS, PP MS 1/IBEA/1/24, 2 December 1890.

[69] France, Archives Diplomatiques, La Courneuve, ADC/F/27a/5 (order as ADC/595), *Questions Monetaires: Zanzibar*, 9 September 1890, note for the English Ambassador to France.

[70] ZNA AC 3/2, 2 January 1892 (Consul-General to Sultan) and 4 January 1892 (Abdul Azizi bin Mohamed replying on behalf of the Sultan).

[71] France, Archives Diplomatiques, Nantes, 748 PO/A 167/1, 11 May 1892, French Consul to Minister.

GEAC territories were no longer part of the Sultanate of Zanzibar, and the second could be ignored since the concession contract allowed for foreign coins (including those of IBEAC) to continue to be used at Zanzibar.[72] Kirk also counter-claimed by arguing that Greffülhe and his partners were now importing such large quantities of copper coin that their actions were damaging the Zanzibar economy.

Kirk's counter-claim was that so many copper pice were being imported at Zanzibar that they had depreciated, and now circulated at around 68 (rather than 64) to the rupee. An order had been issued that British offices were not to accept the copper pice, but this order was often ignored. For example, the Post Office at Zanzibar amassed a surplus of Greffülhe's copper pice that it had accepted in payment but could now exchange only at a 6 per cent loss.[73] British officials at Zanzibar reported to London that it was possible to make money by changing rupees to pice at Zanzibar, picking out the Indian pice and shipping them to Bombay in the Sultan's steamers to exchange back into rupees. However, they suggested that any profits from this would be lost by doubling the rate for freight of copper coin.[74] Compounding British officials' difficulties in understanding the situation at Zanzibar was the fact that they did not know how many copper pice had been imported since Customs House records were only available to them from the 1890 appointment of a British official as Collector of Customs. Previously, the customs had been farmed out to a number of individuals, and their records, if surviving, were not kept at the Customs House. The estimated total number of coins imported in 1891 alone was 1416 cases of copper coin. At 5000 coins per case this totalled 7,080,000 coins.[75]

A particular point of disagreement was the duty to be paid on the increasingly frequent shipments of copper coins. On arrival of one shipment of 120 cases, in May 1892, Greffülhe initially claimed that these should be free of import tax. He then claimed he should pay 5 per cent in kind, as specified in the written concession contract. Ultimately, the Customs Master made him pay 20 of the 120 cases as duty, in line with a verbal agreement of May 1889 that Greffülhe had made with Sultan

[72] ZNA AC 1/2, undated copy of memo by John Kirk to Foreign Office.

[73] ZNA AC 1/6, dispatch no 70, Zanzibar to Foreign Office, 29 January 1891.

[74] ZNA AB 14 28, memorandum from Consul-General Smith to the Marquis of Salisbury, 20 June 1891.

[75] ZNA AC 1/4, anonymous table inserted before Despatch 293, and dispatch no. 309, Zanzibar to Foreign Office, 29 December 1891.

Khalifa.[76] Greffülhe paid the higher amount under formal protest and insisted on receiving a payment that specified both the number of coins paid and their equivalent amount in rupees at the accounting rate of 64 pice per rupee, rather than at the then-current local rate of 68 3/4 pice per rupee.[77] Greffülhe subsequently submitted the receipt to the arbitration proceedings as proof that the importation of copper pice to Zanzibar had not caused depreciation in their value. Since the arbitration was heard in Europe, written evidence—even ephemeral items like receipts—carried more weight than verbal testimony, which would have been proof enough in a Zanzibari legal context. Greffülhe and his partners claimed, "if there is Financial perturbation the cause of it must be found in the illicit coinage and issue of coin by the English and German East African companies".[78] Kirk disagreed, claiming that Greffülhe should be held liable for this economic disturbance because he was importing such large quantities of copper coin that their actions were damaging the Zanzibar economy. Kirk argued that "in no country and under no law" could a concession agreement be "held to cover such a disturbance of the currency, even if [it] were otherwise undisputed, which is by no means the case in the present instance".[79]

The situation became more complicated when the GEAC began efforts to import their copper pice into Zanzibar itself and not just to their concession on the mainland. In June 1892, the GEAC imported 320 cases of copper pice into Zanzibar with the apparent intention of putting them into circulation on the island. The German Consul denied any knowledge of this, and the coins were shipped to the mainland. However, shortly thereafter sacks of copper coin were brought to Zanzibar from the coast. The GEAC claimed that these coins were not intended for wider circulation. Rather, they were to be used by their local agents for payments made in the ordinary course of business. Upon inspection, authorities realized that each sack was full of the new GEAC copper coin covered under a thin layer of Indian and Zanzibar copper pice. As a result, the authorities

[76] ZNA AC 1/7, No. 105, 20 May 1892, and No. 106, 20 May 1892, both Zanzibar to Foreign Office. When later asked about this verbal agreement, the Sultan's former Treasurer, Aben Omani, explained that nothing had been written down, and a search of the palace papers found no trace of it: ZNA AC 1/8, No. 92, 17 March 1893, Zanzibar to Foreign Office.

[77] ZNA AC 1/8, No. 263 Zanzibar to Foreign Office, 3 December 1892.

[78] ZNA AC 1/9, Foreign Office to Zanzibar, 7 January 1893.

[79] ZNA AC 1/8, No. 309 Zanzibar to Foreign Office, 29 December 1891.

rejected the GEAC's justification and sent the shipment of coins back to the mainland.[80]

Though Greffülhe and the British Protectorate government both wanted to prevent the import of GEAC coins, their relationship further deteriorated in 1892.[81] A new low was reached in September 1892, when a notice was published in the *Zanzibar Gazette* that Greffülhe had been appointed as Consul for Holland at Zanzibar, a position which could have given him increased influence, as well as rights and immunities. The British authorities at Zanzibar feared that this appointment would give the French Consul an ally, since he "now frequently stands alone in all measures enacted by the Protecting Power". At the time, there was no treaty between Holland and Zanzibar, and few Dutch interests there. As a result, the Sultan was strongly against the appointment. With support from the British government in London, he withheld his official recognition of the newly appointed Dutch Consul.[82]

In 1893, the arbitration proceedings concluded with a favourable judgement for Greffülhe. The Sultan was ordered to pay £23,500 in damages and the concession was to be ended.[83] In a summary of the decision sent to the Foreign Office, and forwarded to Zanzibar, Kirk was scathing about Bertelin's conduct during the proceedings. He characterized Bertelin's arguments as "of so vague, rambling, and extraordinarily fragmentary a nature that it is practically impossible to reply to it categorically and paragraph by paragraph" and of dealing repeatedly with matters that had been excluded from the scope of the arbitration, including the rate of exchange between the silver riyal and the Indian rupee.[84] Further, Kirk questioned whether some of the statements accepted by the arbiter would have been permissible in a court of law:

> The persistence of such a false statement as this would in any Court of Law have lost the concessionaire their case; it ought to have done so now and would were there a Court to which the error could be referred.[85]

[80] ZNA AC 1/7, No 130 Zanzibar to Foreign Office, 17 June 1892.

[81] See, for example, ZNA AC 19/4, French Consul to Consul-General, 5 December 1892, and ZNA AC 1/7, Customs Master to Consul-General.

[82] ZNA AC 1/8, telegram 259 Foreign Office to Zanzibar, 26 October 1892 and telegram 244 Zanzibar to Foreign Office, 3 November 1892.

[83] ZNA AC 1/14, John Kirk to Foreign Office, 24 July 1893, copy sent to Zanzibar.

[84] ZNA AC 1/19, Foreign Office to Zanzibar, 7 January 1893.

[85] ZNA AC 1/14, John Kirk to Foreign Office, 24 July 1893, copy sent to Zanzibar.

However, there was no possibility of appeal. The British Protectorate government, the Foreign Office, John Kirk, and Sultan Ali, had little choice but to accept the decision. Almost immediately, a loan was arranged in London on the Sultan's behalf to pay the damages. In addition, an announcement was made at Zanzibar that only Indian rupees were to be accepted at the Customs House.[86] At the same time, with the assistance of a "douceur" from the Netherlands Government, Greffülhe was persuaded to renounce his appointment as Consul of the Netherlands at Zanzibar.[87] The Greffülhe arbitration was, it seemed, over.

In his assessment of the arbitration finding, Kirk claimed that, even if it had cost Zanzibar £23,500, it was a good thing for the protectorate that the question was resolved:

> [F]or a Frenchman to have held rights over the currency would have proved a constant source of annoyance to the Sultan's Govt & to us. ... If as the result of the arbitration the Sultan's Govt has to pay a certain sum he is on the other hand to be congratulated for getting rid of a troublesome question in the future.[88]

Coins as Currency and Source of Seigniorage in the Aftermath of the Arbitration Proceedings

During the arbitration proceedings, John Kirk had claimed that the surplus of copper coins at Zanzibar was causing economic problems due to their depreciation. However, the situation quickly changed after shipments of copper coins to Zanzibar stopped in April 1892. By mid-1894, the surplus of copper coin on the island had become a shortage. Though measures had been taken to stop the circulation of GEAC and IBEAC coins at Zanzibar,[89] the scarcity of pice created an incentive for the import

[86] ZNA AC 6/6, listing of telegrams sent, including Zanzibar to Foreign Office, on 6 July 1893, 25 October 1893, 2 and 7 December 1893, 9 and 25 January 1894; Foreign Office to Zanzibar on 25 October 1893, 10 November 1893, 8 January 1894. Payment was made in January 1894, see ZNA AC 2/11, Gray, Dawes & Co to Consul-General, 19 January 1894.

[87] ZNA AC 1/14, No. 164 Foreign Office to Zanzibar, 5 October 1893, enclosing copy of letter from The Hague to London.

[88] ZNA AC 1/14, copy of a letter from John Kirk to Foreign Office, 24 July 1893, copy sent to Zanzibar.

[89] ZNA AA 12/9, Proclamations, notices, regulations, No. 69 of July 5, 1893, Number 70 of 30 August 1893. ZNA AC 3/5 First Minister to Consul General, No. 40, Copy of ordinances, Daressalaam, April 1st and September 18th, 1893.

of the German coins, which soon made up half of the total pice in circulation. General Matthews, First Minister to the Sultan accused German merchants at Zanzibar of taking advantage of the situation by introducing their coinage, "whereby the Germans make a large revenue which ought to belong to the Zanzibar Government". Matthews suggested that that the best course of action would be to introduce a new Zanzibar copper coinage, both to protect Zanzibar from becoming "inundated ... by German coinage" but also to "create a standard value".[90] The views of the Government of India were sought, and they were sceptical, describing it as "both useless and hopeless" to try and reform the copper coinage if there was no established current coinage, which they saw as "beginning currency reform at the wrong end". They instead recommended that the British authorities at Zanzibar should take control of the issue of the copper coin in circulation, securing it by exchanging it for rupees on demand, at a fixed rate, and buying Indian pice to stabilize the rate against the rupee.[91]

This plan was pushed aside in April 1895 when Greffülhe proposed that the Sultan purchase remainder of his stock of copper pice at 87 to the rupee. Greffülhe presented this plan as offering the potential for 13 per cent profit.[92] In light of Greffülhe's offer, Matthews no longer saw why the Zanzibar government should buy Indian coin, and "lose what is regarded by every Government as a means of revenue by the issue of its own coinage". Though Matthew endorsed the purchase and issue of the already-struck coins,[93] Greffülhe's actions nearly sunk the deal. While Matthew had been contemplating the proposal, Greffülhe secretly negotiated a separate deal with the Sultan under which he agreed to purchase the coins at a rate of 85 to the rupee.

[90] ZNA AC 3/5, First Minister, to Consul-General, No. 40, Copper coinage in Zanzibar, report on situation and recommendations, Zanzibar, 18th July 1894.

[91] ZNA AC 1/19, No. 15 of 1895—memorandum from Government of India, Finance and Commerce Department, Accounts and Finance, Mint, 16th January 1895, Calcutta, copy sent to Zanzibar on 15 February 1895.

[92] ZNA AC 19/10, French Consul to Consul-General, forwarding letter from Greffülhe to French Consul, 6 April 1895. Greffülhe also offered 30,000 silver riyals that he had deposited in Bombay to the Sultan at a rate of 100 per 200 rupees: ZNA AC 1/9, Foreign Office to Zanzibar, 7 January 1893.

[93] ZNA AC 1/8, Zanzibar to Foreign Office, typed memorandum by Lloyd Matthews, 2 May 1895.

Under this arrangement with the Sultan, Greffülhe shipped the coins to Zanzibar. The 977 boxes of coins arrived before the British officials had made a final decision about his proposal. However, on their arrival at Zanzibar, the boxes were seized and the original, lower, price of 87 to the rupee was insisted upon by the British authorities. Under pressure, the Sultan relented.[94] Though Sultan Ali professed ignorance of the parallel discussions with Greffülhe, the British Consul General was not convinced. He suspected that the Sultan had been attempting to improve his financial situation, and suggested that he had "made a deliberate attempt to circumvent his European advisors + obtain for his own purse what he knew they were trying to obtain for the public treasury".[95] This assessment of the Sultan's motivations may underplay the complexity of the Sultan's situation. The distinction between Sultan's purse and public treasury was a new one, and before 1890 they were one and the same.[96] However, in 1892 the Zanzibar administration was reorganized. Under the new financial system, the Sultan was allocated a fixed monthly sum for his expenses and was required to keep proper accounts of all income and expenditure.[97]

The Sultan's attempt to deal directly with Greffülhe could have been a simple mistake by a ruler who was still getting used to the new political and financial order of things. Nonetheless, Sultan Ali was well aware of the difficulties of his political position. Though he was careful not to openly defy the British officials at Zanzibar, the Sultan would sometimes act in ways that they disliked, as if to make a point.[98] Officials recognized this pattern. In a deleted draft section of the letter reporting on his conversation with the Sultan, the Consul General emphasized "the independent attitude which the Sultan has attempted to adopt, blaming this on the influence of some leading Arabs at his court".[99] As a result, the attempted purchase of these coins could have been driven by a political, as well as financial, motivation

[94] ZNA AC 2/19, Smith, Mackenzie & Co to Consul-General, 9 October 1895.

[95] ZNA AC 1/8, Zanzibar to Foreign Office, 26 October 1895.

[96] Emilie Ruete, *Memoirs of an Arabian Princess from Zanzibar* (Mineola, New York, Dover Publications, Incorporated, 2009), 121; John Hunwick "Islamic Financial Institutions: Theoretical Structures and Aspects of Their Application in Sub-Saharan Africa," in *Credit, Currencies and Culture: African Financial Institutions in Historical Perspective* (Stockholm, Nordic Africa Institute, 2005) 78–102; Burton, *Zanzibar: The City and the Island*, 270–274.

[97] Lyne, *Zanzibar in Contemporary Times a Short History of the Southern East in the Nineteenth Century*, 191.

[98] Galbraith, 'Italy, the British East Africa Company, and the Benadir Coast, 1888–1893,' 558.

[99] ZNA AC 1/8, Zanzibar to Foreign Office, 26 October 1895.

in that the Sultan could have been attempting to resist the imposition of new political and financial structures under the Protectorate. Interestingly, Greffülhe and his associates explicitly discussed the issue of sovereignty in their correspondence relating to this shipment of copper coins. They suggested that the circulation of these coins would reaffirm the sovereignty of the Sultan because they bore the *thoura* of Sultan Barghash.[100] Whether Sultan Khalifa shared this view is impossible to know, however.

When Henri Greffülhe died in 1898, his business affairs were found to be "in great confusion, and his estate was hopelessly insolvent".[101] The copper coins he had introduced continued to circulate both at Zanzibar and on the mainland. Demand for coinage was growing in the new East Africa Protectorate, which was established when the British government assumed control of the IBEAC.[102] In 1898, the East Africa Protectorate began issuing newly minted copper coins, and preparations were made for stopping the Zanzibar coins from being legal tender there.[103] This proposal did not impress the Zanzibar government, which took the only available action—excluding East African copper coins from circulation on the island. In February 1899, the Zanzibar government proclaimed that only Indian and Zanzibar pice were to be accepted at Zanzibar. Four years later, the administration of Zanzibar was formally separated from that of the British East Africa Protectorate. Subsequently, further steps were taken by the Zanzibar government to exclude from circulation at Zanzibar all silver coin other than the Indian Rupee. For the first time since the Protectorate had been declared 13 years earlier, Zanzibar had a single silver and a single copper currency in circulation. Zanzibar was now clearly separated both in terms of currency and, more broadly, in terms of political rule from the mainland territories.[104]

[100] France, Archives Diplomatiques, Nantes, 748 PO/A 167/1, Bertelin on behalf of all the interested parties, to Greffülhe at Zanzibar, 10 December 1894.

[101] London, National Archives, FO 107/116, includes correspondence relating to water rights, to a wharf that Greffülhe had leased, and to the administration of his estate. The estate took many years to sort out, and was still under consideration by the Sultan in 1903.

[102] Administration of the East Africa Protectorate had passed in 1895 to a Council of Administration at Zanzibar, whose members were most of the senior British officials in the Zanzibar Protectorate government: see ZNA AC 2/118, general papers and correspondence, and ZNA AC 11/47, Minutes of Council of Administration, East Africa Protectorate.

[103] ZNA AC 11/47, Minutes of Council of Administration, East Africa Protectorate, meetings of 29 August 1898 (p. 43) and 31 September 1898 (p. 44).

[104] ZNA AC 4/6, Consul-General to First Minister, 30 October 1903. ZNA 12/9, Proclamations, notices, regulations, No. 131, 15 February 1899, and No. 171, 20 May 1903.

Conclusion and Epilogue

Despite their small value, the Zanzibar copper pice are more than just a numismatic curiosity. They were issued by a French merchant in the name of the Sultan and were circulated widely. Ultimately, they became one of the main circulating coins at Zanzibar and on the mainland, before being replaced on the mainland in the early twentieth century. Throughout, concerns about sovereignty were present, albeit implicitly and indirectly. Sultan Barghash wrote the letter allowing the striking of more copper coins at a time of intense political pressure, when he was losing territory and influence on the mainland. A few years later, Greffülhe invoked the idea of the Sultan's sovereignty when complaining about the actions of the German and British companies. Though for Greffülhe this may of course have been a convenient way to bolster his argument, his decision to frame it this way may have been inspired by tensions between the French and British at Zanzibar. In trying to bolster the authority of the Sultan, even while taking legal action against him in London, the French perhaps were testing the new British Protectorate, and making clear that even though they had signed the 1890 Anglo-French agreement, they were not going to step back and leave the British to have free rein at Zanzibar. Issuing coin, or arguing about who had the right to issue it, can therefore be interpreted as ways of testing the boundaries of the new political order.

The new political boundaries were created in part through disputes about, and definitions of, geographical boundaries in East Africa in this period. The boundaries of Zanzibar's territory on the mainland had been determined by a joint commission of British, French and German representatives—and the disputes about coinage had been handled through an arbitration involving British and French representatives. Moreover, in the coastal areas under the control of the German and British companies, what coins were allowed to circulate was controlled by decrees and proclamations—some excluding particular coins from circulation, and some confirming that others were legal tender. For example, the Imperial British East Africa Company had made explicit their aim to gradually exclude all other currencies from circulation within the borders of their territory, with the aim of excluding all "foreign" coin from those areas. Later, when the British East Africa Protectorate was formed in 1895, one of their first acts was to issue their own coin and to prevent other coin from circulating within their borders—which this time included Zanzibar coinage, despite the fact that the Protectorate was still administered from Zanzibar. These kinds of attempts to limit the circulating currencies had the aim of ensuring that profit from the issuing of coin could be secured, but they can also be seen as a marker of territorial and geographical control, or at claims to control. In this light, they were part of a process of adding additional definition to boundaries that were usually not as powerfully or clearly delineated on the ground as they were on the maps that the European powers drew up and published.[105]

In terms of legal boundaries, the arbitration proceedings also tested the new Protectorate. As soon as the Protectorate had been declared, the French government pressed Greffülhe's case, and agreed with the British government to proceed to arbitration. The Sultan was in theory still the ultimate authority in the Zanzibar legal system, but was represented by proxy in the case against him. The decisions were made in London and Paris, rather than in Zanzibar. Moreover, despite it being common in Zanzibari legal practise to allow the testimony of two witnesses to an agreement to be considered as equivalent to a written document, verbal agreements would have little place in the evidence submitted to the arbitration, being of less importance even than ephemeral documentation like a receipt for a customs payment. Ultimately, even while arguing that the Sultan's political and legal authority must be protected, and despite the fact that the arbitration was not formally a legal proceeding, Henri Greffülhe and his partners undermined that authority by bringing the case against him within European legal frameworks, ensuring that it would be judged by European standards and according to European business practises.

Returning to the issue of sovereignty, the aspect of sovereignty that was at issue in the arbitration proceedings brought by Henri Greffülhe and his partners against the Sultan of Zanzibar was that of the right to issue coin, and how those rights could be protected. Coins often act as a representation of a state or of its ruler, and coinage issued in the name of Sultan Barghash (albeit with his name and genealogy wrongly represented) began to circulate widely at exactly the time when the Sultan's powers were being increasingly limited, in both political and territorial terms. The circulation of these coins may have been seen by the local community as a form of protest against British imperial designs. Though there is scant evidence from the late nineteenth century, there is evidence to this effect from the

[105] Emily Gilbert discusses the spatial dynamics of money in 'Common Cents: Situating Money in Time and Place,' *Economy and Society* 34:3 (2005) 357–88.

period when these coins were withdrawn from circulation, in 1936. These coins, along with the Indian rupee, were to be replaced by new currency issued by the East African Currency Board, but the change met with local protest. A number of petitions were sent to members of the Zanzibar government protesting against the change, with one petition to the Sultan complaining of "strife and quarrelling",[106] and another to the British Resident at Zanzibar stating that the withdrawal of the copper pice would "sever us with the happy past" since they had "been with us and [our] fathers from time immemorial".[107] Another petition, sent to the wife of the Sultan, and decorated at the top with a pencil-rubbing of the two types of Zanzibar copper pice, read:

> In the Official Gazette of Saturday it is published that the 6th of April is the last day of our pice of Zanzibar. Is this fact? If it is true—how this will happen in a town which has its own Sultan who has his own flag—that his pice should be banished. If the pice will be taken away then the Sultan and his flag may also be taken away—there and then we will ascertain that this town is an English town—and this cannot be so. It is true that Zanzibar has no white currency of its own but it has a currency of pice of its own for more than 50 years now and all the Consuls and the Residents who were sent here could not take away our illustrious pice. […] It will do no harm. If he will take away the rupee and replace it by shilling. We know that the rupee is not our coin but the pice are ours.[108]

The petitions were sent from rural areas in the north of Zanzibar, and refer to the pice as "our coin", named along with the Sultan's red flag as symbols of the Sultanate. More powerfully, their withdrawal was seen as a sign that Zanzibar was now British, and that the Sultan and his flag may as well also be taken away—a strong statement of the link between the Sultan's sovereignty and these coins that had been issued 50 years earlier. So, despite all the legal wrangling, and all the debates about currency in the 1890s, the copper pice had become an established part of Zanzibar economic life, and a symbol of the Sultan and his sovereignty. They had endured for 50 years and had, perhaps against the odds, become a symbol of the Sultanate of Zanzibar.

[106] ZNA AB 14/32, undated petition to Sultan.
[107] ZNA AB 14/32, petition of 3 April 1936, to British Resident.
[108] ZNA AB 14/32, petition of 28 March 1936, to Sultan's wife.

CHAPTER 7

The Circulation of Modern Currencies and the Impoverishment of the Red Sea World, 1882–2010

Steven Serels

Over the course of the first half of the twentieth century, European imperial currencies displaced the other currencies used in market transactions in large swaths of the Red Sea world with largely negative effects. Shifts in the currency system were not solely responsible for the dislocations of this period. Local communities were accustomed to their currency system evolving and had previously been able to participate in this evolution in ways that helped to secure the benefits of trade. The currency system that had existed in the region prior to and, in many areas, for decades after the establishment of British, French and Italian colonies was not static. The previous system had a particular kind of dynamism that allowed for the integration of new currencies, including those tied to foreign empires, without producing dramatic negative consequences. For example, the introduction in the Red Sea markets of the Maria Theresa Thaler, which

S. Serels (✉)
Martin Luther Universität Halle-Wittenberg, Halle, Germany

Harvard University, Cambridge, MA, USA

S. Serels, G. Campbell (eds.), *Currencies of the Indian Ocean World*, Palgrave Series in Indian Ocean World Studies,
https://doi.org/10.1007/978-3-030-20973-5_7

had been minted by the Austro-Hungarian Empire since the end of the eighteenth century,[1] lubricated inter- and intra-regional trade throughout the nineteenth century and, in so doing, facilitated the expansion of the export of local products from the Red Sea.[2] However, the introduction of the Italian lira and the French franc, not to mention the expansion of the British-backed Egyptian pound, in the twentieth century resulted in the widespread loss of local capital. During this period, currencies went from relatively stable tools for facilitating trade to unstable media that precipitated the continuous loss of wealth.

European imperial planners did not intentionally render the currency system in the Red Sea unstable, but instability was often the unintended consequence of imperial programmes designed to bring the Red Sea colonial possessions into the metropole's currency zone. Italian officials hoped the lira would become the sole currency of Eritrea and, later, Ethiopia. Similarly, French officials hoped to replace all currencies in the Côte Française des Somalis with the franc. British officials were initially more limited in their plans for imperial currencies. These officials, unlike their French or Italian counterparts, were not immediately interested in replacing the local currencies in their colonial possessions with the British pound. Rather, they were invested both economically and politically in ensuring the continued growth of trade, regardless of the medium of exchange. This flexibility ended in the run-up to the Second World War when British officials started to believe that a supra-imperial currency union based on the pound would ensure the stability and global supremacy of the British economy.[3]

Though officials believed that replacing colonial currencies could be in their own interest, they also realized that colonial subjects and locally active merchants had their own alternative understandings of properly functioning currency systems. In 1904, Gaston Doumergue, the Ministre des Colonies, lamented that "the French currency has not yet taken its leading position that it should occupy in the Côte Française des Somalis" because the Arab, Indian and indigenous merchants who dominate local

[1] For a brief history of this currency, see Adrian E. Tschoegl, 'Maria Theresa's Thaler: A Case of International Money,' *Eastern Economic Journal* 27:4 (Fall 2001) 443–62.

[2] Akinobu Kuroda, 'The Maria Theresa dollar in the Early Twentieth Century Red Sea region: A Complementary Interface between Multiple Markets,' *Financial History Review* 14:1 (April 2007) 108–9.

[3] Allister Hinds, *Britain's Sterling Colonial Policy and Decolonization, 1939–1958* (Westport, CT, Greenwood Press, 2001).

and regional trade have a "repugnance to adopting" this currency. He believed that this repugnance was a result of their misunderstanding of exchange rate fluctuations. Doumergue wrote that these merchants settle their accounts predominantly in rupees because "they are convinced (and it will be very difficult to get them to admit the contrary) that the value of the French currency varies and not that of the rupee".[4] Doumergue's insistence on the stability of the French franc was overly optimistic. The value of the French franc, like other European currencies, was not guaranteed, and the population of the Côte Française des Somalis, like their counterparts elsewhere in the Red Sea region, had reason to avoid its use.

This chapter demonstrates that the weakness of European currency systems undermined imperial plans to transform the Red Sea world. Following the First World War, European currencies became and remained unstable and could not hold their value. There were other, better media of exchange. For local populations, adopting these European currencies at this time meant assuming the instability and risk of devaluation that came with them. For many, this was a risk not worth taking. Unfortunately, others had no choice because they had become poor. Years of political turmoil, ecological fluctuation and economic adjustment had limited the options available to some local communities of producers and merchants to secure their livelihood. Avoiding European currencies, with their associated risks, often meant paying a premium to continue using previous media of exchange. Those who could pay this premium did so and, as a result, were insured against the instability of European currencies. Many could not pay this premium and were forced to use European currencies. These people suffered economically as these currencies lost value. The number of people unable to pay this premium grew after the Second World War. Despite their continued riskiness, the use of these currencies became widespread.

Colonial dependence was not the unique factor that led to the widespread adoption of risky currencies. In territories that were never colonized, such as the Hijaz and parts of Yemen, the options for maintaining the traditional, dynamic currency system also disappeared. In the second half of the twentieth century, the governments of these territories assumed all of the then current prerogatives of governance, including the right to regulate the national currency system. These governments introduced

[4] Ministre des Colonies. *Rapport d'Ensemble sur la Situation Générale du Protectorat de la Côte Française des Somalis et Dépendances en 1904.* FM 1AFFPOL/121 Archives nationales d'outre-mer, Aix-en-Provence (ANOM). Translation by author.

new, national currencies and demonetized all others. Similarly, as colonies gained independence, the newly established governments created their own currencies. However, these currencies were no less risky or more independent than the European imperial currencies introduced by the British, French and Italians. The introduction of these national currencies was often followed by high rates of inflation and currency devaluations. Unfortunately, widespread poverty made the use of these currencies unavoidable and the use of these currencies prevented many from escaping poverty. As a result, the adoption of modern currencies became part of the cycle of poverty from which many communities in the Red Sea world still struggle to escape.

Market-Driven Currency Systems

European imperial agents did not export to the Red Sea the idea that sovereign states could mint their own currencies. The connection between sovereignty and minting currencies was already established in the region before British, French, or Italian agents laid claim to the land. The Ottoman Empire, which long ruled much of the Arabian Red Sea littoral, had its own mints that produced coins whose designs illustrated the power of the Sultan.[5] Local states also expressed their claims to, or at the very least aspirations for, territorial sovereignty by minting their own coins. After Egypt gained its autonomy within the Ottoman Empire at the start of the nineteenth century, the Egyptian government established its own official currency, the Egyptian pound. When religiously inspired Sudanese rebels overthrew the Egyptian colonial administration of Sudan in 1885, officials in the newly independent theocratic state set up a treasury in Khartoum and struck their own coins. The creation of a new Sudanese currency was part of a larger project of developing the visible symbols of authority associated with an autonomous state.[6] A few years later, Menelik II, the emperor of Ethiopia, ordered the creation of a new currency as part of a broader effort to maintain his control over Ethiopia in the face of expanding European influence. Menelik II had the Monnaie de Paris mint over 1.5 million Ethiopian thalers worth of coins, denominated primarily

[5] For a detailed history of money in the Ottoman Empire, see Sevket Pamuk, *A Monetary History of the Ottoman Empire* (Cambridge, Cambridge University Press, 2000).

[6] Kim Searcy, *The Formation of the Sudanese Mahdist State: Ceremony and Symbols of Authority, 1882–1898* (Leiden, Brill, 2011).

at 1, ½, ¼, 1/20th and 1/100th of a thaler.[7] The Monnaie de Paris continued to mint Ethiopian thaler coins until 1905.[8]

In the Red Sea world, the right of a state to establish a new currency did not bring with it the right to determine the role of different currencies in market transactions. As a result, the introduction of a new currency by a state did not radically transform local currency systems, which remained dependent on multiple currencies. For example, between 1840 and the end of the Ottoman rule in the Hijaz during the First World War, the Ottoman lira circulated in Hijazi markets alongside coins from India, Britain, Egypt, Russia, Spain and Mexico.[9] Coins were not the only media of exchange. In Ethiopia, accounts were settled in precious metal currencies of various origins, as well as in salt bars, pieces of cloth, or handfuls of grain.[10] Buyers and sellers were left to determine the mix of media of exchange that they used to settle market transactions. When the interests of the market and the interests of the state did not align, the market won and buyers and sellers determined which currencies circulated. For example, in 1894 Ottoman officials tried to force the dominance of the Ottoman lira in the Hijaz by forbidding the importation of foreign coins. At the time, the relative values of different currencies in Hijazi markets were fluctuating uncontrollably, which was negatively impacting the import-export trade. Nonetheless, people ignored the import restrictions and officials were forced to repeal the prohibition the following year.[11]

Around the same time, vendors in Ethiopia refused to accept the Ethiopian thaler. As a result, this new currency was undervalued in local markets. Merchants exploited this arbitrage opportunity and Ethiopian thalers were withdrawn from circulation as fast as officials could introduce them.[12] The same dynamics shaped the introduction of currencies in most of the newly established European colonies in the Red Sea. Between 1891

[7] The Ethiopian government made ten orders for coins during this period. Each order had to be approved by the French Administration Des Monnaies. Each of these approvals produced a 'Procees-verbal de livraison de monnaies etrangers' contained in FM SG CFS//1. ANOM.

[8] Giovanni Carboneri, *Il Tallero di Maria Teresa e la Questione Monetaria della Colonia Eritrea* (Rome, Tipografia Nazionale di G Bertero E C., 1912) 8.

[9] William Ochsenwald, 'The Commercial History of the Hijaz Vilayet, 1840–1908,' *Arabian Studies* 6 (1982) 57–8.

[10] Richard Pankhurst, *Economic History of Ethiopia, 1800–1935* (Addis Ababa: Haile Sellassie I University Press, 1968) 257–60.

[11] Ochsenwald, 'The Commercial History of the Hijaz Vilayet,' 61–2.

[12] Carboneri, *Il Tallero di Maria Teresa*, 6–8.

and 1896, the new Italian rulers of Eritrea introduced silver coins valued at 10 million Eritrean lire into their new colonial possession. Like the Ethiopian thalers, these coins were undervalued and quickly disappeared from circulation.[13] Similarly, French officials stationed in the Côte Française des Somalis were aware that the biases of merchants against the French franc prevented its widespread acceptance.[14]

At the turn of the twentieth century, the sole territory in which a European-controlled currency gained supremacy was Sudan. In 1896, a British-led force invaded Sudan from Egypt, and a few years later the Mahdist state fell amidst economic chaos. The successor state was officially a condominium under joint British and Egyptian authority. However, this division of authority was more notional than actual. The Egyptian state exerted little oversight and influence over policies pursued by the government of the Anglo-Egyptian Sudan.[15] Moreover, the Egyptian state was itself under the trusteeship of British advisors who had been installed following the 1882 British military occupation of Egypt. These British advisors reformed the Egyptian state's budget, brought Egypt onto the gold standard and made the Egyptian pound a de facto subsidiary currency of the British pound. The reformed Egyptian pound was introduced into Sudan with the establishment of Anglo-Egyptian rule. Under the 1899 Anglo-Egyptian Condominium Agreement that established the formal supervisory roles of Britain and Egypt with respect to the new Sudanese government, all shortfalls in the Sudanese budget were to be met by subventions from the Egyptian Treasury. As a result of this provision, the Egyptian pound became the de facto "official" currency of the Anglo-Egyptian Sudan. In addition, the Anglo-Egyptian government lacked its own, independent armed force and, instead, was dependent on the large contingent of Egyptian Army soldiers stationed in Sudan.

The Egyptian Army, like the Egyptian Treasury, settled accounts in Egyptian pounds. The dependence of the Anglo-Egyptian state on the Egyptian Treasury and the Egyptian Army led large quantities of Egyptian pounds to flow into Sudan in the years immediately following the British-led invasion. Between 1899 and 1912, the Egyptian Treasury granted the

[13] Carboneri, *Il Tallero di Maria Teresa*, 6.

[14] Ministre des Colonies, *Rapport d'Ensemble sur la Situation Générale du Protectorat de la Côte Française des Somalis et Dépendances en 1904*. FM 1AFFPOL/121. ANOM. Translation by author.

[15] Gabriel Warburg, *The Sudan Under Wingate; Administration in the Anglo-Egyptian Sudan, 1899–1916* (London, Frank Cass, 1971) 16–17.

Anglo-Egyptian state a subvention of, on average, 200,000 Egyptian pounds each year.[16] Similarly, the Egyptian Army imported Egyptian pounds to pay soldiers stationed in Sudan, many of whom were Sudanese, and to purchase provisions. The invasionary force was quite large and much of their daily rations had to be bought locally. In 1903 the Egyptian Army purchased 1.7 million kg of wheat in Dongola Province alone, paying for it with Egyptian pounds.[17]

Policies implemented by the new colonial Sudanese state explain the mechanism by which Egyptian pounds were introduced in large quantities but not the reasons why this currency became the overwhelmingly dominant currency in much of northern Sudan. There already was a currency system in the region before the British-led invasion. Until the collapse of the Mahdist state, coins struck by the Mahdist *Bait al-Mal* (Treasury) were in widespread circulation and were used to settle market transactions. Shortly after the establishment of Anglo-Egyptian rule, Mahdist coins were no longer an acceptable currency. They lost their value and became little more than curios that were only of interest to foreigners as tourist mementos.[18] This transition can only be explained by understanding the preferences of market actors. In northern Sudan, the impetus for the widespread acceptance of the Egyptian pound was the preferences of wholesale merchants, retail vendors and itinerant peddlers. The latter two groups of traders played an outsized role in inducing the Sudanese population to use Egyptian pounds in their market transactions. Many of these traders were foreigners of Greek or Levantine origin who arrived in Sudan during the British-led conquest or in the subsequent formative years of the Anglo-Egyptian state.[19] Some of these immigrants made their way south with the advancing Egyptian Army, selling provisions imported from Egypt to

[16] House of Commons, United Kingdom. *Reports by His Majesty's High Commissioner on the Finances, Administration and Condition of Egypt and the Soudan for the Period 1914–1919* (Cmd 957, 1920) 97.

[17] J. H. Neville, 'Annual Report. Agriculture and Lands Department, 1903,' *Reports on the Finances, Administration and Conditions of the Sudan* (RFACS), *1903*, Vol. 3 (1903) 172. Sudan Archive, Durham University (SAD).

[18] H. S. Job. 'The Coinage of the Mahdi and the Khalifa,' *Sudan Notes and Records* 3:3 (1920) 164.

[19] Levantine and Greek merchants had lived and traded in Sudan prior to the Mahdist period. During the Mahdist period, many of these merchants were taken as prisoners in Sudan, though some were allowed to continue to engage in petty trade. *Europeans, Armenians, Syrians, Jews and Copts taken prisoners from different garrisons in the Sudan*, in Intelligence Department, Egyptian Army, *Sudan Intelligence Report*, No. 60 (25 May to 31

recently conquered Sudanese communities.[20] Increasing numbers of migrants came in the years following the establishment of Anglo-Egyptian rule. In 1905 alone, 285 Greeks and 76 Levantines entered Sudan from Egypt to engage in trade and petty crafts.[21] Greek and Levantine traders often travelled to relatively remote regions, where they would sell imported goods, such as sugar and cloth,[22] and purchase grain yields, crop futures,[23] and underutilized agricultural land.[24] These traders had strong commercial and familial ties to Egypt, which they leveraged to ensure access to the capital and goods necessary to engage in trade. As a result, these Greek and Levantine merchants preferred accepting Egyptian pounds as payment when selling goods in Sudan.

These merchants might have also accepted other silver or gold coins with reliable precious metal contents but these were not available in Sudanese markets. The coins minted by the Mahdist *Beit al-Mal* since 1886 were of diminishing fineness. Though the coins struck in 1885 were of a higher fineness than their Egyptian counterparts, the Mahdist mint progressively decreased the precious metal content in newly struck coins. By the early 1890s, Mahdist officials had come to the conclusion that a currency was just a medium of exchange whose value was not inherently tied to the material qualities of struck coins.[25] In 1894, the silver dollars produced by the *Bait al-Mal* were less than 25 per cent silver.[26] Two years later, the silver content had been reduced to just 10 per cent. Officials also stopped changing the date on the coins. As a result, Mahdist coins with the same face value but with radically different precious metal contents were allowed to circulate in the market simultaneously, a state of affairs that eroded confidence in the Mahdist currency even before the collapse of the Mahdist state.[27] Over the same period, the supply of foreign-produced coins in Sudan decreased. Some of Sudan's stock of foreign-produced coins

December 1898) 72–3. SAD; *Statement of Mul Awal Abdalla Eff. Mohammed* [n.d. 1890] SAD179/3/37-41.

[20] Intelligence Department, Egyptian Army, *Sudan Intelligence Report*, No 56 (6 October to 12 November 1897) 6. SAD.

[21] G E Iles, *Annual Report, Halfa Province, 1905* RFACS 67–70. SAD.

[22] Jackson to Civil Secretary, 11 May 1914 CIVSEC2/1/2. National Records Office, Khartoum (NRO).

[23] Phipps to Wingate, 27 August 1905 SAD277/2/67-69.

[24] Cromer to Wingate, 2 February 1906 SAD278/2/2-3.

[25] Job, 166–71.

[26] Wingate to Verme, 20 February 1894 SAD257/1/184-191.

[27] Job, 'The Coinage of the Mahdi and the Khalifa,' 173.

was melted down to produce the precious metal content of coins minted by the Mahdist *Bait al Mal*. Other coins disappeared from circulation as a result of hoarding, a common phenomenon when debased currency coins are introduced.[28] In addition, the resumption of foreign trade resulted in the export of large quantities of foreign-produced coins. At the end of the 1880s, the Mahdist state, British-controlled Egypt and Italian-controlled Eritrea normalized trade.[29] Mahdist Sudan produced few goods in demand in foreign markets. Gum, ivory and slaves could not be exported from Sudan in quantities large enough to offset the demand for imported goods. The negative balance of trade was covered by exports of foreign-minted coins and other gold and silver goods. Merchants arriving from Sudan at Egyptian markets or Red Sea ports often brought gum and relatively large sums of gold and silver. For example, on 29 October three Nilotic Sudanese merchants arrived in Sawakin with 73 camel loads of gum and 1000 silver thalers.[30] As a result, economic policies pursued by the Mahdist state decreased the supply of trustworthy gold and silver coins in Sudan. After the Mahdist state was replaced by the new Anglo-Egyptian government, the only reliable coins circulating in Sudanese markets were recently imported Egyptian pounds.

European Currencies and Economic Instability Before the Second World War

Despite their instrumental role in introducing the Egyptian pound to Sudan, British imperial officials were not specifically committed to a policy of establishing a unitary imperial currency at the start of the twentieth century. British imperial officials did not conceptualize recreating colonial currency systems in the image of the metropole as a necessary part of imperial rule. Until the middle third of the twentieth century, currency policy in the British Empire was one based on expediency. As a result,

[28] The observation that 'bad money drives out good' was first made in the sixteenth century by Thomas Gresham, the financial agent of the British Queen Elizabeth I. For a brief synopsis of Gresham's Law and recent debates about its validity, see its entry in J. Black, N. Hashmizade and G. Myles, *A Dictionary of Economics*, (Oxford, Oxford University Press, 2009).

[29] Steven Serels, *Starvation and the State: Famine, Slavery and Power in Sudan, 1883–1956* (New York, Palgrave Macmillan, 2013) 85.

[30] Intelligence Department, Egyptian Army, *Staff Diary and Intelligence Report, Eastern Sudan*, No. 16 (15 to 31 October 1891). SAD.

India was allowed to remain on a silver standard despite the commitment in Britain to the gold standard. The silver Indian rupee became the currency of the British government of Aden at its inception in 1839 because Aden was ruled through India. However, Aden-based merchants dealt in a number of currencies, including, in the twentieth century, Maria Theresa Thalers,[31] French francs,[32] and Italian lire.[33] Similarly, in certain parts of Sudan, other currencies circulated alongside Egyptian pounds well into the twentieth century. Though Greek and Levantine merchants demanded to be paid in Egyptian pounds, Eritrean and Ethiopian merchants who came to Sudan to trade accepted only Maria Theresa Thalers. In the early years of Anglo-Egyptian rule, the preference of Eritrean and Ethiopian merchants for thalers hurt trade because there were inadequate supplies of this currency in border markets. As a result, thalers were overvalued in border markets by as much as 20 per cent.[34] Anglo-Egyptian officials responded by importing large quantities of thalers and offering to exchange them at favourable rates at these markets. Between October and December 1911 alone, officials purchased 600,000 Maria Theresa Thalers from the mint in Vienna, which were then shipped through Sudan to markets along the Eritrean and Ethiopian frontier.[35] However, the circulation of these coins remained relatively limited in Sudan. Though they facilitated cross-border trade, intra-northern-Sudanese trade continued to be settled in Egyptian pounds. As a result of the initiative of the merchant community, the Egyptian pound, which was a subsidiary currency of the British pound, became the currency of northern Sudan despite the flexible currency policy in the British Empire.

Unlike their British counterparts, French imperial officials believed, at the start of the twentieth century, that the French franc should and would rapidly dominate economic life in the colonies.[36] However, the currency policy of

[31] *Rapport Mensuel. Avril 1917. 2e Partie. Renseignements Economiques. Fascicule No. 4. Abyssinie.* FM 1AFFPOL/122 ANOM.

[32] Copy of Petition of the 16th April 1943 from Scholem Tacoob Attar and Others, Aden FM 1AFFPOL/3699. ANOM.

[33] Jacking to the Secretary of State for Foreign Affairs 18 April 1938 IOR/R/20/2/147 British Library, London (BL).

[34] Slatin to Wingate 7 February 1903 SAD273/2/9-10.

[35] Rowlatt to Oesterreichische Credit Anstalt 30 August 1911 SAD301/2/139-140.

[36] Ministre des Colonies, *Rapport d'Ensemble sur la Situation Générale du Protectorat de la Côte Française des Somalis et Dépendances en 1904.* FM 1AFFPOL/121 ANOM. Translation by author.

the colonial administration of the Côte Française des Somalis was mediated by other local concerns. French officials on the ground did not fully occupy the whole territory. At the end of the nineteenth century, officials determined that holding more than the port of Djibouti and the trade route to Ethiopia was not cost effective. Officials were progressively withdrawn from the remainder of the colony and, by 1909, there was only one government agent stationed outside Djibouti.[37] Officials had in practice relinquished all influence on the economic policy of local rulers that governed the rest of the territory. As the railroad from Djibouti to Addis Ababa was constructed, French influence was again extended into the interior. However, it was limited to the narrow path along which the railroad travelled. As late as 1925, French officials recognized that they did not effectively occupy the vast majority of the Côte Française des Somalis and were, therefore, hampered in shaping political and economic conditions in the interior.[38] Nonetheless, the colonial government was able to use its monopolistic control over the port of Djibouti and the railroad to compel some use of the French francs. Merchants wishing to use these facilities had to pay in francs. As a result, these merchants had to acquire francs, either by using the exchange services of the Banque d'Indochine's local branch or by accepting them from labourers who worked for these facilities and who were paid in francs.

Italian imperial officials initially held positions similar to their British counterparts in so far as currency policy was crafted with economic and political expediency in mind. However, these officials subsequently changed their position and, like their French counterparts, adopted a policy of making the metropolitan currency the sole currency of their colonial possessions. At the end of the nineteenth century, Italian officials tried to intervene in the currency market in Eritrea, but only to replace the Maria Theresa Thaler, which was minted by the Austro-Hungarian Empire, with a similar silver currency minted in Italy. In 1891, Italian officials began minting the Eritrean lira. Over the next five years, officials introduced coins valued at 10 million Eritrean lire into their new colonial possession.[39] However, local traders refused to accept this new currency at face value and they quickly disappeared from circulation.[40] Italian officials

[37] Ministère des Colonies, *Côte Française des Somalis. Rapport Annuel. Situation Générale de la Colonie pendant l'année 1909*. FM 1AFFPOL/133 ANOM.

[38] Merly to le Ministre des Colonies 15 April 1925 FM 1AFFPOL/696. ANOM.

[39] Carboneri, *Il Tallero di Maria Teresa*, 6.

[40] Carboneri, *Il Tallero di Maria Teresa*, 6–8.

allowed the Maria Theresa Thaler to remain the dominant local currency for the next few decades. Following the First World War, officials changed course. Officials in Italy began to believe that there were structural problems in the Italian economy that could only be fixed by adopting a new colonial policy. At the time, Italy was dependent on foreign imports of raw materials and basic foodstuffs. Italy imported annually over 2.5 billion lire's worth of food alone. However, the Italian economy on the whole lacked the foreign currency earning potential to cover the negative trade balance. Following the fascist rise to power, officials conceptualized territorial expansion as the best available solution to Italy's ongoing currency crisis. In particular, Italian fascists came to believe that conquering Ethiopia would lay the groundwork for ending the negative balance of trade. Fascist officials wanted to develop Ethiopia into the breadbasket of Italy by increasing wheat production in the northern highlands and by establishing rigid trade links between Ethiopia and Italy. At the same time, these officials wanted to stimulate the export of coffee, skins, civet and wax from Italy's African colonies to Europe and North America as a way of increasing the government's reserve of pounds, dollars, francs, marks and krone. As a result, colonizing Ethiopia would simultaneously reduce the value of imports from outside the lira zone and increase the earnings of desperately needed foreign currency.[41] The success of this plan was fundamentally dependent upon transforming the currency system of Ethiopia, and with it that of the neighbouring Eritrea, from one based on multiple currencies, with Maria Theresa Thalers serving as the dominant currency in the import/export trade, to one based on the Italian lira.

During the period of fascist rule, the Italian lira thoroughly penetrated the Eritrean economy but failed to take hold in Ethiopia. Following the 1936 invasion of Ethiopia, Italian officials proclaimed the Italian lira to be the only legal currency in all of Africa Orientale Italiana (AOI), the newly agglomerated colony that, at its height, included much of modern-day Ethiopia, Eritrea and Somalia. The local population was required to exchange all Maria Theresa Thalers for Italian lira. The collected thalers were then exported to Italy and used to purchase the foreign currencies needed to settle Italy's negative balance of trade.[42] By 1940, the Italian lira

[41] Alberto Sbacchi, *Ethiopia under Mussolini: Fascism and the Colonial Experience* (New Jersey, Zed Books, 1985) 95.

[42] Jacking to the Secretary of State for Foreign Affairs 14 January 1938 IOR/R/20/2/147 BL.

was effectively the only currency in circulation in Eritrea. However, Maria Theresa Thalers continued to circulate widely in Ethiopia because Ethiopian communities were willing to go to great lengths to avoid using Italian lire. Following the official demonetization of the Maria Theresa Thaler, trade in Ethiopia migrated to areas beyond the supervisory capabilities of newly installed Italian officials. Merchants refused to use market facilities regulated by the colonial government because within these facilities officials could enforce the use of the Italian lira.[43] Instead, merchants sought out other avenues of trade where Maria Theresa Thalers were still dominant. The continued strong demand for thalers despite their reclassification as contraband drove up their price. The value of a thaler in Ethiopia rose under Italian rule, eventually peaking in 1937 at over double its value in London.[44] At the same time, the legal trade in traditional products dried up because merchants refused to sell goods for Italian lira. Private Italian merchants in Ethiopia who were now unable to profit from trade began to exploit the arbitrage opportunity opened up by the disparity in the value of Maria Theresa Thalers. These merchants contracted with Indian merchants in Aden to purchase thalers in exchange for Italian lira. By 1938, Indian merchants were routinely shipping parcels of up to 100,000 lire to London, Paris and Cairo. The profits from this trade were sufficiently large that these Indian merchants continued to send these parcels by steamship even though no insurance agent would insure them.[45]

The Italian lira came to dominate Eritrea, but not Ethiopia, because the local population of Eritrea wanted to earn Italian lira. The period of Italian rule in Eritrea coincided with a series of economic and ecological disasters that permanently and irrevocably disrupted traditional economic practices. The first of these major disasters was the rinderpest epizootic of 1887–1889. Rinderpest is a cattle disease that kills 90 per cent of infected herds in virgin populations, such as those that had existed in Africa prior to this epizootic. During the outbreak, millions of cattle died in Eritrea alone. Cattle were a source of both wealth and agricultural labour. As a result, the epizootic disrupted cultivation and trading practices and set off a deadly famine during which two-thirds of the population in some regions

[43] Vinattieri. *Il Patrimonio zootecnico del Seraè e la sua pastorizia. Adi Ugri*. [n.d. before 1940] FASC524 Istituto agronomico per l'oltremare, Florence (IAO).

[44] Jacking to the Secretary of State for Foreign Affairs 14 January 1938 IOR/R/20/2/147 BL.

[45] Jacking to the Secretary of State for Foreign Affairs 18 April 1938 IOR/R/20/2/147 BL.

died.[46] Though this epizootic and ensuing famine also hit neighbouring communities in Sudan and Ethiopia, Eritrean communities uniquely were unable to recover because of policies pursued by the Italian colonial administration. In the years following the famine, Italian officials confiscated approximately 300,000 hectares in the Eritrean highlands and reserved them for Italian settlement.[47] Though this policy was subsequently reversed, the grain economy of Eritrea was permanently weakened. Eritrea stopped producing sufficient supplies of grain to feed itself. As a result, the colony became structurally dependent on grain imports.[48] In subsequent years, Eritrea was plagued by grain price spikes and repeated food crises.[49] Individual Eritreans ceased to be able to meet their own basic needs and were forced to find other sources of income. The only real substantial demand for wage labour came from the expanding colonial armed forces. Between 1934 and 1940, the indigenous Eritrean military force was expanded from 10,000[50] to 150,000 men.[51] At the time, the total population of Eritrea was slightly larger than 600,000 people.[52] Italian officials were motivated to expand the Eritrean force because Eritrean soldiers were used to conquer and hold Ethiopia and British Somaliland. Eritreans were motivated to enlist because they were impoverished and needed a secure source of income. This income was paid in lira. Each soldier was paid approximately 2 lire per day, with a 1 lira per day bonus for every day of active operations. In rare cases, soldiers with

[46] For descriptions of the famine, see Richard Pankhurst, *The Great Ethiopian Famine of 1888–1892: A New Assessment* (Addis Ababa, Haile Sellassie I University, 1964); Steven Serels, 'Famines of War: The Red Sea Grain Market and Famine in Eastern Sudan 1889–1891,' *Northeast African Studies.* 12:1 (2012) 73–94; Rudolph von Slatin, *Fire and Sword in the Sudan: A Personal Narrative of Fighting and Serving the Dervishes, 1879–1895*, translated by F.R. Wingate (London, Edward Arnold, 1896) 452–7; F. R. Wingate, *Ten Years' Captivity in the Mahdi's Camp 1882–1892* (London, Sampson, Low, Marston and Co, 1892) 284–91; Ferdinando Martini, *Nell'Africa Italiana*, 8th ed. (Milan, Fratelli Treves, 1925) 29–31.

[47] *L'Economia Eritrea; Nel Cinquatennio dell'Occupazione di Assab (1882–1932)* (Florence, Istituto Agricolo Coloniale Italiano, 1932) 7–8.

[48] Michele Checchi, *Movimento Commerciale della Colonia Eritrea*, Istituto Coloniale Italiano, bibliioteca di studi coloniali. No 19. Romer (1912) 32–43.

[49] Governo della Colonia Eritrea to il Ministero delle Colonie 22 September 1915. Pacco 758 Archivio Eritreo, Archivio Storico Diplomatico, Rome (AE)

[50] Alessandro Volterra, *Sudditi Coloniali: Ascari Eritrei 1935–1941* (Milan, FrancoAngeli, 2005) 85–6.

[51] Volterra, *Sudditi Coloniali*, 111.

[52] Fernando Santagata, *La Colonia Eritrea nel Mar Rosso davanti all'Abyssinia.* (Napoli, Libreria Internazionale Treves di Leo Lupi, 1935) 25.

specialty training and higher rank could receive as much as 500 lire per month.[53] As a result, the impoverishment of the Eritrean population at the start of the twentieth century laid the groundwork for the widespread acceptance of the Italian lira during the late 1930s.

The increased circulation of Italian lire, French francs and British-backed Egyptian pounds introduced structural weaknesses into the economy of the Red Sea world. The relative value of these gold-backed currencies and their value relative to the silver currencies in circulation in the region ceased to be stable with the First World War. During the war, Britain, Italy and France each saw their gold reserves plummet and, as a result, the convertibility of their currencies was suspended. At the same time, the Italian lire and French francs lost value relative to the British pound. The nominal exchange rate of 1 British pound increased from 25.86 to 39.67 Italian lire. The lira recovered some lost value in 1918. However, beginning in 1919 the Italian lira began to depreciate rapidly relative to the pound. By December 1923, the nominal exchange rate of 1 British pound had reached 100.48 Italian lire.[54] Similarly, between 1914 and 1919 the coverture in gold of the total mass of circulating French francs decreased from 80 to 18 per cent and France was forced to suspend convertibility. Following the war, the French government sought to rapidly return to convertibility at the pre-war rate. However, this led to speculation against the franc, which resulted in five years of the French franc declining in value against the British pound.[55]

These European currencies experienced another period of volatility in the 1930s. In 1931 Britain devalued both its pound and its satellite currencies. Less than two years later, the United States suspended convertibility and devalued the dollar. As a result, the currencies of the gold area, including the French franc and the Italian lira, were suddenly overvalued.[56] In response, the French government allowed the franc to float beginning in 1937 and within a year the franc had lost nearly one-third of its value relative to the British pound.[57] Similarly, the Italian government responded by reducing the gold content in the Italian lira by nearly 40 per

[53] Volterra, *Sudditi Coloniali*, 174–5.

[54] Michele Fratianni and Franco Spinelli, *A Monetary History of Italy* (Cambridge, Cambridge University Press, 1997) 122.

[55] Jean-Pierre Patat and Michel Lutfalla, *Historie Monétaire de la France au XXe siècle* (Paris, Economica, 1986) 37–8.

[56] Patat and Lutfalla, *Historie Monétaire de la France au XXe siècle*, 67.

[57] Patat and Lutfalla, *Historie Monétaire de la France au XXe siècle*, 82.

cent.[58] Changes in the exchange rate do not completely capture the overall loss of value of these European currencies. Between August 1914 and September 1917, the price of silver in New York and London nearly doubled. Though it subsequently decreased slightly, the price of silver remained elevated for years after the armistice.[59] As a result, even the British pound and its subsidiary currencies, such as the Egyptian pound, lost value relative to the price of silver. During the war and its immediate aftermath, the British pound lost half its value, the French franc lost over 80 per cent of its value and the Italian lira lost nearly 98 per cent of its value relative to silver. As a result, the loss in value of the British pound, Italian lira and French franc relative to silver was on a different order of magnitude to the relatively modest exchange rate fluctuations that had previously occurred in the Red Sea region. For example, between 1887 and 1907, the value of a Maria Theresa Thaler had only fluctuated between 2 and 3 Italian lire.[60]

The decline in the value of the Italian lira, the French franc and the British and Egyptian pounds affected the labour economy in the Red Sea because this decline was not met with an equivalent rise in wages denominated in these currencies. For example, the daily wage for a soldier in the Eritrean force was established in the late 1880s at 1.60 lire per day.[61] This wage did not increase until the 1930s even though the lira had lost most of its value relative to other silver currencies then circulating in the Red Sea. The decline in real wages after the First World War reduced the desirability of wage labour. Local communities with access to other economic strategies avoided entering the labour market because the real value of wages kept declining. Only those with no other choice, such as the exceptionally impoverished communities in Eritrea, took up wage labour. During the first third of the twentieth century, the demand for labour was met by desperate labour migrants, such as those escaping the worsening violence and economic depression in Yemen.[62] As a result, increasing

[58] Fratianni and Spinelli, *A Monetary History of Italy*, 150.

[59] Dickson H. Leavens, *Silver Money* (Bloomington, IN, Principa Press, 1939) 103–6.

[60] *A Relazioni Commerciali fra Trieste e Massaua [nd1888]* Pacco 27 AE. *Apicoltura e commercio della cera e del miele nella colonia Eritrea* (Rome, Istituto Coloniale Italiano, 1910) 11.

[61] Marco Scardigli, *Il Braccio Indigeno: Ascari, irregolari e Bande nella Conquista dell'Eritrea 1885–1911* (Milan, FrancoAngeli, 1996) 46.

[62] R. J. Gavin, *Aden Under British Rule, 1839–1967* (London, C Hurst and Co, 1975) 294.

numbers of Yemeni men migrated across the Red Sea to find work in ports, on farms and in government construction projects. Until 1920, Yemeni men made up the largest group of dockworkers in Massawa.[63] Similarly, between 1924 and 1931 nearly all the stevedores working in Port Sudan were Yemeni.[64] As a result, these migrants spread the effects of the declining value of European currencies from the African to the Arabian littoral of the Red Sea.

The only Red Sea territory to avoid the structural problems that resulted from the expanded circulation of European and European-backed currencies was the Hijaz. However, even this region was vulnerable to economic contractions as a result of its dependence on imports of currency from Britain. In June 1916, British officials began providing Husayn ibn Ali, the *Sharif* of Mecca, with a large stipend paid in gold coins. Between 1916 and 1920, Britain granted Husayn nearly £4 million. The annual subventions were briefly suspended from February 1920 until September 1921, after which they were resumed at a rate of £5000 per month.[65] Husayn used the subvention to provide grants to other local leaders whom he was hoping would support his bid to permanently end Ottoman rule in the Hijaz and to establish himself as Caliph.[66] The subventions came to an end in March 1924, when a Sa'udi force conquered Mecca and 'Abd al-'Aziz al-Sa'ud was subsequently proclaimed King of the Hijaz.[67] The then resource-poor region could not recoup the income lost from the cessation of the subsidy. Oil had yet to be discovered and

[63] Stefano Bellucci and Massimod Zaccaria, 'Wage Labor and Mobility in Colonial Eritrea, 1880s to 1920s,' *International Labor and Working-Class History* 86 (2014) 100–1.

[64] B. A. Lewis, 'Diem el Arab and the Beja Stevedores of Port Sudan,' *Sudan Notes and Records* 43 (1962) 19.

[65] Joseph Kostiner, *The Making of Saudi Arabia 1916–1936: From Chieftaincy to Monarchical State* (Oxford, Oxford University Press, 1993) 57–62.

[66] Joshua Teitelbaum, *The Rise and Fall of the Hashemite Kingdom of Arabia* (London, Hurst and Co, 2001) 76. Husayn came to conceptualize the presence of large quantities of foreign coins in Hijazi markets as an impediment to the full recognition of the legitimacy of his claim to sovereignty. So, Husayn's government began to overstrike foreign coins with a symbol of his rule. When Husyan assumed the Caliphate in 1923, his government began to mint its own coins. Though they were intended to replace all foreign coins in circulation in the Hijaz, the coins were not widely accepted and soon disappeared from circulation. Foreign-minted silver and gold coins continued to be used in market transactions. Teitelbaum, *The Rise and Fall of the Hashemite Kingdom of Arabia*, 207.

[67] For a description of al-Sa'ud's rise to dominance in the Hijaz, see Askar al-Enazy, *The Creation of Saudi Arabia: Ibn Saud and British Imperial Policy, 1914–1927* (London and New York, Routledge, 2010) 129–57.

revenues from the annual Muslim pilgrimage were declining. The average number of annual pilgrims arriving in the Hijaz via the Red Sea declined from 132,109 in 1927 to 21,065 in 1932 and did not recover until after the Second World War. As a result, the annual government revenue from the *hajj* declined from an estimated £1 million to £250,000.[68] Without the regular infusion of large quantities of gold currencies from Britain, the Hijaz sunk into an economic depression that only abated with the post-Second World War expansion of oil exploration.

The Post-War Price of Dependent Currencies

The Second World War precipitated a set of political and economic transformations that further increased the instability of the currency systems that structured trade and, increasingly, market and labour relations in much of the Red Sea world. The war resulted in the end of Italian rule in Ethiopia and Eritrea. In 1941, British troops invaded the AOI and the Italian administration collapsed. The new British rulers of Ethiopia and Eritrea were military officers and their primary concerns were tactical and not economic. As a result, these officers did not craft a coherent plan for the reconstruction of the economy of newly conquered territories and the rebuilding of their currency systems. Decisions about which currency to use for official business and which currencies to recognize as legal tender were driven by expediency. Officials recognized all currencies in circulation as legal tender, including the Italian lira and Maria Theresa Thalers.[69] For settling official accounts British officials used subsidiary currencies of the British pound. Initially, the invading British-led forces made payments in Egyptian pounds because this was the currency used at the base of operations in Sudan. The use of Egyptian pounds continued through April 1941 when British officials switched to the East African shilling for settling payments in occupied territories.[70] In July 1941, British officials contracted with Barkley's Bank to ensure adequate supplies of East African shillings in the region.[71] As a result, Eritrea and Ethiopia were brought

[68] Roger Owen and Sevket Pamuk, *A History of Middle East Economies in the Twentieth Century* (London, I. B. Tauris Publishers 1998) 81.

[69] Lewin to Lynch 3 January 1952 FO371/96766 National Archives, London (NA); Tschoegl, 'Maria Theresa's Thaler,' 450–1.

[70] Lewin to Lynch 3 January 1952 FO371/96766 NA.

[71] Barkley's Bank continued to provide banking and exchange services in Ethiopia until April 1943. Befekadu Degefe. 'The Development of Money, Monetary Institutions and

into the Sterling Area, a group of independent countries, colonial territories and militarily administered regions that either pegged their currencies to the British pound or used the pound or a subsidiary currency as the official currency.

By 1942, nearly all of the Red Sea was within the Sterling Area. The sole holdouts were Arabia and Yemen, which continued to use silver and gold currencies, and the Côte Française des Somalis, which used the French franc. However, French officials stationed in Djibouti quickly realized that it was in their political and economic interest to join this currency union. The economy of Djibouti and the solvency of the railroad to Addis Ababa were dependent on capturing a large share of Ethiopia's foreign trade. With both Ethiopia and Eritrea in the Sterling Area, French officials feared that Ethiopia's trade would gravitate to the Eritrean ports of Assab and Massawa in order to avoid the expense and uncertainty that comes with exchanging currencies. In 1943, French officials decided to introduce a new currency, the Djibouti franc, which would be pegged to the British pound, at a rate of 176.625 Djibouti francs to the pound. This made Djibouti unique within the French Empire, as the only territory in the empire within the Sterling Area.[72]

The expansion of the Sterling Area in the Red Sea was itself unstable and the Côte Française des Somalis did not stay in the Sterling Area for long. The change in local currency policy in the Côte Française des Somalis was again motivated by events in Ethiopia. In 1945, Ethiopia left the Sterling Area. The newly reinstated Ethiopian government under Haile Selassie was suspicious of British designs on the region. Hoping to limit British involvement, the Ethiopian government sought closer association with the United States. In keeping with this goal, Ethiopian officials decided to establish their own currency, the Ethiopian birr, with a fixed exchange rate of 1 Ethiopian birr equal to US $0.4025.[73] Since Ethiopia was now in the Dollar Zone, there was no longer a reason for the Côte Française des Somalis to stay in the Sterling Area. As the Ethiopian dollar was being introduced, French officials decided to withdraw the Djibouti franc and replace it with the Colonies Françaises d'Afrique (CFA) franc, a

Monetary Policy, 1941–75,' *An Economic History of Ethiopia: Volume 1: The Imperial Era, 1941–74.* Shiferaw Bekele, ed. (Oxford, CODESRIA, 1995) 235.

[72] Le Comissaire aux Colonies to le Commissaire aux Finances 27 November 1943 FM 1AFFECO/237 ANOM.

[73] Mr. de Blesson [Ministre de France en Ethiopie] to Mr. Georges Bidault [Ministre des affaires etrangers a paris] 5 July 1945. FT CFS 2E8 ANOM.

currency in use in all of France's African colonies that was pegged to the metropolitan franc. However, the CFA francs' use as the official currency in the Côte Française des Somalis was short-lived. Officials again became concerned that fluctuating exchange rates would impede Djibouti's role in servicing Ethiopia's import/export trade. So, only one year after it was introduced, the CFA was replaced with a new Djibouti franc pegged to the US dollar.

The rapid transition between currencies in Eritrea, Ethiopia and the Côte Française des Somalis resulted in large economic losses for local communities. The end of Italian rule in the AOI led the lira to lose nearly all of its value. Merchants and vendors refused to accept lira and its value became more notional than real. By the end of 1943, 1 Maria Theresa Thaler was worth 2106 Italian lire.[74] Since the lira had thoroughly penetrated Eritrea's economy, the currency crisis set off a food crisis in Eritrea. People whose incomes and savings were denominated in lira stopped being able to purchase basic necessities and started to starve. To cope with the crisis, British officers initiated a food aid programme in May 1941[75] and began encouraging impoverished Italian settlers to return to Italy. The introduction of the East African shilling introduced a level of stability that was short-lived. In 1951, Eritrea was federated with Ethiopia under the sovereignty of Haile Selassie. As part of this federation, the Ethiopian birr was made the only legal tender in Eritrea. During the conversion, exchange rates were set at unfavourable levels, as they had been when the birr was first introduced in Ethiopia.[76] As a result, the introduction of the birr in Eritrea, as it had in Ethiopia, resulted in economic losses for all holders of hard currencies.[77]

In the Côte Française des Somalis, the transition from metropolitan francs to the first Djibouti franc in 1943 was designed by the newly established Free French administration to economically punish people perceived to have benefited from Vichy rule. During the period of Vichy-loyalist rule in the Côte Française des Somalis, merchants in Aden and other Red Sea markets amassed large quantities of French francs. By

[74] British Military Administration. Eritrea, *Annual Report by the Chief Administrator on the British Administration of Eritrea, Report V, for Period 1 January to 31 December 1943*, 10.

[75] *The Control of Finance and Accounts, Occupied Territory Administration, Middle East Command to the Permanent Under Secretary of State, War Office* 19 May 1942. FO 1015/69. NA.

[76] de Blesson to Bidault 29 November 1946. FT CFS 2E8 ANOM.

[77] *Eritrea Annual Report for 1951*. 1952 FO 371/96719. NA.

1942, 31 merchants in Aden alone collectively held nearly 6 billion francs.[78] In 1943, the newly established Free French administration believed that these merchants had amassed these holdings by engaging in contraband trade with the Vichy-loyalist regime. To punish the owners of these reserves, officials implemented a rapid conversion from metropolitan to Djibouti francs. The timeline was purposefully so tight that merchants outside of the city of Djibouti did not have enough time to convert their metropolitan francs before they stopped being recognized as legal tender. As a result, the metropolitan francs still in private possession after the conversion lost much of their value.[79] Two years later, the withdrawal of the Djibouti franc and the introduction of the CFA franc resulted in a sudden 30 per cent increase in the cost of living in Djibouti. This transition occurred just before currency traders in Europe began speculating against the metropolitan franc. This currency market speculation forced France to devalue the franc and its subsidiary currencies in 1948. Following this devaluation, market prices in Djibouti rose another 80 per cent.[80]

This history of lost wealth associated with changes to the currency systems of the Red Sea did not prevent further politically motivated changes in the second half of the twentieth century. Between 1956 and 1997, new currencies were introduced in Sudan, Eritrea, Saudi Arabia and Yemen, in part, as expressions of national self-determination. Concerns about sovereignty led the newly installed revolutionary Yemen Arab Republic to demonetize the Maria Theresa Thaler in 1962 and replace it with a national currency.[81] In 1990, the Yemen Arab Republic, which ruled northern Yemen, and the People's Democratic Republic of Yemen were united and their respective currencies were replaced with a single currency, the Yemeni riyal. Similar concerns resulted in the severing of the currency union between Sudan and Egypt, on the one hand, and Eritrea and Ethiopia, on the other. The movement towards Sudanese independence was propelled by Egyptian nationalist assertions of a natural right to rule in Sudan. When the by-now independent Egyptian government began making claims on Sudan, British officials in the Anglo-Egyptian government pushed back and helped usher in the establishment of an

[78] Copy of Petition of the 16th April 1943 from Scholem Tacoob Attar and Others, Aden FM 1AFFPOL/3699. ANOM.

[79] Ibid.

[80] Virginia Rhompson and Richard Adloff, *Djibouti and the Horn of Africa* (Stanford, CA, Stanford University Press, 1968) 180–1.

[81] Tschoegl, 'Maria Theresa's Thaler,' 451.

independent Sudan in 1956. The new government, which was created to curtail Egyptian influence in Sudan, subsequently established its own currency, the Sudanese pound. Similarly, in 1991, Eritrea won its independence after a protracted civil war with Ethiopia and, a few years later, the newly independent government introduced its own national currency, the Eritrean nakfa.

The newly established currency systems were neither more independent nor more stable than their predecessors. Since their establishment, the Saudi riyal, the Eritrea nakfa, the Ethiopian birr, the Djibouti franc and the Sudanese pound have, at least for some time, been pegged to the US dollar. In Sudan, Ethiopia and Eritrea this peg came at a steep price. In Ethiopia in the 1950s and 1960s, the commitment to maintaining convertibility with the US dollar limited investment in local industries, exacerbated the negative balance of trade and led to increased inflation. Economic instability in Ethiopia led to the widespread protests that brought the *Derg* to power in 1974, which, in turn, escalated the military conflict between the Ethiopian government and Eritrean nationalist rebels.[82] Similarly, currency policy in independent Sudan prevented the government from restraining inflation. After the United States went off the gold standard in 1971, inflation in Sudan rose dramatically. Between 1972 and 1977, the average annual inflation rate was 24 per cent. In 1979, the Sudanese government ended its dollar peg and subsequently implemented a series of currency devaluations. When these did not have their desired effects, the government was forced to remove price subsidies, reduce public expenditures, lower wages and limit nonessential imports. Despite these measures, the annual inflation rate continued to rise, reaching 300 per cent in 1991.[83] Yemen suffered similar levels of uncontrolled inflation. The Yemeni riyal, which has been freely convertible with the US dollar since its introduction in 1993, has seen its value drop from 12.01 to 215 riyals to the dollar between 1993 and early 2015.

The instability of the newly introduced national currencies further contributed to the cycle of poverty that, in turn, left communities with no choice but to try and earn unstable currencies. The southern half of the

[82] Mulatu Wubneh and Yohannis Abate, *Ethiopia: Transition and Development in the Horn of Africa* (Boulder, CO, Westview Press, 1988) 87. For a description of the escalation of this armed conflict, see Africa Watch. *Evil Days: Thirty Years of War and Famine in Ethiopia* (New York, Human Rights Watch, 1991).

[83] Mohamed Hassan Fadlalla, *A Short History of Sudan* (Lincoln, iUniverse, 2004) 126.

Red Sea world is one of the poorest regions in the world. Sudan, Eritrea, Djibouti, Yemen and Ethiopia all have a low Human Development Index according to the United Nations Development Programme.[84] Over the course of the twentieth century, many communities in the region experienced the decline of their traditional economic strategies. Large numbers of cultivators lost access to their land and were forced to become tenants or labourers on plantations that produced cash crops for internal markets and for the export trade. Others were forced by necessity to move to cities in search for work.[85] Similarly, pastoralism stopped being an option for many, who were subsequently compelled to settle and/or take up wage labour.[86] As the rural countryside stopped being able to retain its population, the population of cities grew. For example, the population of Kassala in Sudan grew from 45,000 to 245,000 between 1956 and 1986. The largest group of settlers to this town was former pastoralists from Eastern Sudan and Eritrea who had lost their animals as a result of repeated droughts and the 1984–1985 famine.[87] The process of urbanization was the outcome of spreading poverty and was further intensified by regional conflicts that led millions to flee their homes. Regional conflicts on the African Red Sea littoral pushed many refugees to resettle in Sudan and Djibouti.[88] Most refugees resettled on the outskirts of growing regional

[84] The United Nations, *Human Development Index*, 2013.

[85] Tony Barnett, *The Gezira Scheme: An Illusion of Development* (London, Frank Cass, 1977); James McCann, *People of the Plow: AN Agricultural History of Ethiopia, 1800–1990* (Madison, University of Wisconsin Press, 1955); Serels, *Starvation and the State*, 172–6; Abdel Ghaffar Muhammad Ahmad, *Changing Systems of Livelihood in Rural Sudan* (Addis Ababa, Organization for Social Science Research in Eastern and Southern Africa, 2002).

[86] Lewis, 'Diem el Arab and the Beja Stevedores of Port Sudan,' 16–49; Janet C.M. Milne, 'The Impact of Labour Migration on the Amarar in Port Sudan,' *Sudan Notes and Records* 15 (1974) 70–87; Muneera Salem-Murdock, *The Impact of Agricultural Development on a Pastoral Society: The Shukriya of the Eastern Sudan: A Report Submitted to the Agency for International Development* (New York, Institute for Development Anthropology, 1979) 1–10.

[87] Walter Kok, 'Self-Settled Refugees and the Socio-Economic Impact of their Presence on Kassala, Eastern Sudan,' *Journal of Refugee Studies* 2:4 (1989) 421.

[88] Economic and Social Research Council, National Council for Research. Ministry of the Interior, Republic of the Sudan, *Social and Economic Survey of South Tokar District Eastern Region Sudan (with Special Reference to Refugees and Self-Reliance)* (1989) 15–16; Maknun Gamaledin, 'The Decline of Afar Pastoralism,' *Conflict and the Decline of Pastoralism in the Horn of Africa*, John Markakis (ed.) (London, Macmillan Press, 1993) 56–7.

towns and tried to support themselves through the informal economy.[89] The ever-increasing urban and refugee population lacked the access to domesticated animals and agricultural land necessary to support basic subsistence. As a result, these communities were compelled to seek out other ways of earning the income necessary to purchase food and other necessities. This income was paid in the unstable currencies then in circulation. Poverty demands that these communities work to earn these currencies and the instability of these currencies helped ensure that these communities remain poor.

Acknowledgements Researching and writing this chapter was made possible by grants from the Gerda Henkel Foundation, Social Studies and Humanities Research Council of Canada, the Alexander von Humboldt Foundation, the VolkswagenStiftung, the Andre W. Mellon Foundation and Harvard University's Weatherhead Initiative on Global History.

[89] Kok, 'Self-Settled Refugees and the Socio-Economic Impact of their Presence on Kassala, Eastern Sudan,' 419–20.

CHAPTER 8

Gilding the Waves: Gold Smuggling and Monetary Policies Around the Arabian Sea, 1939–1967

Johan Mathew

For several decades, histories of the Indian Ocean have highlighted the ways in which this maritime space was one of dense financial interconnection. The movement of capital from the Early Modern period through the era of European imperial rule, particularly by diasporic Indian financiers, is well documented. Recent scholarship has made a strong case for the role of "intermediary capital" as functioning in concert with European imperialism and globalized capital as drivers of regional economic history.[1] This chapter builds upon this important work and the larger scholarship that

[1] Rajat Kanta Ray, 'Asian Capital in the Age of European Domination: The Rise of the Bazaar, 1800–1914,' *Modern Asian Studies* 29:3 (July 1995) 449–554; Sugata Bose, *A Hundred Horizons: The Indian Ocean in the Age of Global Empire* (Cambridge, MA, Harvard University Press, 2006), chapter 3; Claude Markovits, *The Global World of Indian Merchants, 1750–1947: Traders of Sind from Bukhara to Panama* (Cambridge, UK, Cambridge University Press, 2000); Pedro Machado, *Ocean of Trade: South Asian Merchants, Africa and the Indian Ocean, c.1750–1850* (Cambridge, UK, Cambridge University Press, 2014).

J. Mathew (✉)
History Department, Rutgers University, New Brunswick, NJ, USA

S. Serels, G. Campbell (eds.), *Currencies of the Indian Ocean World*, Palgrave Series in Indian Ocean World Studies,
https://doi.org/10.1007/978-3-030-20973-5_8

highlights connectivities across the ocean in the colonial and post-colonial periods. In particular, this chapter focuses on the financial networks that connected South Asia and the Arabian Peninsula from the Second World War through the decades of decolonization. What emerges from this evidence is not just a further application of this concept of intermediary capital, but the suggestion that merchant networks were both more powerful and more problematic than this term might suggest. These intermediary networks did not merely facilitate or resist state policies; they actively redirected these policies through their engagements in illicit trade.

Monetary and financial histories downplay or ignore this interregional world of smuggling networks. Most monetary histories of these regions tend to focus on the challenges of a particular national currency like the Indian Rupee. Examinations of international financial flows focus almost exclusively on the relationships between local currencies and their European counterparts.[2] Of particular interest to scholars is the tumultuous twentieth-century history of the Sterling Area. The Sterling Area was a set of procedures initially implemented in the early twentieth century to coordinate monetary policies across the British Empire. Though they were established within the framework of imperial rule, these policies and procedures continued to operate even after decolonization as a means of facilitating trade between former colonies and Britain. As a result, scholarship on the Sterling Area has naturally focused on Britain and tends to highlight Britain's reasons for creating and maintaining Sterling as an international reserve currency, its efforts to manage the increasingly precarious position of the Sterling and the impact of Sterling Area policies on the economy of Britain.[3] While this scholarship is excellent, it largely neglects the intermediary financial flows that connected economies around the Indian Ocean without the mediation of Britain.

[2] R.K. Seshadri, *From Crisis to Convertibility: The External Value of the Rupee* (Madras, Orient Blackswan, 1993); S.K. Verghese, 'International Monetary Crises and the Indian Rupee,' *Economic and Political Weekly* 8:30 (July 28, 1973) 1342–8; G. Balachandran, *John Bullion's Empire: Britain's Gold Problem and India Between the Wars* (Richmond, UK, Curzon, 1996).

[3] See for example: Phillip W. Bell, *The Sterling Area in the Postwar World: Internal Mechanism and Cohesion, 1946–52* (New York, Oxford University Press, 1956); Susan Strange, *Sterling and British Policy: A Political Study of an International Currency in Decline* (Oxford, Oxford University Press, 1971); Catherine Schenk, *Britain and the Sterling Area: From Devaluation to Convertibility in the 1950s* (London, Routledge, 1994); Catherine Schenk, *The Decline of Sterling: Managing the Retreat of an International Currency, 1945–1992* (New York, Cambridge University Press, 2010).

Colonial archives as well as British business records naturally highlight the actions of bureaucrats and British firms, and yet when read creatively the historian can glean evidence of the weakness of financial authorities and the reactive quality of monetary policy. The merchant networks that operated across the Indian Ocean world were resilient against increased regulation and were adaptive to the European competition that penetrated the region in the twentieth century. The cooperation of Indian Ocean mercantile networks was consequently essential to the successes of colonial monetary policy and their subversions were equally essential to the failures of monetary policy. We must then see monetary policy as a conjoined process between merchants and colonial authorities. Policies that assumed bounded economies and tried to maintain divergent valuations of money and specie were quickly exploited for arbitrage profits. Financial regulators had little ability to control merchant networks that were dispersed across multiple jurisdictions. Merchants capitalized on the differences in law, enforcement and market conditions between the shores of the Arabian Sea and became the arbiters of how monetary policies impacted ordinary exchange. Thus, merchant networks were largely responsible for the rejection and subversion of new currency forms and for prompting the development of new policies and currencies that might be accepted in the broader markets of the Arabian Sea.

Viewed from the perspective of the Arabian Sea, an alternate intra-Indian Ocean monetary history comes into focus. By highlighting smuggling and arbitrage within this part of the Indian Ocean world, this chapter brings to light the historically significant, innovative efforts of merchant networks to exploit and redirect monetary policy as the sun set on the British Empire. The first section of this chapter outlines the financial world of the Arabian Sea in the early twentieth century by tracing both the dense networks of diasporic capital that held these regions together and the structures of banking and monetary policy that overlaid these networks. The second section of the chapter focuses on the Second World War and details both the increasing currency controls necessitated by the conflict and the phenomenal expansion of arbitrage and gold smuggling that subverted these regulations. The final section examines the ways that persistent illicit currency flows in the post-war period led to official reforms in the Sterling Area. Throughout this period, I argue that the tumultuous history of monetary policy around the Arabian Sea was intimately tied to the arbitrage and smuggling of diasporic networks.

Diasporic Networks and Imperial Policies

Since the 1870s the cornerstone of British monetary policy and, indeed, global capitalism was the gold standard. However, much of the Indian Ocean world maintained silver currencies which existed in a complicated and often confused relationship with the gold-based currencies of Europe. But as Britain's power declined in the twentieth century, the gold standard also faltered. The First World War caused the first interruption to this regime, and a little over a decade later, the Great Depression rendered the gold standard ineffective in facilitating international trade. When Britain abandoned the gold standard in 1931, shifting to a soft Sterling standard became unavoidable for Britain's colonies, as well as its semi-imperial trading partners. These governments responded by pegging their currencies to the now floating British Pound Sterling. The Sterling Area as an official currency bloc would not be created until after the Second World War. However, its real origins can be located in these informal arrangements implemented in the 1930s. The Great Depression and the need for a coordinated monetary standard in the absence of gold were, therefore, at the origins of the Sterling Area.[4]

In the Arabian Sea, the Sterling Area operated through particularly complex and opaque circuits. This currency block inherited from earlier monetary policies the trans-oceanic circulation of the Indian Rupee and the reliance on the diasporic trading networks that dominated interregional finance. Though Indians, Arabs and Persians had crossed this sea for millennia, Hindu traders from the state of Gujarat known as *banias*, came to dominate the financial activities of this region during the nineteenth century with the support of the British Empire. While these *banias* had developed advanced forms of accounting and commercial acumen, their success was substantially the result of political patronage. Loans to rulers, customs farms and contracts to provision armies were central to the rise of many financial diasporas over the history of the Indian Ocean. *Banias* worked closely with sheikhs, sultans, nawabs and European officials along the Indian

[4] Balachandran, *John Bullion's Empire*; Lawrence Officer, 'Gold Standard,' *EH.Net Encyclopedia*, Robert Whaples, ed., March 26, 2008, http://eh.net/encyclopedia/article/officer.gold.standard; Barry Eichengreen, *Golden Fetters: The Gold Standard and the Great Depression, 1919–1939* (New York, Oxford University Press, 1996); Ian M. Drummond, *The Floating Pound and the Sterling Area, 1931–1939* (Cambridge, UK, Cambridge University Press, 1981).

Ocean littoral.[5] *Bania* networks were the key vector in the dispersion of the British-Indian Rupee around the Arabian Sea.[6] Over the course of the nineteenth century, the combination of British imperial influence and Indian mercantile dominance led the rupee to be established as legal tender in all of the states of the Arabian Peninsula except Saudi Arabia. And in Saudi Arabia the rupee was a de facto legal tender.[7] Yet the British-Indian Rupee did not displace other currencies, rather it operated as the currency of trade and taxation, constantly in need of conversion into locally circulating currencies.[8] Therefore official monetary policies around the Arabian Sea were decided by bureaucrats in London, New Delhi and Nairobi. But their actual implementation was carried out by networks of Hindu merchant bankers operating in Mandvi, Muttrah and Massawa. These merchant bankers were also important because of their ability to connect the policies of rulers to the everyday transactions of people around the Indian Ocean littoral. They provided loans, money transfer and currency conversion services to agriculturalists, fishermen, traders and artisans across these regions.[9]

From the end of the nineteenth century, the expanding power of *banias* was not only a function of their knowledge of local trade conditions and their connections to state power; it was also a result of their access to

[5] Johan Mathew, 'Moral Economies of Violence along the Arabian Sea Littoral,' in *Trading Circuits, Mobile Cultures: Port Cities and Littoral Societies of the Indian Ocean* (unpublished manuscript); Lakshmi Subramanian, *Indigenous Capital and Imperial Expansion: Bombay, Surat and the West Coast* (New Delhi, Oxford University Press, 1996); Sanjay Subrahmanyam and C.A. Bayly, 'Portfolio Capitalists and the Political Economy of Early Modern India,' *Indian Economic & Social History Review* 25:4 (December 1988) 401–24; Mohammed Reda Bhacker, *Trade and Empire in Muscat and Zanzibar: The Roots of British Domination* (London, Routledge, 1992).

[6] Ray, 'Asian Capital in the Age of European Domination'; Wambui Mwangi, 'Of Coins and Conquest: The East African Currency Board, the Rupee Crisis, and the Problem of Colonialism in the East African Protectorate,' *Comparative Studies in Society and History* 43:4 (October 2001) 763–87; Charles Schaefer, 'Selling at a Wash: Competition and the Indian Merchant Community in Aden Crown Colony,' *Comparative Studies of South Asia, Africa and the Middle East* 19:2 (1999) 16–23.

[7] National Archives of India: Department of Commerce and Industry, Sept. 1905, Commerce and Trade Branch, Proceedings 11–23, File 19, Report of H.W. Maclean on the Conditions and Prospects of British Trade in Persia &c. in Secretary of State for India to Government of India 22/7/1904.

[8] Regarding this "complementarity" of currencies see Akinobu Kuroda, 'The Maria Theresa Dollar in the Early Twentieth-Century Red Sea Region: A Complementary Interface between Multiple Markets,' *Financial History Review* 14:01 (2007) 89–110.

[9] See Machado, *Ocean of Trade*, chapter 1.

European capital markets. *Banias* could access larger pools of capital through British banks and also facilitate transactions with suppliers and consumers in Europe and North America. They kept close ties with these banks by opening accounts with their branches in Bombay and by working as the local agents of these banks in various ports and market towns throughout the Arabian Sea.[10] The relationship of dependence went both ways. European banks were reliant on the networks of these *banias* to expand the reach of their capital.

Similarly, British officials also benefited from their association with these *banias* in so far as they were dependent on these *banias* to expand the circulation of the British-Indian Rupee. Nonetheless, officials could rarely monitor much less control how this was being achieved.

Bania firms were happy to expand the rupee's circulation because it was profitable. Given that these firms were generally headquartered in India, it would seem obvious that they preferred to use rupees to avoid the uncertainties of exchange rate fluctuations and to simplify accounting practices. Yet there is no indication that these trading diasporas limited themselves to working with rupees or forced others to eliminate competing currencies. In fact, *bania* merchants were actively involved and dependent on revenues from money-changing and currency arbitrage. Much, if not most, of the sizeable profits that they accrued came from this business rather than from more mundane trading activities. Charles Schaeffer has detailed the ways in which Indian merchants spread into remote corners of Ethiopia and the Red Sea littoral, selling textiles and other commodities at or below cost in order to maintain access to currency arbitrage opportunities.[11] What Schaefer observed for this particular corner of the Indian Ocean was true generally for the region. From Cape Delgado to Colombo, Indian merchants in particular, but also Arab, Iranian and African traders keenly appraised the arbitrage opportunities resulting from the sheer variety of circulating monies and their constantly varying demand.

These opportunities only expanded following the demonetization of silver in Europe and America at the end of the nineteenth century. In the

[10] Guildhall Library, Eastern Bank Records: 39, 010/20 N.S. Golder, Eastern Bank London to M. Gunn, Eastern Bank Bahrain 9/4/1948; Report by Mr. Findlay 1/10/1947; British Library, India Office Records (Henceforth IOR): R/15/6/189 Said bin Taimur, Sultan of Muscat, to Hickinbotham, Political Agent in Muscat 10/10/1939, p. 208; Government of India Foreign Department to Secretary of State for the Commonwealth, Memorandum No. 5978, 28/5/1948, p. 120; Mathew, *Margins of the Market*, chapter 4.

[11] Schaefer, 'Selling at a Wash.'

decades that followed, silver flowed into the Indian Ocean world, progressively undermining the British-Indian Rupee, the Qajar Kran and the Maria Theresa Thaler as units of account and stores of value. Subsequently South Asian populations, in particular, began to see gold as the *only* secure store of value. Instability in the silver market and the rising demand for gold created the impetus for the development of widespread currency smuggling.

Indian Hoards, Arab Dhows and Nazi Gold

The Second World War reversed the normal flows of currency circulations. Whereas gold and silver were imported into India before the war, suddenly India's hoards became a supply for the enormous hard currency demands of war-time production in Europe. Indian and Arab merchants engineered extraordinarily subtle and ingenious systems to profit from the surge in prices for precious metals in Europe. Gold bars and sovereign coins were hidden in food, in Qur'ans and in human digestive systems. They were also shipped on dhows in the cover of night.[12] Dhows carried these illicit cargoes from India to Arabia and then up the Persian Gulf to Iraq. These cargos were then transported overland to Syria's Mediterranean ports, where they were again trans-shipped onto boats for the final leg of their journey to Europe. In just two months in 1940 at least 250,000 British sovereigns made the journey from India to Iraq where they could be sold for twice the value.[13] This war-time smuggling makes abundantly clear that the Asian desire for gold was not an irrational hoarding of the yellow metal, but rather a very calculated and astute judgement of how to maintain the value of their savings and when to cash them in.

Smugglers particularly exploited opportunities presented by points of cultural sensitivity. At this time it would not have been out of place to see a South Asian woman wearing substantial amounts of jewellery. While for some this might have been motivated by conspicuous consumption, for many others a woman's body presented the most secure space to store a family's savings. In the context of travel, female bodies were largely exempt from search and seizure and thus proved to be excellent vehicles for the

[12] IOR: R/15/5/309 Political Agent in Kuwait to Political Resident in the Persian Gulf 6/1/1941; MSS Eur C446 Anecdotes of Smuggling in Bombay in the 1930s.

[13] IOR: R/15/2/352 Report from Cairo Censorship, 6/3/1941m p. 69; C.G.L. Grenier, Customs Director Bahrain to Alban, Political Agent in Bahrain 6/5/1941.

illicit importation of gold. Smugglers routinely enlisted their wives, daughters and other female relatives in their activities by having them wear cargoes of gold. Customs officials, cautious about violating norms of propriety, hesitated to interfere as these women boarded or disembarked. Even if they suspected this jewellery was an item of trade rather than fashion, customs officials were wary of trespassing on issues of cultural sensitivity.[14] Smugglers took advantage of precisely this hesitancy, arranging to meet their female couriers outside the customs house where they were relieved of their heavy but highly profitable burdens.

A less burdensome system of smuggling involved the exploitation of royal privileges. Arab and Indian royals were immune from customs searches and consequently their luggage—as well as that of their entourages—became a useful conduit for evading the war-time colonial prohibition on the export of gold from India. British officials suspected that one notorious smuggler, Muhammad Ismail, had convinced the King of Saudi Arabia, the Sultan of Muscat and the Emir of Kuwait to help him transport gold out of India during the war. Muhammad Ismail allegedly used the entourage of King Abdul Aziz to smuggle tens of thousands of gold sovereigns out of India on a single trip. This trip was supposedly a small component of a massive operation that moved hundreds of thousands of gold sovereigns a week, charging 3 Rupees for each smuggled sovereign.[15] These reports were undoubtedly exaggerated, but certainly an element of truth inhered in them as royal entourages provided a perfect conveyance for illicit goods of all sorts. These sheikhs and sultans may or may not have known that their privileges were being abused to facilitate smuggling, but they may just as well have turned a blind eye in protest against colonial regulations which drove profits to British firms rather than Arab merchants.

Another tried and true method of gold smuggling was the use of remote ports and poorly monitored coastlines. Most Gulf merchants were based in Bombay or Karachi and much of the initial smuggling of gold out of India during the Second World War occurred out of these ports.[16] As colonial authorities became more effective at stopping exports from Bombay, merchants began shipping gold from ports with less diligent

[14] Patrick B. Sweeney, 'A Game Warden's Permit for a Corpse: The Life and Times of a Customs Officer' (Unpublished MSS in British Library, n.d.) 155.

[15] IOR: R/15/2/351 Special Report by A.B. 4/3/1941, p. 217.

[16] IOR: R/15/3/309 Chancery, British Embassy Baghdad to Intelligence Bureau, Government of India 30/4/1940; Anonymous letter to Financial Secretary, British Embassy Baghdad 27/4/1940.

customs administrations, such as in the nearby princely states in Gujarat and the Portuguese territory of Goa.[17] When those ports were restricted, gold was taken over land to Iran from where it could more easily be spirited across the Gulf to Kuwait.[18] A particularly dramatic instance of this shifting geography of smuggling emerges in the case of a prominent Kuwaiti merchant named Yusuf Sagar.

Yusuf Sagar was based out of the port of Calicut on the Malabar Coast of southwestern India. Compared to Bombay or Gujarat, Calicut was hundreds of miles in the wrong direction from the Gulf. However the local Muslim population had historic links with the Arab world, as well as dense jungles and winding backwaters capable of sheltering vessels and hiding illicit activities. The additional costs of shipping from this distant region were easily offset by the enormous profits of war-time smuggling. Sagar managed to capitalize on this unexpectedly convenient location to engineer a successful traffic smuggling gold from India to Kuwait and Iraq. He may have even gotten away with it except that British officials discovered that this gold was making its way from Iraq to Europe and was feeding the German war machine.[19] Gold was the only currency acceptable on both sides of the battle lines and thus was in high demand. British officials were willing to put extreme efforts to stop any smuggling that helped the Nazis and thus Sagar's telegrams were monitored and his elaborate traffic was thwarted.[20]

War-time censorship was a useful tool in fighting smuggling networks, but diasporic merchants also developed means of throwing censors off their tracks. To prevent detection by the authorities, merchants and dhow captains started to use special codes in their correspondence that could not be deciphered by military intelligence. In addition, they regularly shifted their cargoes between different dhows. This was assisted by the fact

[17] IOR: R/15/3/309 VG Matthews, Collector of Customs Bombay to Central Board of Revenue, Simla, 3/6/1944.

[18] IOR: R/2/596/7 Maneklal Lallubhai, Member of State Council Junagadh to McClenaghan, Collector of Salt Revenue, Bombay 29/3/1941; Report from anonymous informer 14/3/1941; Reports by Customs Agents 18/3/1941.

[19] IOR: R/15/2/352 Report from Cairo Censorship, 6/3/1941, p. 69; C.G.L. Grenier, Customs Director Bahrain to Alban, Political Agent in Bahrain 6/5/1941; R/15/3/309 Collector of Excise and Salt Revenue Madras Presidency to Political Agent in Kuwait 20/5/1942.

[20] British Library, India Office Records (IOR): R/15/3/309 Collector of Central Excises and Salt Revenue, Madras, Order No. D351, 28/5/1943.

that almost all dhows shared maybe a dozen auspicious names. An intercepted message that a dhow named *Fath-al Rahman* was carrying illicit cargo would still require searching dozens or even hundreds of vessels with the same name. As a result, the intercepted messages from smugglers would only marginally help British officials actually find and stop diasporic smuggling networks.[21]

Smuggling gold out of India was immensely profitable, but it was ultimately useless if the smugglers could not find a way to repatriate their profits. Fortunately for these smugglers there was a large build-up of British and Indian troops stationed in Iraq during the war, and they brought with them a large quantity of rupee notes. So, Indian merchants and sailors sold British gold sovereigns to money-changers or *sarrafs* in Basra for Iraqi Dinars and then used their dinars to purchase rupee notes.[22] The supply of rupee notes in war-time Iraq was so large that smugglers had to accept an 8–10 per cent discount against the official exchange rate for the dinar. British banks in Iraq were happy to deal with the smugglers, who were the only significant local source of demand for rupees. These banks often performed this transaction and pocketed the perfectly legal profits. In fact, bank officials even pushed customs officials to keep open this dinar-rupee exchange despite the fact that it mostly existed to facilitate smuggling.[23] The lobbying of legitimate business to keep open this trade ensured that smugglers would be able to bring their profits back to India.

However, as risks increased and profits tightened, gold smugglers became frustrated with giving British banks an 8–10 per cent discount on the exchange. Increasingly, Indian smugglers took their gold to Arab *sarrafs* in Bahrain and Kuwait who would provide rupee drafts for a smaller discount. The smugglers ultimately wanted rupee coins which were more liquid, and in Bahrain, these rupee drafts could be exchanged for silver rupee coins at only a 2 per cent discount at the Eastern Bank. By drawing

[21] IOR: R/15/5/309 Collector of Central Excises and Salt Revenue, Madras, Order No. D351, 28/5/1943; Political Agent in Kuwait to Political Resident in the Persian Gulf 16/5/1944; Indian Censor intercept—Fahad Khalifah Shaheen Al-Ghanim, Bombay to Abdul Latif Mohammad Thaniyan, Kuwait 25/3/1944.

[22] IOR: R/15/5/309 Anonymous letter to Financial Secretary, British Embassy, Baghdad 27/4/40.

[23] IOR: R/15/2/352 Capt. J.B. Howes to Political Agent in Kuwait 16/8/1941, p. 58; R/15/2/351 Political Agent in Bahrain, Memorandum No. 148, 21/5/1940; R/15/2/352 Conclusions of a conference regarding gold and silver smuggling in Bahrain 28/2/1942, pp. 200–2; A. Gunn, Eastern Bank to Political Agent in Bahrain 7/4/1942.

on the exchange monopoly of the Eastern Bank in Bahrain, Indian merchants were able to gain an extra increment of profit on this smuggling circuit. The coordination between Indian smugglers, Arab *sarrafs* and the Eastern Bank was not set in stone. Arab *sarrafs* also sought to independently exploit currency arbitrage opportunities, even if this undermined some of their partners.

By the summer of 1941, anti-smuggling measures were increased, making smuggling out of India a less enticing proposition. Arab *sarrafs* discovered that they could cut out Indian merchants altogether by looking to the black gold of Saudi Arabia. Saudi Bedouin received gold coins as their share of the country's growing oil windfall, and they brought this gold to Bahrain and Kuwait. Bahraini and Kuwaiti *sarrafs* purchased Saudi gold coins at a discount and exchanged them for dinar and rupee currency notes. They obtained these notes by going up to Iraq where they could sell those same Saudi gold coins at a premium. Their Saudi clients were happy because they now had silver denominated notes which they needed in order to buy foreign commodities in the markets of the Gulf.[24] However the *sarrafs* had made profits on both sides of this arbitrage circuit.

Subsequently, the *sarrafs* discovered that they could actually exploit the Eastern Bank's exchange monopoly for a different form of arbitrage. The Eastern Bank was required to exchange rupee notes for silver coins at a discount of 1.5 per cent, but the exchange rate on the black market was far lower. So *sarrafs* brought rupee notes to the Eastern Bank and obtained silver coins at a small loss, they then went to black market dealers and exchanged those coins for a much larger amount of rupee notes than they had originally exchanged. They could then return to the Eastern Bank and repeat this process ad infinitum. As a result, Bahrain began haemorrhaging hundreds of thousands of rupees worth of silver coins, which British exchange banks were providing. Eventually British officials prohibited the export of both gold and silver from Bahrain in an attempt to stanch these incredibly complex currency exchange circuits.[25]

As the Second World War drew to a close, yet another arbitrage opportunity opened up. As the Nazi defeat was becoming apparent, the

[24] IOR: R/15/2/351 Political Agent in Bahrain, Memorandum No. 148, 21/5/1940; R/15/2/352 Capt. J.B. Howes to Political Agent in Kuwait 16/8/1941, p. 58; R/15/5/309 Political Agent in Kuwait to Collector of Customs, Karachi 7/2/1942; Imperial Bank of Persia, Kuwait Branch to Imperial Bank of Persia, Basra Branch 6/5/1942.

[25] IOR: R/15/2/352 p. 25, Political Agent in Bahrain to Hickinbotham, Political Agent in Kuwait 11/5/1942.

demand for gold dropped in Iraq and prices began to rise in India. Many merchants were able to double their profits by smuggling the same gold back into India as the war came to a close.[26] Smuggling networks were so nimble and efficient that they made profits by sending gold to Iraq at the beginning of the war and then made additional profits by bringing the same gold back to India at the end of the war. Some of these transactions were legal; others were illegal and still more exposed the blurred boundary between the two. The agility of merchant networks to exploit arbitrage opportunities constantly pushed war-time regulation to adapt.

Those British officials who were not directly profiting from bribes always seemed one step behind the evolving methods of the smugglers. In a rather sportsmanlike vein, one British official summed up the situation as follows:

> Now that the export of silver from Bahrain to Kuwait is restricted to the comparatively small amounts that can be smuggled through, new methods of "playing the money market" will certainly be devised by Kuwait and Basrawi and Bahraini merchants and brokers, and we shall have to be on the look out for their next move. It is an interesting kind of game that we play with these gentlemen; their great skill in playing the game is balanced by the authority that we have to alter the rules![27]

This quote captures perfectly the evolution of smuggling and financial regulation in the Arabian Sea. As British administrators began to understand the structure of black market trade and smuggling, they initiated new regulations to curtail this illegal activity. These regulations were not based on a preconceived notion of the proper war-time functioning of trade and finance. Rather, the regulations were reactive. They evolved in response to the activities of the smugglers and illegal currency traders. As a result, the actions of the smugglers and traders to circumvent official regulation shaped subsequent changes to official regulation.

[26] IOR: MSS Eur C446 Anecdotes of Smuggling in Bombay in the 1930s.

[27] IOR: R/15/2/352 Political Agent in Bahrain to Hickinbotham, Political Agent in Kuwait 11/5/1942, 25.

Contraband and the Origins of Post-Colonial Currencies

Measures implemented by the British during the Second World War laid the foundations for the post-war Sterling Area. During the war, Britain had cajoled its trading partners and coerced its colonies into providing Sterling-denominated loans to support the imperial war effort. For years after the war ended, Britain was not in a position to pay back these debts. As colonies gained their independence, the successor states kept their currencies tied to the pound in the hope of eventual repayment of these British debts. Official treaties were signed and international institutions were set up to coordinate monetary policies and shore up the strength of the British pound. In effect Britain and its former colonies put in place a number of complex fiscal and trade policies that worked to artificially elevate the value of the British pound. The exigencies of war financing consequently perpetuated the Sterling Area as an imperial hangover in a post-colonial world.[28] Though Sterling Area monetary policies were focused on the pound, their implementation in the Arabian Sea was mediated by the regional dependence on Indian Rupees.

When India and Pakistan became independent in 1947, the Arabian Peninsula was awash with rupees. Independent India had inherited the colonial Reserve Bank of India and as a result assumed responsibility for managing the circulation of rupees in the Arabian Peninsula. Though much of the Arabian Peninsula was still formally under British imperial rule, independent India was responsible for the region's currency system. This unusual monetary structure was made possible by the larger umbrella of the Sterling Area, which facilitated close cooperation between officials in the Reserve Bank of India and the Bank of England.

The Sterling Area, as a whole, was dependent on Arabian oil exports in order to function. The value of Sterling currencies was constantly undermined by the desire of businesses in India, Pakistan and Britain itself to purchase manufactured goods from the United States and other non-Sterling currencies. This would ultimately require the Bank of England or the Reserve Bank of India to pay the US Federal Reserve in gold or dollars for the commodities purchased. Unless there was an equal amount of goods that US firms wanted from the Sterling Area, these reserves would be depleted and the value of Sterling currencies would fall. Thus the entire

[28] Bell, *The Sterling Area in the Postwar World*; Schenk, *Britain and the Sterling Area*.

Sterling system was underwritten by the growing export of oil from Gulf states within the Sterling Area.

The ruling sheikhs in the Gulf agreed to their inclusion in this complex currency system in part because the system opened arbitrage opportunities for their subjects. Along with Hong Kong, Kuwait was permitted to operate as a de facto "gap" in the strict regulatory cordon that controlled trade between Sterling Area and non-Sterling Area regions. This gap effectively meant that the normal rules did not apply in Kuwait and specifically individuals and firms from across the Sterling Area could purchase dollar securities with their Sterling currencies in Kuwait. Kuwaiti merchants and bankers profited from this business, and as a result the Sheikh was satisfied to remain within this unwieldy semi-colonial currency regime. Kuwaitis continued to profit from this line of business until 1957 when these transactions threatened to exceed the earnings Kuwait brought to the Sterling Area.[29]

Arab sheikhs were not the only ones who sought official concessions to engage in these kinds of arbitrage. In the late 1940s, a young Indian trader named Dhirubhai Ambani noticed that the price of silver bullion had recently spiked in the London market, and simultaneously the Maria Theresa Thaler—an almost pure silver coin used widely around the Red Sea—was trading well below its normal value. So Ambani put out a standing order to purchase thalers in the neighbouring Imamate of Yemen, which he then exported for resale in London. Even though the populations of British Aden and Imamate Yemen were historically and culturally the same, Aden was in the Sterling Area and Yemen was outside it. The import of vast quantities of silver thalers raised concerns with officials in Aden who feared that they might have to provide gold in exchange for this silver, thus undermining imperial currency reserves. Ambani consequently recruited the aid of his employer Antonin Besse, the most powerful businessman in Aden, who managed to convince colonial officials that this arbitrage would not exhaust currency reserves.[30] Having secured official sanction, Ambani sold hundreds of thousands of thalers on the London market and single-handedly contracted the monetary supply in Yemen. Ambani made a small fortune, but on recalling the incident he merely

[29] Schenk, *Britain and the Sterling Area*, 10, 25–26.

[30] IOR: R/20/B/1622 Governor of Aden to Secretary of State for the Colonies 24/7/1948; Secretary of State for the Colonies to Governor of Aden 12/10/1948; R/20/B/1623 Note from A. Besse 10/10/1955.

noted: "I don't believe in not taking opportunities".[31] Ambani subsequently went on to become the founder of Reliance Industries, now India's largest private-sector company. His genius, exhibited for the first time in Aden, was knowing how to exploit the arbitrage opportunities produced by the labyrinthine regulations of the post-colonial economic order.

The complexities of the Sterling zone did not provide the only opportunity for currency arbitrage in the Arabian Sea after the Second World War. Into the 1950s, Saudi Arabia maintained perhaps the last pure metallic currency in the world. The Wahhabi interpretation of Islamic law prohibited interest-bearing loans and speculative financial transactions, which meant that Saudi Arabia did not issue currency notes or maintain a central bank. So Saudi Arabia presented a unique opportunity for merchant networks in the Arabian Sea. Saudi Arabia had a very unusual monetary policy, was in close proximity to dense Arabian Sea trading networks and received enormous amounts of gold and US dollars for its vast oil production. Saudi consumers looked to purchase consumer goods from India and Pakistan with their gold earnings, and the Indian and Pakistani governments anxiously captured this gold for state development projects. The Reserve Bank of India took Saudi payments in gold and dollars and passed on their rupee equivalents to the actual South Asian firms doing business with the Saudis.

Indian and Pakistani firms however knew that rupees were unreliable, and they looked for ways to circumvent government restrictions. They appear to have turned to the French imperial world to find a workaround. A wealthy Lebanese businessman Michel Dumit and a Monsieur Milhomme of the French Banque de l'Indochine joined forces to take advantage of this situation. They appear to have organized a long complex chain of legal transactions, flowing through Switzerland and Lebanon which permitted South Asian firms to convert their Indian Rupees back into gold without the knowledge of British financial authorities.[32] When British officials discovered these banking activities, they did their utmost to stop them but

[31] Hamish McDonald, *The Polyester Prince: The Rise of Dhirubhai Ambani* (St. Leonards, Australia: Allen & Unwin, 1999) 15.

[32] IOR: R/15/5/310 R.H. Newall, Commercial Secretary, British Legation, Beirut to Under-Secretary, Commercial Relations and Exports Department, Board of Trade 23/9/1949.

succeeded only temporarily.[33] Thus at every opportunity firms across the globe found opportunities to exploit this vortex of trade and financial transactions and ultimately undercut the Sterling regulations.

Money was incredibly challenging to manage not only for the incredibly subtle and complex Sterling monetary system but also for the strikingly simple Saudi monetary system. Money traders all around the Arabian Sea developed complex licit, semi-licit and illicit means of exploiting the structural weaknesses in Saudi monetary policy. By the early 1950s silver was worth 70 per cent more in Bombay than the official value of the riyal in Saudi Arabia. Riyals were extensively minted, but rather than staying in the country they disappeared across the ocean. At the same time, the copper-nickel Saudi *qirsh* was becoming an object of hoarding and speculation within the kingdom. The silver riyal was officially equivalent to 22 copper *qirsh*, but as a result of these financial pressures the effective exchange rate rose from 22 *qirsh* to 20 *qirsh* per riyal.[34] The unpredictable fluctuations in the value of the *qirsh* and the riyal, as well as the inability of the Saudi state to control the value of the British gold sovereign to which the value of the riyal was pegged, ultimately led to the minting of a Saudi gold coin. This gold *guineah* was based on the dimensions of the British sovereign. However the Saudi government decided not to let its value float. Rather, its value was fixed against the silver riyal at a rate of 40:1.[35] Thus, at least in part, the vicissitudes of smuggling and arbitrage had led to the creation of a new coin to ease the pressures on Saudi metal currency.

Moreover, in 1952, the Saudi Arabian Monetary Agency was established as a quasi-central bank in response to these frustrating conditions. However it took some time and effort to actually get the upper hand against diasporic smuggling networks. Almost immediately after the introduction of the gold *guineah*, counterfeits came into circulation and forced the withdrawal of the coin. Two years later another surge in the global

[33] National Archives of the United Kingdom: FO371/4978 Political Resident in the Persian Gulf to Foreign Office, Eastern Department 6/5/1949.

[34] Saudi Arabian Monetary Agency, 'Saudi Currency,' The Historical Framework of the Currency of Saudi Arabia, 2014, http://www.sama.gov.sa/sites/samaen/Currency/Pages/HistoricalInfo.aspx.

[35] IOR: L/E/8/7831 Commonwealth Relations Office to E.A. Midgley, Office of the High Commissioner, New Delhi, April 1949; Foreign Office to British Middle East Office, Cairo and Jedda, 6/5/1949; Michael E. Edo, "Currency Arrangements and Banking Legislation in the Arabian Peninsula," *Staff Papers—International Monetary Fund* 22:2 (July 1, 1975) 510–38, https://doi.org/10.2307/3866487.

market for silver vacuumed riyals out of circulation and forced the Saudi Arabian Monetary Agency to issue a "pilgrims' receipt" in lieu of hard currency. These pilgrims' receipts would open the door to relaxing restrictions on the issuance of paper money and are thus the origin of Saudi Arabia's current paper currency. Though Islamic scholars in Saudi Arabia had argued that paper currencies were in contravention of the *Shari'a*, the strength of smuggling networks gave the Saudi government no other option but to create its own. Eventually, as oil revenues increased and paper notes became an accepted form of currency, the riyal became a more stable currency with fewer temptations to arbitrage and smuggling.[36] This process was possibly also facilitated by the founding of Saudi Arabia's first domestic bank by a powerful firm of *sarrafs*. King Abdulaziz ibn Saud gave permission to Salem bin Mahfouz and his partners to establish the National Commercial Bank. Salem bin Mahfouz gave up his previous occupation and the profits from currency exchange, and we might speculate that the shift of such prominent merchants from money-changing to money-lending also helped to reduce the pressures and insure the stabilization of the riyal.

Saudi Arabia was not alone in inventing new currencies to prevent illicit monetary flows. Large numbers of Muslims from India and Pakistan wished to make the Hajj pilgrimage to Mecca each year. In order to pay for food, lodging and other sundries in Saudi Arabia, they still paid in rupees, which had been accepted by businesses in Jeddah and Mecca since the nineteenth century. As the post-colonial Sterling regulations took effect, smugglers were able to use the pilgrimage as an opportunity to circumvent monetary regulations and export large quantities of rupees in exchange for gold which South Asian savers would purchase at a premium. Arab firms, such as the National Commercial Bank of Saudi Arabia, subsequently demanded that the Reserve Bank of India provide hard currency to redeem the rupee notes that merchants had presented at their branches. As a result, this trans-regional circuit ultimately resulted in gold moving from state coffers into the much-maligned hoards of South Asian families.

This situation became even more pronounced in Pakistan when Britain devalued the pound in 1949. Officials at the newly created State Bank of Pakistan believed that they could avoid a devaluation of the Pakistani Rupee because their large jute and cotton exports propped up international confidence in the Pakistani Rupee. Therefore, Pakistan was the only

[36] Edo; Saudi Arabian Monetary Agency, 'Saudi Currency.'

member of the Sterling Area that did not follow Britain's lead and devalue its currency. However, the elevated value of the Pakistani Rupee made it a much more attractive target for smuggling circuits because they could get more gold for Pakistani Rupees than any other currency. The Hajj was a key conduit of this illicit traffic and ultimately Pakistani officials had to respond in 1951 by issuing special Hajj Rupee notes that could only be used in Saudi Arabia. Only this specialized and limited quantity of notes could be used in Saudi Arabia and thus the State Bank of Pakistan hoped to eliminate smuggling and limit the volume of transactions to only those legitimately undertaken by pilgrims. The State Bank limited the number of notes issued to a minimum and would no longer redeem normal Pakistani Rupee notes if they were spent in Saudi Arabia.[37] Thus Pakistan had created a special currency note that only circulated outside of Pakistan in order to address the persistent problem of smuggling.

When Pakistan was finally forced to devalue its currency in 1955, the Indian Rupee became the focus of Arabian Sea arbitrageurs. By the late 1950s India was haemorrhaging rupees, which were being sent by smugglers to the Gulf in exchange for gold. In 1959, the Reserve Bank of India also began to issue Hajj Rupee notes for use in Saudi Arabia as well as Iraq where many Shi'a pilgrims also travelled. In addition, the Reserve Bank simultaneously introduced Gulf Rupees to replace the Indian notes used far more widely in Oman, Kuwait and the United Arab Emirates as ordinary currency. These new rupees were printed in different colours and had special serial numbers beginning with the letter Z.[38] These special new rupees were still backed by gold reserves. However, these reserves were provided by the Gulf Sheikhs and not the Indian government.[39] Yet another currency system was designed explicitly to prevent gold smuggling.

[37] State Bank of Pakistan, *Annual Report* (1951) 7; James Russell Andrus and Azizali F. Mohammed, *The Economy of Pakistan* (Stanford: Stanford University Press, 1958) 373; Peter Symes, 'The Haj Notes of Pakistan,' Banknotes of Pakistan, May 1999, http://www.pjsymes.com.au/.

[38] Reserve Bank of India Act (Amendment) May 1, 1959; Republic of India, "The Foreign Exchange Regulation Act" (1973); J. O. Ronall, "Banking Developments in Kuwayt," *Middle East Journal* 24:1 (January 1, 1970) 87–90.

[39] 'Gold Smuggling from Kuwait Ends: Indian Currency May not be Withdrawn,' *The Times of India*, November 12, 1958, 1; 'Reserve Bank Bill Passed: Bid to Curb Smuggling,' *The Times of India*, April 30, 1959, 8; Pranay Gupte, *Dubai: The Making of a Megapolis* (Penguin Books India, 2011) 413; Peter Symes, 'Gulf Rupees,' Banknotes of the Arab World, December 1999, http://www.pjsymes.com.au/.

The Bretton Woods system established in the aftermath of the Second World War gave a new lease on life to the gold standard. But if Bretton Woods institutions fostered western economies in the post-war period, it was built on shifting sand around the Arabian Sea. Sterling Area exchange controls relied on the cooperation of merchant networks and were thus consistently undermined. Certainly many of the problems of the Sterling Area were derived from wars and poorly formulated import-substitution industrialization policies. Yet the failure of these policies was in important ways the result of persistent smuggling. The desire of populations to hold wealth in the form of gold contradicted the desire of state bureaucracies to monopolize hard currency for the purchase of foreign capital goods. Merchant diasporas carefully managed both licit and illicit flows of currency and gold across borders and capitalized on the profits from these competing desires. In this way the ultimate effects of monetary policy were always mediated by mercantile profits. Milton Friedman famously had to imagine dropping money out of a helicopter to avoid the complications of injecting money into the US economy through banks. In the Arabian Sea, the challenges of monetary policy were even greater, involving multiple jurisdictions, mobile populations and entrenched mercantile power. Far more than a helicopter would be needed for state officials to dictate monetary policy and circumvent the power of merchant networks across the Arabian Sea.

The rupee was finally withdrawn from the Arabian Peninsula in 1966, the gold standard collapsed in 1971 and the Sterling Area ended with a whimper in 1972. Since the 1973 oil crisis, petroleum revenues have protected Gulf currencies from the threats of devaluation. However, Dubai remains a key node in the international gold trade because of its history and continuing role as an entrepôt for illicit gold and financial flows. The smuggling of gold remains a serious concern for the Reserve Bank of India and the State Bank of Pakistan. I hope that this brief history has shown that gold smuggling and currency arbitrage are not simply salacious or even peripheral aspects of economic history. These illicit and informal financial circuits are drivers of monetary policy. Colonial era monetary policy was built on the shifting sands of diasporic financial networks. The Second World War created an exceptionally powerful demand for gold, equally strong efforts to regulate gold flows and ever more creative efforts to subvert these regulations. The post-war world saw independent states around the Arabian Sea try to assert increasing control over their borders and finances. Yet they were simply incapable of overpowering the dense mercantile networks that thrived on arbitrage. Monetary policy in South Asia and the Arabian Peninsula was thus as much a reaction to the innovations of smugglers as smuggling was a response to new rules and regulations. While nation-states are increasingly powerful in the twenty-first century, I believe that they cannot afford to ignore the dense networks and vigorous innovations that keep gilding the waves of the Arabian Sea.

CHAPTER 9

Dollar, Sovereign and Rupee: Money in Mauritius

Amenah Jahangeer Chojoo and Gorah Beebeejaun

The lens of monetary history reveals the ways in which a society is intimately constructed through the constant negotiations of interpersonal transactions. The acceptance or rejection of a currency as a standard of value, a store of wealth or a medium of exchange is based on perception and trust. These social processes are even more complicated in a colonial context, where the colonized may engage in acts of symbolic or effective resistance against those imperial structures that back the currency system. In the particular case of Mauritius, this history is overlaid by repeated imperial transitions from Dutch, to French and, finally, to British rule. Each colonizing power attempted to govern the monetary system according to its colonial objectives. However, the distance of the island from Europe and the realities on the ground in the colony opened spaces of agency for the local population to creatively improvise and contest the imposition of imperial hegemony. The success of this resistance allowed

A. Jahangeer Chojoo (✉)
Mahatma Gandhi Institute, Moka, Mauritius

G. Beebeejaun
Mauritius Research Council, Port Louis, Mauritius

S. Serels, G. Campbell (eds.), *Currencies of the Indian Ocean World*, Palgrave Series in Indian Ocean World Studies,
https://doi.org/10.1007/978-3-030-20973-5_9

the inhabitants of the island to actively participate in directing the development of the Mauritian society, in general, and the local monetary system in particular.[1]

This chapter reconstructs the history of currencies in Mauritius in order to examine two cases in which the official imperial monetary policy was successfully resisted. The first one concerns the symbolic use of the Spanish dollar, locally known by its French name *piastre*, in every auctioneering transaction in Mauritius. This reflects the contestation against British imperial rule by the Franco-Mauritian elite after the conquest of the former French colony. Despite British efforts to impose their own currencies, the colonial elite managed to integrate customs and traditions of the French period into the cultural and economic life of the island, albeit at times only symbolically. The continued life of the French *piastre* on the island points to an ambivalence at the heart of all colonizer/colonized relations in which the nature of authority is not actually that clear-cut.[2] According to Robert Young, the marginalized periphery responds to it being rendered as such by the centre with an equivocal, indefinite, indeterminate ambivalence.[3] In Mauritius this played itself out through the creation of new transcultural forms within the contact zone produced by colonization. On this "Creole Island",[4] cultural difference has produced an empowering hybridity in which mimicry is never very far from mockery.[5]

The second case study is the refashioning of the British sovereign by the Indian indentured labourers into a symbolic signifier of social status. These labourers used this symbol of high British imperial rule to create the "*guirni* necklace", a string of gold and/or silver coins worn as jewellery. In this case study, we listen to Arjun Appadurai's call to "follow the things themselves, for their meanings are inscribed in their forms, their uses, their trajectories".[6] By following the surprising trajectories of the *guirni*

[1] R.B. Allen, *Slaves, Freedmen and Indentured Laborers in Colonial Mauritius* (London, Cambridge University Press, 1999).

[2] H.K. Bhabha, 'Of Mimicry and Man: The Ambivalence of Colonial Discourse,' *October* 28 (1984) 125–33.

[3] R.J.C. Young, *Colonial Desire: Hybridity in Theory, Culture and Race* (London, Routledge, 1995).

[4] M. Vaughan, *Creating the Creole Island: Slavery in Eighteenth Century Mauritius* (Durham, NC, Duke University Press, 2005).

[5] Bhabha, 'Of Mimicry and Man.'

[6] A. Appadurai, 'Introduction: Commodities and the Politics of Value,' in *The Social Life of Things: Commodities in Cultural Perspective*, A. Appadurai, ed. (Cambridge, Cambridge University Press, 1988) 5.

necklace, we find another case in which the use of a colonial currency is turned into an act of symbolic subversion. Indian indentured labourers were drawn to Mauritius with the promise of wages, free lodgings, food and clothing rations and a return ticket home upon completion of their five year contract.[7] They laboured under strict labour laws that further rendered them the subaltern other in a strictly stratified colonial society. Despite their social position, these labourers were able to create for themselves spaces of empowerment.

These two case studies demonstrate that in Mauritius, as was likely the case in other lands peripherally linked to the globalized colonial world, resistance was possible for many segments of society. At times, resistance was oppositional to all colonial institutions. However, at other times it took the form of selectively defending some of them. Homi Bhabha has shown that this selective defence was not a direct "imitation" of colonial domination. Rather, it was a strategy used by colonized people to cope with their status as such.[8] In Mauritius, the popular maintenance of conventions associated with colonial currencies was part of a broader strategy to contest and oppose the imperial order.

Colonial Monetary Systems of Mauritius

During the early colonial rule, monetary transactions in Mauritius were limited. The colonial period began in 1638 when the Dutch East India Company (VOC) established a small outpost on the island to serve as both a stopover on the way to Batavia and a base for exploiting ebony and other resources of the island. Though the company made the rijksdaler the official currency, there was little need for currencies. The company granted colonists land, supplies, slaves, animals and tools. In exchange, colonists were required to sell their produce to the company.[9] However, the VOC could not maintain the outpost, which was constantly under threat from passing pirates, competing imperial powers, marooned slaves and pests. In 1710 the VOC withdrew from the island after burning down their forts and huts.

[7] M. Carter, *Servants, Sirdars & Settlers: Indians in Mauritius, 1834–1874* (New Delhi, Oxford University Press, 1995).

[8] H.K. Bhabha, *The Location of Culture* (London and New York, Routledge, 1994).

[9] See: See LyThioFane Pineo, *Ile de France*, 2 Vols. (Moka, Mahatma Gandhi Institute, 1993/1999); Baron d'Unienville, *Statistique de l'Ile Maurice et ses Dépendances*, Vol. 1 (Paris, Gustave Barba, 1830).

Five years later, the French East India Company (FEIC) took over the abandoned island and renamed it Ile de France. The FEIC, which already had a presence in the neighbouring island of Bourbon, established a small colony on their new possession in 1721. The new colony was run along lines similar to that of the previous VOC one; the company provided the land and inputs and acted as the monopoly purchaser of the produce.[10] The FEIC settled accounts on the island with paper coupons redeemable only at the company's headquarters in Paris. Settlers managed to get around this quasi-feudal system by clandestinely selling their produce to pirates and passing ships.[11] This illegal trade brought hard currency to the island. Though settlers accepted gold and silver coins of various origins for the black market sale of their produce, they preferred piasters from Spain and Portugal.[12] This propensity to flout the laws imposed by the ruling classes when they ran against the interests of the settlers remained an enduring feature on the island.[13]

In 1767, the French Crown took over the bankrupt company's territories and subsequently strengthened the colonial government of Ile de France. French officials wanted to shore up their control over the route to India by developing the island into a dependable naval base. The crown invested between 265,000 and 462,000 piasters per year on the island. To further encourage trade, the government fixed the exchange rate of the piaster at 5 *livres* 6 *sols*, and in 1771 increased it to 10 *livres*.[14] The resulting trade boom favoured exports and, as a result, the hard currency stocks of the island made their way to the island's major commodity providers—India, China and Madagascar.[15]

To meet the needs of the island's domestic economy, the government issued paper money and cash vouchers known as *Billets Hulot*. Repeated emissions of paper money resulted in confusion and inflation, which

[10] J.M. Paturau, *Histoire Economique de l'Ile Maurice* (Les Pailles, Henry & Cie, 1988) 277.

[11] P. de Sornay, *Isle de France—Ile Maurice: Sa Géographie, son Histoire, son Agriculture, ses Industries et ses Institutions* (Port Louis, General Printing and Stationery Co., 1950) 299.

[12] d'Unienville, *Statistique de l'Ile Maurice et ses Dépendances*, 243.

[13] In the early nineteenth century, 1 Spanish dollar was valued at 3 livres 12 sous in the colony while in Europe its value stood at 5 livres 5 sous. The livre was struck at Tours and known as la livre tournois and was subdivided into 240 deniers.

[14] d'Unienville, *Statistique de l'Ile Maurice et ses Dépendances*, 243. It was actually the *livre coloniale* which was only legal tender in the French colonies.

[15] d'Unienville, *Statistique de l'Ile Maurice et ses Dépendances*, 244.

motivated the growing population of settlers to once again turn to black market trading. During the War of American Independence (1775–1783), some of these activities were granted official sanction. Officials allowed the colony to become a base for piracy aimed against France's enemies.[16] Following the outbreak of the French Revolution, these activities became the main way for the island to import hard currency. During the revolution settlers on Ile de France established their own government with an *Assemblée Coloniale*. During the period of quasi-independence, the new government introduced *assignats*, a form of fiduciary money, which soon lost its value due to inflation. Gold and silver coins became the only stable money on the island. Meanwhile, the government of France stopped sending its annual injections of currencies. As a result, privateering and trade with foreign vessels became the sole means of importing new coins. Though France re-established its control over the island in 1803, the settlers had learned from years of ineffective governments and unreliable monetary policies to distrust both local and French currencies. Instead, settlers began to hold the Spanish silver dollar as the only truly dependable hard currency.

In 1810 Britain conquered the island to curtail the activities of the corsairs that had been operating from Ile de France since the start of the Napoleonic Wars. British officials inherited a monetary system in chaos on the island, which they renamed Mauritius.[17] Gold, silver and copper coins plundered from ships circulated on the island alongside large quantities of paper money and the exchange rates between all of these various currencies were extremely volatile. Over the next 15 years, colonial officials took a number of vigorous measures to rationalize the island's monetary system and bring it in line with that of British India. The Sicca rupee was made the official currency of the Island and the official exchange rate was fixed at 2 Sicca or 2.5 Arkot rupees per Spanish dollar.[18] In addition, the government opened a bank to issue new money, minted special silver coins in Calcutta and struck 50,000 silver coins equal in value to the Spanish dollar but with a different design.

[16] During the war, seven French corsairs operated in the Indian Ocean, bringing in takes of around 11 million livres, Paturau, *Histoire Economique de l'Ile Maurice*, 77.

[17] From 1793 to 1802, more than 51 corsair ships were involved and they brought 126 prizes, estimated at £2.5 million. A. Toussaint, *Port Louis: Deux siècles d'histoire, 1735–1935* (Port Louis, La Typographie Moderne, 1936).

[18] Robert Chalmers, *A History of Currency in the British Colonies* (London, H.M. Stationery Office, 1893) 361.

These efforts were undermined when Britain shifted to the gold standard in 1816. Officials fixed the exchange rate on the island at 4 British shillings to the dollar, which created the opportunity for currency arbitrage. Throughout the middle third of the nineteenth century, British colonial officials tried in vain to curtail currency speculation on the island. The colonial government changed and adjusted the official exchange rates in 1836 and again in 1838. In 1849, it established a Currency Board, which issued paper currency in the form of 10 and 5 rupee notes. However, the discrepancy between the official and market exchange rates for gold and silver persisted and with it the opportunity for arbitrage. Nonetheless, speculation continued as a result of arbitrage opportunities created by the official exchange rate of gold currencies for silver ones. The board was eventually forced to withdraw the rupee notes and replace them with sterling notes. This measure did not have the expected result, and by the 1860s the government of Mauritius ended its efforts to bring the island under the gold standard by establishing the Indian silver rupee as the official currency.

The Indian rupee remained the legal tender for Mauritius into the first third of the twentieth century in no small part because India was the island's main trading partner. Under British rule, the sugar economy of the island grew. With the encouragement and support of the British government, Mauritius plantation owners began in 1834 using Indian indentured servants to work the fields. Over the next 40 years over 453,000 workers were brought from India under this system to work on the expanding sugarcane plantations. Many of these Indian servants settled permanently on the island after their contracts had run up. Much of the sugar they produced was exported to India. In the mid-1920s, this ended. In 1924, officials abolished the practice of indentured servitude. The bulk of the former indentured labourers settled on the island. Many bought small plots of land and began growing sugarcane and various food crops.[19] Britain had meanwhile, become the major purchaser of the island's sugar yield since the First World War. In 1934, the government established a new Currency Board, which subsequently recommended switching to a sterling exchange standard. This recommendation resulted in the creation of a new Mauritian rupee.[20] This remains the currency of the country to this day, though it is now pegged to a flexible basket constituted of the currencies of major trading partners.

[19] See Allen, *Slaves, Freedmen and Indentured Laborers in Colonial Mauritius.*
[20] See Paturau, *Histoire Economique de l'Ile Maurice.*

The Auction and the Franco-Mauritians

Although the rupee has been the only legal tender in Mauritius for decades, the Spanish dollar, or piaster, remains a symbolic currency. The piaster does not circulate but is used in every auctioneering activity, whether conducted by individuals, private companies or government agencies. Cultivators sell their produce on the market by auction. Companies use auctions to dispose of used goods or unsold stock. Government agencies use auctions to sell seized goods or unclaimed articles. No matter the auction, bids are always denominated in piasters. For this purpose, a piaster is set at 2 rupees. This is the value first established by British colonial officials in 1824. However, the practice of sale by auction predates British rule. It began on the island during the early French period and was transmitted from generation to generation within a few Franco-Mauritian families. The unique local auctioneering practices developed by these Franco-Mauritian families form a part of the island's unique folk traditions.

The continued use of the piaster in auctioneering reflects the legacy of earlier forms of colonial resistance dating back to the British capture of Mauritius in 1810. The new British rulers of the island promised through the Treaty of Capitulation to allow the French settler population to continue to keep their assets, religion, traditions and customs.[21] Throughout the period of British rule, the Franco-Mauritian population repeatedly used this clause to stave off the imposition of British institutions.[22] The Franco-Mauritian elite were sufficiently self-confident to pose a serious challenge for the island's British governors. As Smith-Simmons puts it "for the first century of British rule, the administration could not afford to cross the Franco-Mauritians, who were considered the only politically significant 'indigenous inhabitants'".[23]A British governor remarked that "it require(d) a very great deal of courage, I will say a great deal of self-reliance, to stand up against (the Franco-Mauritian planters') influence".[24] This resistance allowed these Franco-Mauritians

[21] The Treaty of Capitulation can be viewed in the annex of Ly-Thio-Fane Pineo, 1993.

[22] To date the Civil Code of Napoleon still forms the basis of law and several niche areas, such as notarial deeds, still use French, while all subsequent laws and administrative functioning are in English.

[23] Smith-Simmons, *Modern Mauritius*, 18.

[24] A. Hamilton-Gordon, *Mauritius: Records of Private and Public Life, 1871–1874*, Vol. II (Edinburg, R. R. Clark, 1894) 176.

to maintain their elite status throughout the period of British colonial rule and into the post-independence period.[25]

Some of the cultural forms created and maintained by the Franco-Mauritians elite have become "socially relevant" for non-elite groups on the island. As Appadurai suggests, "the commodity situation in the social life of any 'thing' can be defined as the situation in which its exchange-ability (past, present, or future) for some other thing is its socially relevant feature".[26] One of these "socially relevant things" is the piaster as a unit of account in auctioneering. Nowadays, auctioneering companies are owned by members of a diverse range of ethnicities. Nonetheless, the ritual of the auction follows the form first established and maintained by the Franco-Mauritian elite. When the actors of this ritual are asked about the reason for the use of the piaster, they say that it is the tradition. The perceived long history of this practice leads to widespread respect and lends an aura of authority to the practice of auctioneering.

Guineas and Sovereigns, a Post-Colonial Paradox

The British gold sovereign is another coin that has made a lasting imprint on Mauritian culture, especially amongst the descendants of Indian indentured labourers. The gold sovereign was first minted in 1816 when Britain officially went on the gold standard. Its weight and value were set precisely at £1 and it replaced the guinea which held the inconvenience of being worth 21 shillings (£1 and 1 shilling).[27] The gold sovereign held the effigy of the British monarch on the obverse and either St George slaying the dragon or a shield on the reverse. When the sovereign was introduced to Mauritius, the indentured Indian servants did not differentiate between it and the guinea. They called the new coin the same name as the old one, that is, the *guirni*. British sovereigns are still called *guirnis* in the Indian languages in use in Mauritius.

The Victoria sovereigns played a particularly important role in the social economy of the indentured labourers. Victoria reigned from 1834 to 1901, roughly the period of indentured immigration to Mauritius. These bonded labourers came with the objective of remitting money back

[25] T. Salverda, *The Franco-Mauritian Elite: Power and Anxiety in the Face of Change* (New York, Berghahn Books, 2015) 103.

[26] Appadurai, 'Introduction,' 13.

[27] P.L. Bernstein, *The Power of Gold: The History of an Obsession* (New York, Wiley, 2012).

to their families in India or returning home with their hard-won savings. The most convenient way to send remittances was to send precious metal coins that were easily redeemable in India's rural areas. The most stable currency in the Victorian period was the sovereign. The labourers were aware of the fact that the British made special efforts to ensure the integrity and accuracy of fineness, weight and diameter of the sovereign in order to sustain the gold standard.[28] As a result, they preferred these coins even though many other gold and silver coins were in circulation in Mauritius and India at that time.

Given the precarious dwellings on the plantations, the labourers found that the safest place to secure their saved silver or gold coins was on their bodies. They therefore strung the *guirnis* on a thread and transformed them into a necklace. They were able to add or remove coins as required by their fluctuating fortunes. Ideally, women wore the *guirni* necklace, but as the sex ratio among indentured labourers tipped heavily in favour of men, it was not rare to see male Indians wearing gold or silver coin necklaces. The *guirni* necklace became all in one a social signifier, a marker of status, a personal bank and a cultural item of embellishment. While the sovereign was meant by the imperial administration to be a circulating symbol of its power as a necklace, it was diverted from its original nexus and given a new meaning by a subaltern group. It became a valued commodity and helped empower women.

In fact, although Mauritius was a part of the British Empire, the laws regarding inheritance and ownership of property were (and still are) governed by Napoleon's Civil Code. As a result, Indian migrants to the island found themselves in a system where men and women could own land in full property, which, on their death, would be divided equally among their heirs, male and female. This must have constituted a motivation to settle down and many did, especially at the end of the nineteenth century. At that time, the sugar industry faltered and many plantations were forced to parcel and sell out the land. Between 1880 and 1904 some 44,588 sales contracts for small plots were drawn mostly to the name of former indentured Indians, which brought the proportion of land cultivated by the Indians/Indo-Mauritians to 32 per cent by 1910.[29] Many women had put to good use their *guirni* necklaces by investing in plots of land or animals and had improved their socio-economic status.

[28] *Ibid.*

[29] Paturau, *Histoire Economique de l'Ile Maurice*, 117–18.

Though literature often depicts Indian women of all social classes as irrationally in love with gold,[30] for women jewellery was traditionally the only tangible asset that could be claimed as their own within the traditional system of patriarchy and inheritance. In Mauritius, women could play a more active role in family investments and gain a higher status by managing their *guirni* necklaces.[31]

The disappearance of sovereigns in personal hoards became a preoccupation for the authorities. The colonial government set up a Government Savings Bank in 1837, with a head office in Port Louis and branch offices in eight districts so as to encourage deposits from small earners. However, the success of these efforts was limited as for the largely illiterate Indian labourers it was difficult to gain confidence in and interact with a British institution. Further, the restrictions on their movement outside the plantation deterred them from using this institution.[32] Widespread hoarding of sovereigns made the British authorities stop circulating them in 1932. However, the demand for *guirnis* in Mauritius did not cease as the upwardly mobile wanted to parade their *guirni* necklace as higher status women. This demand led to the appearance of imitation coins on the market and curiously, the counterfeit coins typically bore the Golden Jubilee head of Victoria.

Guirnis have become a well-entrenched aspect of folk traditions among Indo-Mauritian families, as attested by oral history. In addition, *guirnis* have integrated into Indo-Mauritian life-cycle rituals. Coins are also gifted during marriage rituals. Brides are still made to carry some coins along with some rice and grains wrapped in a handkerchief when they go to the in-laws' home as a symbol of wealth.

Though precious metal coins have long been replaced by paper money, *guirnis* are still an element of jewellery worn by brides of some families at their wedding. Gold jewellery forms part of the dowry given to daughters

[30] N. Mehrotra, 'Gold and Gender in India: Some Observations from South Orissa,' *Indian Anthropologist* 34:1 (2004) 27–39.

[31] See A. Jahangeer Chojoo, 'The Yamse and Horse-Racing: Integration and Contestation in a Stratified Society,' in *Angaje: Explorations into the History, Society and Culture of Indentured Immigrants and their Descendants in Mauritius*, Vol. 3 (Port Louis, AGTF, 2013) 67–88.

[32] The Savings Bank had some 18,000 depositors in 1911, and the sum deposited was small compared to the assets held by Indo-Mauritians. See A. Macmillan (ed.), *Mauritius Illustrated: Historical and Descriptive, Commercial and Industrial Facts, Figures, and Resources* (New Delhi, Asian Educational Services, 2000 reprint of 1914 edition) 258.

and daughters-in-law. It denotes the status of the families being united. The dearth of girls during the indenture period brought some modifications to the traditional Hindu dowry system, where the bride's family gave a negotiated amount to the groom. Here, the dowry is given to the bride by both parties, generally in the form of jewellery. This will remain her property, which she can dispose of as she wishes. In fact, during a marriage settlement each family used to declare the amount of gold to be given in dowry in terms of the number of *guirnis*. To date the sovereign is still a measure of gold weight in common parlance.

Though present-day Mauritian inhabitants of Indian origin are fourth to seventh generation, there is some continuity in attitudes towards the *guirni* necklace in particular and to gold or silver jewellery in general. Despite the fact that the country has undergone profound socio-economic changes, jewellery is still a valued investment and gifts of jewels are still ritually given on life-cycle events. Many men and women still wear a Victoria sovereign pendant, especially the Golden Jubilee issue. Elderly women still wear their *guirni* necklaces on special occasions. However, these are becoming rare because they are often split among heirs. Brides still display gold jewellery given by the families. Nonetheless, there have been many changes both in attitude and in practice. For instance, the trend among many Hindu brides is the use of fancy jewellery made out of base metals as part of the bridal outfit. This fashion started in the 1960s under the influence of Hindustani movies. Some brides do not even buy gold jewels for the wedding. This evolution relates to the contestation of patriarchal norms related to gender roles and dowries, especially as women have entered the job market as holders of professional degrees. In addition, gold has lost its former role in family savings or as a sign of social status. Jewellery has likewise lost its paramount importance in social functions or in inheritance matters. Women are emancipating themselves from the shackles of gold tradition and are contesting former attachment to the gold sovereigns.

Conclusion

The people of Mauritius have actively participated in shaping and reshaping the role currencies have played on the island. They did not just passively receive the value system imposed by colonial rulers. Currencies, which have been fundamental to the functioning of the island's economy, have also been used in everyday acts of political resistance. The material form of money has been used to contest the dominant order by both elites and subaltern groups on the island, each in their own way. The peculiar history of the Spanish dollar and the British sovereign in Mauritius illustrates the ways in which "things" gain social and cultural value different from their originally intended economic uses.

Bibliography

Abu-Lughod, Janet. *Before European Hegemony: The World System A.D. 1250–1350*. New York: Oxford University Press, 1989.

Africa Watch. *Evil Days: Thirty Years of War and Famine in Ethiopia*. New York: Human Rights Watch, 1991.

Ahmad, Abdel Ghaffar Muhammad. *Changing Systems of Livelihood in Rural Sudan*. Addis Ababa: Organization for Social Science Research in Eastern and Southern Africa, 2002.

Allen, Calvin H. 'The State of Masqat in the Gulf and East Africa, 1785–1829.' *International Journal of Middle East Studies*. 14:2 (1982) 117–27.

Allen, Richard. *Slaves, Freedmen and Indentured Laborers in Colonial Mauritius*. London: Cambridge University Press, 1999.

Alpern, Stanley. 'What Africans Got for Their Slaves: A Master List of European Trade Goods.' *History in Africa*. 22 (1995) 5–43.

Alpers, Edward A. 'The French Slave Trade.' *Historical Association of Tanzania Paper* 3 (1967).

———. *The Indian Ocean in World History*. New York: Oxford, 2014.

Andrus, James Russell, and Azizali F. Mohammed. *The Economy of Pakistan*. Stanford: Stanford University Press, 1958.

Apicoltura e commercio della cera e del miele nella colonia Eritrea. Rome: Istituto Coloniale Italiano, 1910.

Appadurai, Arjun, ed. *The Social Life of Things: Commodities in Cultural Perspective*. Cambridge: Cambridge University Press, 1986. 3–63.

Atwell, William S. 'International Bullion Flows and the Chinese Economy, circa 15300–1650.' *Past and Present*. 95:1 (1982) 68–90.

S. Serels, G. Campbell (eds.), *Currencies of the Indian Ocean World*, Palgrave Series in Indian Ocean World Studies,
https://doi.org/10.1007/978-3-030-20973-5

———. 'Time, Money and the Weather: Ming China and the "Great Depression" of the Mid-Fifteenth Century.' *The Journal of Asian Studies*. 61:1 (2002) 83–113.

Austen, Ralph. 'Patterns of Development in Nineteenth-century East Africa.' *The Journal of African History*. 4:3 (1971) 645–57.

Balachandran, G. *John Bullion's Empire: Britain's Gold Problem and India between the Wars*. Richmond, UK: Curzon, 1996.

Barendse, R. J. *Arabian Seas: 1700–1763. Volume 3: Men and Merchandise*. Leiden: Brill, 2009.

Barnett, Tony. *The Gezira Scheme: An Illusion of Development*. London: Frank Cass, 1977.

Baron, Richard. 'Malagasy Terms of Monetary Values.' *Antananarivo Annual and Madagascar Magazine*. 14 (1890) 191–2.

Beachey, Raymond. *The Slave Trade of Eastern Africa*. London: Rex Collings, 1966.

Beaujard, Philippe. 'The Indian Ocean in Eurasian and African World-Systems before the Sixteenth Century.' *Journal of World History*. 16:4 (2005) 411–65.

———. *Les Mondes de l'océan Indien, tome II. L'ocean Indien, au coeur des globalisations de l'ancien monde (7e-15e siècles)*. Paris: Armand Colin, 2012.

Becker, Jerome. *La Vie en Afrique ou trois ans dans l'Afrique Centrale*. Paris: J. Lebègue, 1887.

Bell, Phillip W. *The Sterling Area in the Postwar World: Internal Mechanism and Cohesion, 1946–52*. New York: Oxford University Press, 1956.

Bell, Stephanie. 'The Role of the State and the Hierarchy of Money.' *Cambridge Journal of Economics*. 25 (2001) 149–63.

Bell, Stephanie and John H. Henry. 'Hospitality versus Exchange: The Limits of Monetary Economies.' *Review of Social Economy*. 59:2 (June 2001) 203–26.

Bellucci, Stefano and Massimod Zaccaria. 'Wage Labor and Mobility in Colonial Eritrea, 1880s to 1920s.' *International Labor and Working-Class History* 86 (2014) 89–106.

Bennett, Norman Robert. 'Americans in Zanzibar: 1865–1915.' *Tanganyika Notes and Records*. 60 (1963) 49–66.

———. 'France and Zanzibar, 1775–1844.' *Eastern African History*. Daniel F. McCall, Norman Robert Bennett, and Jeffrey Butler, eds. New York: Praeger, 1969. 148–75.

———. 'France and Zanzibar, 1844 to the 1860s.' *The International Journal of African Historical Studies*. 6:4 (1973): 602–32.

———. ed. *Stanley's Despatches to the New York Herald 1871–1872, 1874–1877*. Boston: Boston University Press, 1970.

Bennett, Norman Robert and George E. Brooks. *New England Merchants in Africa: A History through Documents, 1802 to 1865*. New York: Africana, 1965.

Bernstein, Peter L. *The Power of Gold: The History of an Obsession*. New York: Wiley, 2012. Accessed February 2015, Questia.com.

Bhabha, Homi K. *The Location of Culture*. London and New York: Routledge, 1994.

Bhacker, Mohammed Reda. *Trade and Empire in Muscat and Zanzibar: The Roots of British Domination*. London: Routledge, 1992.

Blake, Robert P. 'The Circulation of Silver in the Moslem East down to the Mongol Epoch.' *Harvard Journal of Asiatic Studies*. 2 (1937) 291–328.

Blandare, Shailendra. 'Money on the Move: The Rupee and the Indian Ocean Region.' *Cross Currents and Community Networks: The History of the Indian Ocean World*. Himanshu Prabha Ray and Edward A. Alpers, eds. Oxford: Oxford University Press, 2007. 205–25.

Bontnick, François. ed. *L'Autobiographie de Hamed ben Mohammed el-Murjebi Tippo Tip (ca. 1840–1905)*. Bruxelles: Académie Royale des Sciences d'Outre-Mer, 1974.

Bose, Sugata. *A Hundred Horizons: The Indian Ocean in the Age of Global Empire*. Cambridge, MA: Harvard University Press, 2006.

Bouchon, Genevieve and Denys Lombard. 'The Indian Ocean in the Fifteenth Century.' *India and the Indian Ocean, 1500–1800*. Ashin Das Gupta and Michael N. Pearson, eds. Calcutta: Oxford, 1987. 46–70.

Bromber, Katrin. *The Jurisdiction of the Sultan of Zanzibar and the Subjects of Foreign Nations*. Würzburg: Ergon, 2001.

Brown, Beverley. 'Muslim Influence in the Lake Tanganyika Region.' *African Historical Studies*. 4:3 (1971) 617–29.

———. *Ujiji: History of a Lakeside Town*, PhD Thesis, University of Boston, 1973.

Burton, Richard Francis. 'The Lake Regions of Central Equatorial Africa.' *Journal of the Royal Geographical Society*. 29 (1859) 1–454.

———. *Zanzibar: The City and the Island*. London: Tinsley, 1872.

Callet, François. *Histoire des Rois*. Tananarive: Éditions de la Librairie de Madagascar, 1974.

Cameron, Verney L. *Across Africa*. Daldy: Isbister, 1877.

Campbell, Gwyn. 'The Adoption of Autarky in Imperial Madagascar, 1820–1835.' *Journal of African History*. 28:3 (1987) 395–411.

———. *An Economic History of Imperial Madagascar, 1750–1895: The Rise and Fall of an Island Empire*. Cambridge: Cambridge University Press, 2005.

———. 'Gold Mining and the French Takeover of Madagascar, 1883–1914.' *African Economic History*. 17 (1988) 99–126.

———. 'Labour and the Transport Problem in Imperial Madagascar, 1810–1895.' *Journal of African History*. 21:3 (1980) 341–56.

———. 'Madagascar and the Slave Trade, 1810–1895.' *Journal of African History*. 22:2 (1981) 203–27.

———. *The Role of the London Missionary Society in the Rise of the Merina Empire, 1810–1861*, PhD dissertation, University of Wales, Swansea, 1985.

———. 'Toamasina (Tamatave) and the Growth of Foreign Trade in Imperial Madagascar, 1862–1895.' *Figuring African Trade*. Gerhard Liesegang et al., eds. Berlin: Dietrich Reimer Verlag, 1986. 525–56.

Carboneri, Giovanni. *Il Tallero di Maria Teresa e la Questione Monetaria della Colonia Eritrea*. Rome: Tipografia Nazionale di G Bertero E C, 1912.

Carter, Marina. *Servants, Sirdars & Settlers. Indians in Mauritius, 1834–1874*. New Delhi: Oxford University Press, 1995.

———. 'Of Mimicry and Man: The Ambivalence of Colonial Discourse.' *Discipleship: A Special Issue on Psychoanalysis*. 28 (1984) 125–33.

Case, Karl, Ray Fair, Manfred Gärtner, and Ken Heather. *Economics*. London: Prentice Hall, 1996.

Catat, Louis. *Voyage à Madagascar, 1889–90*. Paris: Hachette, 1895.

Chaffee, John. 'Song China and the Multi-state and Commercial World of East Asia.' *Crossroads: Studies on the History of Exchange Relations in the East Asian World*. 1/2 (2010) 33–54.

Chakravarti, Ranabir. India and the Indian Ocean—Issues in Trade and Politics (up to c. 1500 CE). Mumbai: Maritime History Society, 2014.

———. 'Merchants, Merchandise and Merchantmen in the Western Seaboard of India (c. 500 BCE—1500 CE).' *The World of Indian Ocean Commerce 1500–1800*. Om Prakash, ed. New Delhi: Pearson, 2011. 53–171.

———. 'Monarchs, Merchants and a Matha in Northern Konkan (c. 900–1053 AD).' *Indian Economic and Social History Review*. 27:2 (1990) 189–208.

———. *Trade and Traders in Early Indian Society*. Delhi: Manohar, 2007.

———. 'The Pull towards the Coast: Politics and Polity in India (ca. 600–1300 CE).' *Proceedings of the Indian History Congress, 72nd Session*. Patiala (2011) 22–42.

Chalmers, Robert. *A History of Currency in the British Colonies*. London: H.M. Stationery Office, 1893.

Chapelier, Louis Armand. 'Lettres adressées au citoyen préfet de l'ile de France, de décembre 1803 en mai 1805.' *Bulletin de l'Académie Malgache*. 4 (1905–1906) 1–56.

Chapman, Anne. 'Barter as a Universal Mode of Exchange.' *L'Homme*. 22:3 (1980) 33–83.

Chapus, G.-S. 'Le soin du bien-être du peuple sous le règne d'Andrianampoinimerina.' *Bulletin de l'Académie Malgache*. 30 (1951–1952) 1–11.

Chapus, G.S. and G. Mondain. 'Un chapitre inconnu. Des rapports de Maurice et de Madagascar.' *Bulletin de l'Académie Malgache*. 30 (1951–1952) 111–30.

Chattopadhyay, Pranab K. 'In Search of Silver: Southeast Asian Sources for the Coinage of Bengal.' *Kalhar—Studies in Art, Iconography, Architecture and Archaeology of India and Bangladesh*. Gouriswar Bhattacharya, et al., eds. New Delhi: Kaveri Books, 2007. 296–305.

Chaudhuri, K. N. *Trade and Civilisation in the Indian Ocean: An Economic History from the Rise of Islam to 1750*. Cambridge: Cambridge University Press, 1985.

Chauvicourt, J. 'Les premières monnaies de Madagascar.' *Bulletin de Madagascar*. 261 (1968) 146–71.

Checchi, Michele. *Movimento Commerciale della Colonia Eritrea*. Rome: Istituto Coloniale, 1912.

Chen, Hailian. *Zinc for Coin and Brass Bureaucrats, Merchants, Artisans, and Mining Laborers in Qing China, ca. 1680s–1830s* [Monies, Markets, and Finance in East Asia, 1600–1900, vol. 11]. Leiden: E. J. Brill, 2018.

Chen Jie 陳捷, trans. *ZhongRi jiaotong shi* 中日交通史 (Taibei, no date; Japanese original by Kimiya Yasuhiko 木宮泰彥), 2 vols.

Cheng Wing-cheong (Zheng Yongchang) 鄭永昌. 'Mingmo Qingchu de yingui qianjian xianxiang yu xiangguan zhengzhi jingji sixiang.' 明末清初的銀貴錢賤現象與相關政治經濟思想, *Taiwan Shifan daxue lishi yanjiu yuan zhuankan* 台灣師範大學歷史研究院專刊, no. 24 (1994), 65, MA Thesis, 1993.

Copland, Samuel. *A History of Madagascar*. London: Burton and Smith, 1822.

Coupland, Reginald. *East Africa and Its Invaders: From the Earliest Times to the Death of Seyyid Said in 1856*. Oxford: Clarendon Press, 1938.

Crossland, Zoë. *Ancestral Encounters in Highland Madagascar: Material Signs and Traces of the Dead*. Cambridge: Cambridge University Press, 2014.

Curtin, Philip D. 'Africa and the Wider Monetary World 1350–1850.' *Precious Metals in the Late Medieval and Early Modern Worlds*. J.F. Richards, ed. Durham: Carolina Academic Press, 1983. 231–68.

———. *Economic Change in Pre-colonial Africa: Senegambia in the Era of the Slave Trade*. Madison: University of Wisconsin Press, 1975.

Cusack, Igor. 'Tiny Transmitters of Nationalist and Colonial Ideology: The Postage Stamps of Portugal and Its Empire.' *Nations and Nationalism*. 11:4 (2005) 591–612.

Dahle, Lars. 'The Influence of Arabs on the Malagasy Language.' *Antananarivo Annual and Madagascar Magazine*. 2 (1876) 203–19.

Davies, C. Colin. *An Historical Atlas of the Indian Peninsula*. Madras: Oxford University Press, 1959.

Decary, Raymond. 'L'ancien régime de l'or à Madagascar.' *Bulletin de l'Académie Malgache*. 40 (1962) 83–96.

Degefe, Befekadu. 'The Development of Money, Monetary Institutions and Monetary Policy, 1941–75.' *An Economic History of Ethiopia: Volume 1: The Imperial Era, 1941–74*. Shiferaw Bekele, ed. Oxford: CODESRIA, 1995. 232–76.

Desan, Christine. 'Money as a Legal Institution.' *Money in the Western Legal Tradition: Middle Ages to Bretton Wood*. David Fox and Wolfgang Ernst, eds. Oxford: Oxford University Press, 2016. 18–35.

Deyell, John S. 'The China Connection: Problems of Silver Supply in Medieval Bengal.' Reprinted in *Money and the Market in India 1100–1700*. Sanjay Subrahmanyam, ed. Delhi: Oxford University Press, 1994. 112–36.

———. 'Cowries and Coins: the Dual Monetary System of the Bengal Sultanate.' *Indian Economic and Social History Review*. 47:1 (2010) 63–106.

———. *Living Without Silver: The Monetary History of Early Medieval North India*. Delhi: Oxford University Press, 1990.

———. 'Monetary and Financial Webs: The Regional and International Influence of Pre-modern Bengali Coinage.' *Pelagic Passageways: The Northern Bay of Bengal before Colonialism*. Rila Mukherjee, ed. Delhi: Primus, 2011. 279–314.

———. 'Precious Metals, Debasement and Cowrie Shells in the Medieval Indian Monetary Systems (ca. 1200–1575).' *Money in the Pre-Industrial World: Bullion, Debasements and Coin Substitutes*. John H. Munro, ed. London: Pickering & Chatto, 2012. 163–82.

Dez, Jacques. 'Considérations sur les prix pratiqués à Tananarive en 1870.' *Bulletin de l'Académie Malgache*. 40 (1962) 42–61.

Digby, Simon. 'The Maritime Trade of India (c. 1200–1500).' *The Cambridge Economic History of India, Vol 1, c. 1200–1750*. Tapan Raychauduri and Irfan Habib, eds. Cambridge: Cambridge University Press, 1982. 125–59.

Drummond, Ian M. *The Floating Pound and the Sterling Area, 1931–1939*. Cambridge, UK: Cambridge University Press, 1981.

Dubois, Henri. *Monographie des Betsileo (Madagascar)*. Paris: Institut d'ethnologie, 1938.

Dunstan, Helen. 'Safely Duping with the Devil: The Qing State and Its Merchant Suppliers of Copper.' *Late Imperial China*. 13:2 (1992), 42–81.

Eagleton, Catherine and John Williams. *Money: A History*. London: British Museum Press, 2007.

Eaton, Richard M. *Essays on Islam and Indian History*. New Delhi: Oxford, 2001.

———. *The Rise of Islam and the Bengal Frontier 1204–1760*. New Delhi: Oxford University Press, 1994.

L'Economia Eritrea: Nel Cinquatennio dell'Occupazione di Assab (1882–1932). Florence: Istituto Agricolo Coloniale Italiano, 1932.

Edo, Michael E. 'Currency Arrangements and Banking Legislation in the Arabian Peninsula.' *Staff Papers—International Monetary Fund*. 22:2 (1975, July 1) 510–38.

Eichengreen, Barry. *Golden Fetters: The Gold Standard and the Great Depression, 1919–1939*. New York: Oxford University Press, 1996.

Ellis, William. *History of Madagascar*. 2 vols. London: Fisher, 1838.

al-Enazy, Askar. *The Creation of Saudi Arabia: Ibn Saud and British Imperial Policy, 1914–1927*. London and New York: Routledge, 2010.

Fadlalla, Mohamed Hassan, *A Short History of Sudan*. Lincoln: iUniverse, 2004.

Fane-Pineo, Huguette Ly Tio. *Île de France, 1715–1746. Tome I. L'émergence de Port Louis*. Moka: Mahatma Gandhi Institute, 1993.

Ferrand, Gabriel, trans. *Voyage du marchand arabe Sulaymân en Inde et en Chine, rédigé en 851, suivi de remarques par Abû Zayd Hasan (vers 916)*. Paris: Brossard, 1922.

Flynn, Dennis O and Arturo Gíraldez. 'Born with a "Silver Spoon": The Origins of World Trade in 1571.' *Journal of World History*. 6:2 (1995) 201–21.

———, eds. *Metals and Monies in an Emerging Global Economy*. Aldershot: Variorum Books, 1997.

Frank, Andre Gunder. *Re-orient: Global Economy in the Asian Age*. Berkeley: University of California Press, 1998.

Fratianni, Michele and Franco Spinelli. *A Monetary History of Italy*. Cambridge: Cambridge University Press, 1997.

Freeman-Grenville, G.S.P. *The French at Kilwa Island*. Oxford: Clarendon Press, 1965.

Freitag, Ulrike. *Indian Ocean Migrants and State Formation in Hadhramaut: Reforming the Homeland*. Leiden: Brill, 2003.

Frere, W.E. and Williamson, V.A. *Report of the Commission to Enquire into the Condition of Indian Labourers in the Island of Mauritius*. London: HM Stationery Office, 1875.

Galbraith, John S. 'Italy, the British East Africa Company, and the Benadir Coast, 1888–1893.' *Journal of Modern History*. 42:4 (1970) 549–63.

Gamaledin, Maknun. 'The Decline of Afar Pastoralism.' *Conflict and the Decline of Pastoralism in the Horn of Africa*. John Markakis, ed. London: Macmillan Press, 1993. 45–63.

———. *Mackinnon and East Africa 1878–1895: A Study in the "New Imperialism"*. Cambridge: Cambridge University Press, 2008.

Gates, Hill. 'Money for the Gods.' *Modern China*. 13:3 (1987, July) 259–77.

Gavin, R.J. *Aden Under British Rule, 1839–1967*. London: C Hurst and Co, 1975.

Gereffi, Gerold, and Korzeniewicz, Miguel, eds. *Commodity Chains and Global Capitalism*. Westport: Greenwood Press, 1994.

Gilbert, Emily. 'Common Cents: Situating Money in Time and Place.' *Economy and Society*. 34:3 (2005) 357–88.

Gilbert, Emily and Erik Helleiner, eds. *Nation-States and Money: The Past, Present and Future of National Currencies*. London: Routledge, 1999.

Gilbert, Erik. *Dhows and the Colonial Economy of Zanzibar: 1860–1970*. Oxford: James Currey, 2004.

Glassman, Jonathon. *Feasts and Riot. Revelry, Rebellion, and Popular Consciousness on the Swahili Coast, 1856–1888*. Portsmouth: Heinemann, 1995.

Goitein, Shelomoh Dov and M.A. Friedman. *India Traders of the Middle Ages: Documents from the Cairo Geniza*. Leiden: Brill, 2008.

Goron, Stan and J.P. Goenka. *The Coins of the Indian Sultanates*. New Delhi: Munshiram Manoharlal, 2001.

Gramlich-Oka, Bettina. 'Shogunal Administration of Copper in the Mid-Tokugawa Period (1670–1720).' *Metals, Monies, and Markets in Early Modern Societies: East Asian and Global Perspectives.* Thomas Hirzel and Nanny Kim, eds. Berlin: LitVerlag, 2008. 65–105.

Grandidier, Alfred. 'Property among the Malagasy.' (trans. James Sibree). *Antananarivo Annual and Madagascar Magazine* 22 (1898).

Grandidier, Alfred and Guillaume Grandidier. *Histoire Physique, Naturelle et Politique de Madagascar. Tome 4: Ethnographie de Madagascar.* Paris: Imprimérie Nationale, 1908.

Green, Jeremy and Zae Geun Kim. 'The Shinan and Wando Sites, Korea: Further Information.' *The International Journal of Nautical Archaeology and Underwater Explorations.* 18:1 (1989) 33–41.

Greffülhe, Henri. 'Voyage de Lamoo a Zanzibar.' *Bulletin de la Société de géographie de Marseille.* (1878) 209–17.

Grierson, Philip. 'The Origins of Money.' *Research in Economic Anthropology.* 1 (1978) 1–35.

Griffiths, David. *Hanes Madagascar.* Machynlleth: R. Jones, 1843.

Guha, Ranajit. 'On Some Aspects of the Historiography of Colonial India.' *Subaltern Studies.* 1 (1982) 1–8.

Gupta, Parmeshwari Lal. *Coin Hoards from Gujarat State.* Varanasi: Numismatic Society of India, 1969.

———. *Coins.* New Delhi: National Book Trust, 1969.

Gupte, Pranay. *Dubai: The Making of a Megapolis.* Penguin Books India, 2011.

Guyer, Jane. *Marginal Gains. Monetary Transactions in Atlantic Africa.* Chicago: University of Chicago Press, 2004.

———, ed. *Money Matters. Instability, Values and Social Payments in the Modern History of West African Communities.* Portsmouth: Heinemann, 1995.

Haider, Najaf. 'International Trade in Precious Metals and Monetary Systems of Medieval India: 1200–1500.' *Proceedings of the Indian History Congress, 59th Session*, Patiala (1998) 237–54.

———. 'The Network of Monetary Exchange in the Indian Ocean Trade, 1200–1700.' *Cross Currents and Community Networks: The History of the Indian Ocean World.* Himanshu Prabha Ray and Edward A. Alpers, eds. Oxford: Oxford University Press, 2007. 181–205.

Hakansson, Thomas N. 'The Human Ecology of World Systems in East Africa: The Impact of the Ivory Trade.' *Human Ecology.* 32 (2004) 561–91.

———. 'Socio-Ecological Consequences of the Ivory Trade.' *Ecology and Power: Struggles over Land and Material Resources in the Past, Present and Future.* A. Hornborg, B. Clark, and K. Hermele, eds. Routledge: New York, 2014. 124–42.

Hall, Kenneth. 'Coinage Trade and Economy in Early South India and Its Southeast Asian Neighbours.' *Indian Economic and Social History Review*. 36:4 (1999) 449–50.

———. *Networks of Trade, Polity and Societal Integration in Chola-Era South India, c. 875–1400*. New Delhi: Primus, 2014.

Hamashita, Takeshi. *China, East Asia and the Global Economy. Regional and Historical Perspectives*. Linda Grove and Mark Selden, eds. London and New York: Routledge, 2008.

Hammett, Daniel and Paul Nugent. *Making Nations, Creating Strangers: States and Citizenship in Africa*. Leiden: Brill, 2007.

Hanson, Holly E. *Landed Obligations. The Practice of Power in Buganda*. Portsmouth: Heinemann, 2003.

Haring, L. 'Buried Treasure.' *Journal of Mauritian Studies*. 4:1 (1992) 22–35.

Hay, Margaret Jean. 'Changes in Clothing and Struggles over Identity in Colonial Western Kenya.' *Fashioning Africa. Power and the Politics of Dress*. J. Alleman, ed. Bloomington: Indiana University Press, 2004. 67–83.

Heimann, J. 'Small Change and Ballast: Cowry Trade and Usage as an Example of India Ocean Economic History.' *South Asia*. 3:1 (1980) 48–69.

Helleiner, Eric. *The Making of National Money: Territorial Currencies in Historical Perspective*. Ithaca, NY: Cornell University Press, 2003.

Henry, John H. 'The Social Origins of Money: The Case of Egypt' Money.' *Credit and State Theories of Money: The Contribution of A. Mitchell Innes*. L. Randall Wray, ed. Cheltenham, UK: Edward Elgar, 2004. 79–98.

Herbst, Jeffrey. *States and Power in Africa: Comparative Lessons in Authority and Control*. Princeton, NJ: Princeton University Press, 2000.

Hinds, Allister. *Britain's Sterling Colonial Policy and Decolonization, 1939–1958*. Westport, CT: Greenwood Press, 2001.

Hobley, Charles Kenya. *From Chartered Company to Crown Colony. Thirty Years of Exploration and Administration in British East Africa*. 2nd edn. London: Frank Cass, 1929.

Hogendorn, Jan. *The Shell Money of the Slave Trade*. Cambridge: Cambridge University Press, 1986.

Hogendorn, Jan and Henry A. Gemery. 'Continuity in West African Monetary History? An Outline of Monetary Development.' *African Economic History*. 17 (1989) 127–46.

Hogendorn, Jan and Marion Johnson. *The Shell Money of the Slave Trade*. New York: Cambridge University Press, 1986.

Holmes, Charkes F. 'Zanzibari Influence at the Southern End of Lake Victoria: the Lake Route.' *African Historical Studies*. 4:3 (1971) 477–503.

Hopkins, Anthony G. *An Economic History of West Africa*. London: Longman, 1973.

Hopper, Matthew. *Slaves of One Master: Globalization and Slavery in Arabia in the Age of Empire*. New Haven: Yale University Press, 2015.

Hore, Edward. *Eleven Years in Central Africa*. London: Stanford, 1892.

———. 'On the Twelve Tribes of Lake Tanganyika.' *Journal of the Anthropological Institute of Great Britain and Ireland*. 12 (1883) 2–21.

Horn, Alfred. *The Waters of Africa*. London: Jonathan Cape, 1929.

Humphery, Caroline. 'Barter and Economic Disintegration.' *Man*. 20 (1985) 48–72.

Hunwick, John. 'Islamic Financial Institutions: Theoretical Structures and Aspects of Their Application in Sub-Saharan Africa.' *Credit, Currencies and Culture: African Financial Institutions in Historical Perspective*. Endre Stiansen, ed. Stockholm: Nordic Africa Institute, 2005. 72–99.

Husain, Mahdi, trans. *The Rehla of Ibn Battuta*. Baroda: Oriental Institute, 1976.

Hussain, Syed Ejaz. *The Bengal Sultanate: Politics, Economy and Coins, AD 1205–1576*. Delhi: Manohar, 2003.

Ichihara, M. 'Coinage of Old Korea.' *Transactions of the Korea Branch of the Royal Asiatic Society*. 4:2 (1913) 45–74.

Ingham, Geoffery. *The Nature of Money*. Cambridge: Polity Press, 2004.

Inikori, Joseph. 'Africa and the Globalization Process: Western Africa, 1450–1850.' *Journal of Global History*. 2:1(2007) 63–86.

Innes, A. Mitchell. 'What is Money.' Reprinted in *Credit and State Theories of Money: The Contribution of A. Mitchell Innes*. L. Randall Wray, ed. Cheltenham, UK: Edward Elgar, 2004. 14–49.

Innes, Robert L., *The Door Ajar: Japan's Foreign Trade in the Seventeenth Century*, PhD dissertation, University of Michigan, 1980.

Jackson, Frederick J. *Early Days in East Africa*. London: E. Arnold: 1930.

Jackson, Peter. *The Delhi Sultanate: A Political and Military History*. Cambridge: Cambridge University Press, 1999.

Jahangeer Chojoo, Amenah. 'The Yamse and Horse-Racing: Integration and Contestation in a Stratified Society.' *Angaje. Explorations into the History, Society and Culture of Indentured Immigrants and their Descendants in Mauritius*, AGTF Vol 3. Port Louis: AGTF, 2013. 67–88.

Jahangeer Chojoo, Amenah and D. Daworaz. *The Guirni Necklace: A Shining Heritage of Mauritius*. Moka: MGI Multimedia Production, 2017.

Jevons, William Stanley. *Money and the Mechanism of Exchange*. New York: D. Appleton & Co, 1875.

Job, H. S. 'The Coinage of the Mahdi and the Khalifa.' *Sudan Notes and Records*. 3:3 (1920) 164–71.

Jørgensen, Jan Jelmert. *Uganda: A Modern History*. London: Croom Helm, 1981.

Kieran, A. 'The Origins of the Zanzibar Guarantee Treaty of 1862.' *Canadian Journal of African Studies*. 2:2 (1968) 147–66.

Kindleberger, Charles P. *Spenders and Hoarders: The World Distribution of Spanish American Silver, 1550–1750*. Singapore: Institute of Southeast Asian Studies, 1989.

Kobata, Atsushi. 'The Production and Uses of Gold and Silver in Sixteenth and Seventeenth Century Japan.' *Economic History Review*. 18:2 (1965) 245–66.

Kok, Walter. 'Self-Settled Refugees and the Socio-Economic Impact of their Presence on Kassala, Eastern Sudan.' *Journal of Refugee Studies*. 2:4 (1989) 419–41.

Kostiner, Joseph. *The Making of Saudi Arabia 1916–1936: From Chieftaincy to Monarchical State*. Oxford: Oxford University Press, 1993.

Krahl, Regina, John Guy, J. Keith Wilson, and Julian Raby, eds. *Shipwrecked: Tang Treasures and Monsoon Winds*. Washington, DC: Arthur M. Sackler Gallery, 2010.

Kulke, Hermann, K. Kesavapany, and Vijay Sakhuja. *Nagapattinam to Suvarnadwipa: Reflections on the Chola Naval Expeditions to Southeast Asia*. Delhi: Manohar, 2010.

Kuroda Akinobu. 'The Maria Theresa Dollar in the Early Twentieth Century Red Sea Region: A Complementary Interface between Multiple Markets.' *Financial History Review*. 14:1 (2007, April) 89–110.

———. 'What is Complementarity among Monies? An Introductory Note.' *Financial History Review*. 15:1 (2008) 7–15.

Lamusse, R. *Supremacy and Twilight of Mauritian Sugar Industry*. Rose Hill: Osman Books, 2011.

Lê Tành Khôi. *Histoire du Vietnam des origines à 1858*. Paris: Sudestasie, 1981.

Leakey, Louis S.B. *The Southern Kikuyu before 1903*. London: Academic Press, 1977.

Leavens, Dickson. *Silver Money*. Bloomington, IN: Principa Press, 1939.

Leminier, N. 'Notes sur une excursion faite dans l'intérieur de l'Île de Madagascar en 1825.' *Bulletin de Madagascar*. 292 (1970).

Lewis, B.A. 'Diem el Arab and the Beja Stevedores of Port Sudan.' *Sudan Notes and Records*. 43 (1962) 16–49.

Li, Kangying. 'A Study on the Song, Yuan and Ming Monetary Policies Within the Context of Worldwide Hard Currency Flows during the 11th–16th Centuries and Their Impact on Ming Institutions.' *The East Asian Maritime World 1400–1800. Its Fabrics of Power and Dynamics of Exchange*. Angela Schottenhammer, ed. Wiesbaden: Otto Harrassowitz, 2007. 99–136.

Liebner, Horst Hubertus. *The Siren of Cirebon. A Tenth Century Trading Vessel lost in the Java Sea*, PhD dissertation submitted to the University of Leeds, 2014, March.

Lin, Man-houng, 'The Shift from East Asia to the World: The Role of Maritime Silver in China's Economy in the Seventeenth to Late Eighteenth Centuries.' *Maritime China in Transition 1750–1850*. Gungwu Wang and Chin-Keong Ng, eds. Wiesbaden: Otto Harrassowitz, 2004. 77–96.

Liu Hsü-feng (Liu Xufeng) 劉序楓. 'Qing Kangxi~Qianlong nianjian yangtong de jinkou yu liutong wenti' 清代康熙乾隆年間洋銅的進口與流通問題. Zhongguo haiyang fazhanshi lunwenji 中國海洋發展史論文集. vol. 7. T'ang Hsi-yung (Tang Xiyong) 湯熙勇, ed. Taibei: Nankang, 1999. 93–144.

———. 'Qingdai de Zhapu gang yu ZhongRi maoyi.' 清代的乍浦港與中日貿易. *Zhongguo haiyang fazhanshi lunwenji* 中國海洋發展史論文集, vol. 5. Chang Pin-ts'un 張彬村 and Liu Shih-chi 劉石吉, eds. Taibei: Zhongyang yanjiuyuan, 1993. 187–244.

Louis, Francois, 'Metal Objects on the Belitung Shipwreck.' *Shipwrecked. Tang Treasures and Monsoon Winds.* Regina Krahl, John Guy, J. Keith Wilson, and Julian Raby, eds. Washington, DC: Arthur M. Sackler Gallery, 2010. 85–91.

Lovejoy, Paul. 'Interregional Monetary Flows in the Precolonial Trade of Nigeria.' *The Journal of African History.* 15 (1974) 563–85.

Lucassen, Jan, ed., *Wages and Currency: Global Comparisons from Antiquity to the Twentieth Century.* Bern: Peter Lang, 2007.

Ly-Tio-Fane Pineo, H. *Ile de France, 1715–1746, Vol. I; Ile de France, 1747–1767, Vol. II; Port Louis base navale.* Vol. III. Moka: Mahatma Gandhi Institute, 1993/1999.

Lyne, Robert. *Zanzibar in Contemporary Times: A Short History of the Southern East in the Nineteenth Century.* London: Hurst and Blackett, 1905.

Ma, Debin. 'Money and Monetary Systems in China, in the 19th and 20th Century: an Overview.' *Economic History Working Paper London School of Economics and Political Science.* 159:12 (2012).

Machado, Pedro. *Ocean of Trade: South Asian Merchants, Africa and the Indian Ocean, c.1750–1850.* Cambridge, UK: Cambridge University Press, 2014.

Macmillan, Allistair. *Mauritius Illustrated: Historical and Descriptive, Commercial and Industrial Facts, Figures, and Resources.* Originally published by Collingridge, 1914, London, New Delhi: Asian Educational Services, 2000.

Maheshwari, K.K. *Imitations in Continuity: Tracking the Silver Coinage of Early Medieval India.* Mumbai: IIRNS Publications, 2010.

Mair, Lucy, *An African People in the Twentieth Century.* London: Routledge, 1934.

Major, R.H., ed. *India in the Fifteenth Century: Being a Collection of Narratives of Voyages to India.* London: Hakluyt Society, 1858.

Malcolm, W.E. ed., *England's East African Policy. Articles on the Relations of England to the Sultan of Zanzibar, and on the Negotiations of 1873, Etc.* London: Simpkin, Marshall & Co., 1875.

Malekandathil, Pius. *Maritime India: Trade, Religion and Polity in the Indian Ocean.* Delhi: Primus, 2010.

Markovits, Claude. *The Global World of Indian Merchants, 1750–1947: Traders of Sind from Bukhara to Panama.* Cambridge, UK: Cambridge University Press, 2000.

Martini, Ferdinando. *Nell'Africa Italiana.* 8th ed. Milan: Fratelli Treves, 1925.

Marx, Karl, *Capital. A Critique of Political Economy.* Moscow: Progress Publishers, Reprint 1986.

Mathew, Johan. *Margins of the Market: Trafficking and Capitalism across the Arabian Sea*. Oakland: University of California Press, 2016.

Maunder, Peter and Danny Myers, *Nancy Wall and Roger LeRoy Miller. Economics Explained*. 3rd edn. London: Harper Collins, 1991.

Maxon, Robert. 'The Kenya Currency Crisis, 1919–21 and the Imperial Dilemma.' *Journal of Imperial and Commonwealth History*. 17 (1989) 323–48.

McCann, James. *People of the Plow: An Agricultural History of Ethiopia, 1800–1990*. Madison, WI: University of Wisconsin Press, 1995.

McDonald, Hamish. *The Polyester Prince: The Rise of Dhirubhai Ambani*. St. Leonards, Australia: Allen & Unwin, 1999.

Médard, Henri. *Le Royaume du Buganda au XIXe siècle: mutations politiques et religieuses dans un ancien état d'Afrique*. Paris: Khartala, 2007.

Mehrotra, Nilika. 'Gold and Gender in India: Some Observations from South Orissa.' *Indian Anthropologist*, 34:1 (2004) 27–39.

Merritt, H.P. 'Bismarck and the German Interest in East Africa, 1884–1885.' *Historical Journal*. 21:1 (1978) 97–116.

Middleton, John. *African Merchants of the Indian Ocean: Swahili of the East African Coast*. Long Grove, IL: Waveland Press, 2004.

Milne, Janet. 'The Impact of Labour Migration on the Amarar in Port Sudan. *Sudan Notes and Records*. 15 (1974) 70–87.

Ministere des Finances, Tresorerie, Monnaie Royale de Belgique. *Catalogue des poincons & matrices du musee de l'hotel des monnaies*. Brussels: Monnaie Royale, 1977.

Molesworth Macpherson, John and Albert Williams. *British Enactments in Force in Native States*. 2nd edn. Calcutta: Office of the Superintendent of Government Printing, 1899.

Mommsen, Wolfgang J. and Jaap de Moor. *European Expansion and Law: The Encounter of European and Indigenous Law in Nineteenth- and Twentieth-Century Africa and Asia*. New York: Oxford University Press, 1992.

Moosvi, Shireen. 'Numismatic Evidence and the Economic History of the Delhi Sultanate.' *Proceedings of the Indian History Congress, 50th Session*. Gorakhpur (1991) 208–15.

Munro, J Forbes. 'Shipping Subsidies and Railway Guarantees: William Mackinnon, Eastern Africa, and the Indian Ocean, 1860–1893.' *Journal of African History*. 28:2 (1987) 209–30.

Mwangi, Wambui. 'The Lion, the Native and the Coffee Plant: Political Imagery and the Ambiguous Art of Currency Design in Colonial Kenya.' *Geopolitics*. 7:1 (2002): 31–62.

———. 'Of Coins and Conquest: the East African Currency Board, the Rupee Crisis and the Problem of Colonialism in the East African Protectorate.' *Comparative Studies in Society and History*. 4:4 (2001) 763–87.

Naanen, Ben. 'Economy within an Economy: The Manilla Currency, Exchange Rate Instability and Social Conditions in South-Eastern Nigeria 1900–48.' *The Journal of African History*. 34 (1993) 425–46.

al-Naqar, Umar. 'Arabic Materials in the Government Archives of Zanzibar.' *History in Africa*. 5 (1978) 377–82.

Nicholls, Christine S. *The Swahili Coast: Politics, Diplomacy and Trade on the East African Littoral, 1798–1856*. London: Allen and Unwin, 1971.

Nolan, Francis P. *Christianity in Unyamwezi 1878–1928*, PhD Thesis, University of Cambridge, 1977.

Ochsenwald, William. 'The Commercial History of the Hijaz Vilayet, 1840–1908.' *Arabian Studies*. 6 (1982) 57–77.

Ofonogoro, Walter I. 'From Traditional to British Currency in Southern Nigeria: Analysis of a Currency Revolution, 1880–1948.' *The Journal of Economic History*. 39:3 (1979) 623–54.

Oliver, Samuel. *Madagascar: An Historical and Descriptive Account of the Island and Its Former Dependencies*. 2 vols. London: Macmillan, 1886.

———. 'General Hall and the Export Slave Trade from Madagascar: A Statement and a Vindication.' *Antananarivo Annual and Madagascar Magazine*. 12 (1888) 473–9.

Ōta Yukio 大田由紀夫. '12–15 seiki shotō Higashi Ajia ni okeru dōsen no ryufu: Nihon, Chūgoku o chūshin toshite.' 12–15 世紀初頭東アジアにおける銅錢 の流布:日本中國を中心として. *Shakai keizaishi gaku* 社會經濟史學 (1995) 61–2.

Owen, Roger and Sevket Pamuk. *A History of Middle East Economies in the Twentieth Century*. London: I. B. Tauris Publishers, 1998.

Pakistan, State Bank of. *Annual Report*, 1951.

Pallaver, Karin. 'The African native has no Pocket': Monetary Practices and Currency Transitions in Early Colonial Uganda.' *The International Journal of African Historical Studies*. 48:3 (2015) 471–99.

———. 'Currencies of the Swahili World.' *The Swahili World*. S. Wynne-Jones and A. La Violette, eds. London and New York: Routledge, 2018. 447–57.

———. 'Paying in Rupees, Paying in Cents. Colonial Currencies, Labour Relations and the Payment of Wages in Kenya (1890–1920).' *Colonialism, Institutional Change and Shifts in Global Labour Relations*. K. Hofmeester and P. de Zwart, eds. Amsterdam: University of Amsterdam Press, 2018. 295–325.

———. 'A Recognized Currency in Beads': Glass Beads as Money in 19th-Century East Africa: the Central Caravan Road.' *Money in Africa*. C. Eagleton, H. Fuller, and J. Perkins, eds. London: British Museum Research Publications, 2009. 20–9.

———. 'From Venice to East Africa: History, Uses and Meanings of Glass Beads.' *Luxury in Global Perspective: Commodities and Practices, c. 1600–2000*. K. Hofmeester and B.S. Grewe, eds. Cambridge: Cambridge University Press, 2016. 192–217.

Pamuk, Sevket. *A Monetary History of the Ottoman Empire*. Cambridge: Cambridge University Press, 2000.

Pankhurst, Richard. *Economic History of Ethiopia, 1800–1935*. Addis Ababa: Haile Selassie I University Press, 1968.

———. *The Great Ethiopian Famine of 1888–1892: A New Assessment*. Addis Ababa: Haile Sellassie I University, 1964.

Parkin, Michael and David King. *Economics*. 2nd edn. London: Addison-Wesley, 1995.

Parsons, H.A. *The Colonial Coinages of British Africa, with the Adjacent Islands*. London: Spink & Son, Ltd., 1950.

Patat, Jean-Pierre and Michel Lutfalla. *Historie Monétaire de la France au XXe siècle*. Paris: Economica, 1986.

Paturau, J. Maurice. *Histoire Economique de l'Ile Maurice*. Les Pailles: Henry & Cie Ltée, 1988.

Pawelczak, Marek. *The State and the Stateless: The Sultanate of Zanzibar and the East African Mainland: Politics, Economy and Society, 1837–1888*. Warsaw: SOWA, 2010.

Pearce, Francis Barrow. *Zanzibar: The Island Metropolis of Eastern Africa*. London: T Fisher Unwin, 1920.

Pearson, Michael. *The Indian Ocean*. London: Routledge, 2003.

Peng Xinwei 彭信威. *Zhongguo huobi shi*中國貨幣史. Shanghai: Shanghai renmin chubanshe, 1958.

———. *Zhongguo huobishi* 中國貨幣史*: A Monetary History of China*. Edward H. Kaplan, trans. Washington, DC: Western Washington University, 1993.

Penrose, Jan. 'Designing the Nation: Banknotes, Banal Nationalism and Alternative Conceptions of the State.' *Political Geography*. 30 (2011) 429–40.

Pfieffer, Ida. *Voyage à Madagascar*. Paris: Librarie Hachette, 1881.

Pokharna, Prem Lata. 'A Huge Hoard of Gadhaiya Coins from Kasindra.' *Journal of the Numismatic Society of India*. 46 (1984) 51–2.

Pomeranz, Kenneth and Roy Bin Wong. 'China and Europe, 1500 to 2000 and Beyond: Was it "Modern?".' Accessed March 29, 2015. http://afe.easia.columbia.edu/chinawh/web/s5/s5_4.html.

Porkonowski, Ila. 'Beads and Personal Adornment.' *The Fabrics of Culture: The Anthropology of Clothing and Adornment*. Justine M. Cordwell and Ronald A. Schwarz, eds. New York: Mouton Publishers, 1979. 103–18.

Prakash, Om. 'Foreign Merchants and Indian Mints in the Seventeenth and the Early Eighteenth Century.' *The Imperial Monetary System of Mughal India*. J.F. Richards, ed. Delhi: Oxford University Press, 1987. 171–92.

Prestholdt, Jeremy. *Domesticating the World. African Consumerism and the Genealogies of Globalization*. Berkley: University of California Press, 2008.

Prud'homme. 'Contribution à l'histoire de l'Imerina.' *Bulletin de l'Académie Malgache*. 14 (1931) 55–73.

Quan Hansheng 全漢昇. 'Qingdai Yunnan tongkuang gongye' 清代雲南銅礦工業. *Xianggang Zhongwen daxue Zhongguo wenhua yanjiusuo xuebao* 香港中文大學中國文化研究所學報. 7:1 (1974) 155–82.

———. 'Ming Zhongye hou taicang suiru yinliang de yanjiu' 明中葉後太倉歲入銀兩的研究. *Xianggang Zhongwen daxue Zhongguo wenhua yanjiusuo xuebao* 香港中文大學中國文化研究所學報. 1 (1972), 136–39.

Quiggin, Mary Alison. *A Survey of Primitive Money. The Beginnings of Currency.* New York: Barnes & Noble, 1970 [1949].

Rasoamiaramanana, Micheline. *Aspects économiques et sociaux de la vie à Majunga entre 1862 et 1881*, PhD dissertation, Université de Madagascar, 1973.

Ray, Rajat Kanta. 'Asian Capital in the Age of European Domination: The Rise of the Bazaar, 1800–1914.' *Modern Asian Studies.* 29:3 (1995, July) 449–554.

Reid, Anthony. *Southeast Asia in the Age of Commerce 1450–1680.* New Haven: Yale University Press, 1993.

Reid, Richard. *Political Power in Precolonial Buganda: Economy, Society and Warfare in the Nineteenth Century.* Oxford: James Currey, 2002.

Reddy, D. Raja. 'Hyderabad Museum Collection of Treasure Trove Coins of Bahmani, Vijayanagara, and Yadava Dynasties.' *Journal of the Numismatic Society of India.* 71 (2009) 105–14.

Renaudot, Eusebius, trans. *Ancient Accounts of India and China.* London: Harding, 1733.

Rhompson, Virginia and Richard Adloff. *Djibouti and the Horn of Africa.* Stanford, CA: Stanford University Press, 1968.

Richardson, David. 'West African Consumer Patterns and Their Influence on the Eighteenth-century English Slave Trade.' *Uncommon Markets: Essays in the Economic History of the Atlantic World.* H.A. Gemery and J.S. Hogendorn, eds. London: Academic Press, 1979. 303–30.

Rigby, Christopher Palmer. *General Rigby, Zanzibar, and the Slave Trade: With Journals, Dispatches, Etc.* London: Allen & Unwin, 1935.

Risso, Patricia. *Merchants and Faith: Muslim Commerce and Culture in the Indian Ocean.* Boulder, CO: Westview Press, 1995.

Roberts, Andrew. 'The Nyamwezi.' *Tanzania before 1900. Seven Area Histories.* A.D. Roberts, ed. Nairobi: East African Publishing House, 1968. 117–50.

Rockel, Stephen. *Carriers of Culture. Labor on the Road in Nineteenth-century East Africa.* Portsmouth: Heinemann, 2006.

Ronall, J. O. 'Banking Developments in Kuwait.' *Middle East Journal.* 24:1 (1970, January 1) 87–90.

Rowe, John A. *Revolution in Buganda 1856–1900. Part One: Reign of Mukabya Mutesa 1856–1884*, PhD Thesis, University of Wisconsin, 1966.

Ruete, Emilie. *Memoirs of an Arabian Princess from Zanzibar.* Mineola, NY: Dover Publications, Incorporated, 2009.

Salem-Murdock, Muneera. *The Impact of Agricultural Development on a Pastoral Society: The Shukriya of the Eastern Sudan*. New York: Institute for Development Anthropology, 1979.

Salmon, Claudine. 'Srivijaya, la Chine et les marchands chinois (Xe–XIIe s.): Quelques réflexions sur la société de l'empire sumatranais.' *Archipel*. 63 (2002) 57–78.

Salverda, Tijo. *The Franco-Mauritian Elite. Power and Anxiety in the Face of Change*. New York: Berghahn Books, 2015.

Santagata, Fernando. *La Colonia Eritrea nel Mar Rosso davanti all'Abyssinia*. Naples: Libreria Internazionale Treves di Leo Lupi, 1935.

Saudi Arabian Monetary Agency. "Saudi Currency." The Historical Framework of the Currency of Saudi Arabia, 2014. http://www.sama.gov.sa/sites/samaen/Currency/Pages/HistoricalInfo.aspx.

Sbacchi, Alberto. *Ethiopia under Mussolini: Fascism and the Colonial Experience*. New Jersey: Zed Books, 1985.

Scardigli, Marco. *Il Braccio Indigeno: Ascari, irregolari e Bande nella Conquista dell'Eritrea 1885–1911*. Milan: FrancoAngeli, 1996.

Schaefer, Charles. '"Selling at a Wash": Competition and the Indian Merchant Community in Aden Crown Colony.' *Comparative Studies of South Asia, Africa and the Middle East*. 19:2 (1999) 16–23.

Schafer, Edward H., *The Golden Peaches of Samarkand. A Study of T'ang Exotics*. Berkeley and Los Angeles: University of California Press, 1963.

Schenk, Catherine. *Britain and the Sterling Area: From Devaluation to Convertibility in the 1950s*. London: Routledge, 1994.

———. *The Decline of Sterling: Managing the Retreat of an International Currency, 1945–1992*. New York: Cambridge University Press, 2010.

Schneider, Harold K. 'Livestock as Food and Money.' *The Future of Pastoral Peoples*. J.G. Galaty et al., eds. Ottawa: International Development Research Center, 1981. 210–33.

———. *Livestock and Equality in East Africa. The Economic Basis for Social Structure*. Bloomington: Indiana University Press, 1979.

Schottenhammer, Angela. 'China's Gate to the South: Iranian and Arab Merchant Networks in Guangzhou During the Tang-Song Transition (c.750–1050), PART II: 900–c.1050.' *AAS Working Papers in Social Anthropology/ÖAW Arbeitspapiere zur Sozialanthropologie* 29 (2015) 1–30.

———. 'The Emergence of China as a Maritime Power.' *The Cambridge History of China, vol. 5, part Two, The Five Dynasties and Sung China, 960–1279*. John W. Chaffee and Paul J. Smith, eds. Cambridge: Cambridge University Press, 2014. 437–525.

———. 'Chūgoku keizaishi no kenkyū ni okeru kahei to kahei seisaku: futatsu no jiri to sore ni kansuru kenkai 中国経済史の研究における貨幣と貨幣政策: 二つの事例とそれに関する見解.' [Money and Monetary Policy in the Study of Chinese Economic History: Two Examples and Some Related Observations]. *宋銭の世界』 [The World of Song Money].* Ihara Hiroshi, ed. Tōkyō: Bensei shuppansha, 2009. 219–50.

———. 'Brokers and "Guild" (*huiguan* 會館) Organizations in the Sino-Japanese Copper Trade during the Qing Dynasties.' 明清時期江南市場經濟的空間、制度與網絡 *The Market Economy of the Lower Yangzi Delta in Late Imperial China: Space, Institutions and Networks.* Billy So Kee Long et al., eds. London: Routledge, 2011. 278–99.

———. 'The Role of Metals and the Impact of the Introduction of Huizi Paper Notes in Quanzhou on the Development of Maritime Trade during the Song Period.' *The Emporium of the World: Maritime Quanzhou, 1000–1400.* Angela Schottenhammer, ed. Leiden: E. J. Brill, 2001. 95–176.

———. *Das songzeitliche Quanzhou im Spannungsfeld zwischen Zentralregierung und maritimem Handel. Unerwartete Konsequenzen des zentralstaatlichen Zugriffs auf den Reichtum einer Küstenregion.* Wiesbaden: Otto Harrassowitz, 2000.

Schwartzberg, Joseph E. *A Historical Atlas of South Asia.* Chicago: University of Chicago, 1978.

Schweinfurth, Georg A. et al., eds. *Emin Pasha in Central Africa, Being a Collection of his Letters and Journals*, London: Philip & Son, 1888.

Scrutton, Thomas Edward, ed. *The Commercial Laws of the World: Comprising the Mercantile, Bills of Exchange, Bankruptcy and Maritime Laws of Civilised Nations.* London: Sweet & Maxwell Ltd., 1911.

Searcy, Kim. *The Formation of the Sudanese Mahdist State: Ceremony and Symbols of Authority, 1882–1898.* Leiden: Brill, 2011.

Sen, Tansen. *Buddhism, Diplomacy and Trade: The Realignment of Sino-Indian Relations 600–1400.* Delhi: Manohar, 2003.

———. 'The Formation of Chinese Maritime Networks to Southern Asia, 1200–1450.' *Journal of the Economic and Social History of the Orient.* 49:4 (2006) 421–53.

Serels, Steven. 'Famines of War: The Red Sea Grain Market and Famine in Eastern Sudan, 1889–1891.' *Northeast African Studies.* 12:1 (2012) 73–94.

———. *Starvation and the State: Famine, Slavery and Power in Sudan, 1883–1956.* New York: Palgrave Macmillan, 2013.

Servet, Jean-Michel. 'Démonétisation et remonétisation en Afrique-Occidentale et Équatoriale (XIXe-XXe siecles).' *La Monnaie Souveraine.* Michel Aglietta and AndrÉ Orléans, eds. Paris: Odile Jacob, 1998. 289–324.

Seshadri, R.K. *From Crisis to Convertibility: The External Value of the Rupee.* Madras: Orient Blackswan, 1993.

Sheriff, Abdul. 'Ivory and Economic Expansion in East Africa in the Nineteenth Century.' *Figuring African Trade. Proceedings of the Symposium on the Quantification and Structure of the Import and Export and Long-distance Trade in Africa 1800–1913.* G. Liegesang, H. Pasch, and A. Jones, eds. Berlin: Dietrich Reimer Verlag, 1986. 415–50.

———. *Slaves, Spices and Ivory in Zanzibar*. Oxford: James Currey, 1987.

Shiba Yoshinobu 斯波義信. Sōdai shōgyōshi kenkyū 宋代商業史研究. Tōkyō: Kazama Shobō, 1968.

Shimada, Ryuto. *The Intra Asian Trade in Japanese Copper by the Dutch East India Company During the Eighteenth Century*. Leiden: E. J. Brill, 2006.

Sissons, Carol J. *Economic Prosperity in Ugogo, East Africa, 1860–1890*, PhD Thesis, University of Toronto, 1984.

Smith, Adam. *The Wealth of Nations*. New York: Bantam Dell, 2003.

Smith, George Herbert. *Among the Menabe; or, Thirteen Months on the West Coast of Madagascar*. London: SPCK, 1896.

Smith, MacKenzie and Company, Ltd. *The History of Smith, MacKenzie and Company, Ltd*. London: East Africa, Ltd., 1938.

Smith-Simmons, Adele. *Modern Mauritius: The Politics of Decolonization*. Bloomington: Indiana University Press, 1982.

de Sornay, Pierre. *Isle de France- Ile Maurice. Sa Géographie, son Histoire, son Agriculture, ses Industries et ses Institutions*. Port Louis: Printed by General Printing and Stationery, 1950.

Spivak, Gayatri. 'Can the Subaltern Speak? Speculations on Widow Sacrifice.' *Wedge*. 7:8 (1985) 120–30.

Stanley, Henry Morton. *How I Found Livingstone*. Vercelli: White Star, 2006 [1872].

———. *Through the Dark Continent*. London: Sampson Low, 1878.

Stieglitz, Joseph and John Dariffill, *Economics*. New York: W. W. Norton, 2000.

Strange, Susan. *Sterling and British Policy: A Political Study of an International Currency in Decline*. Oxford: Oxford University Press, 1971.

Subrahmanyam, R. *A Catalogue of Yadava Coins in the Andhra Pradesh State Museum, Hyderabad*. Hyderabad: Government of Andhra Pradesh, 1965.

Subrahmanyam, Sanjay and C.A. Bayly. 'Portfolio Capitalists and the Political Economy of Early Modern India.' *Indian Economic & Social History Review*. 25:4 (1988, December) 401–24.

Subramanian, Lakshmi. *Indigenous Capital and Imperial Expansion: Bombay, Surat and the West Coast*. New Delhi: Oxford University Press, 1996.

Sundström, Lars. *The Exchange Economy of Pre-colonial Tropical Africa*. New York: St. Martin's Press, 1974.

Symes, Peter. 'Gulf Rupees.' Banknotes of the Arab World (1999, December). http://www.pjsymes.com.au/.

Teitelbaum, Joshua. *The Rise and Fall of the Hashemite Kingdom of Arabia*. London: Hurst and Co, 2001.

Thompson, E.P. 'The Moral Economy of the English Crowd in the Eighteenth Century.' *Past and Present.* 50 (1971, February) 76–136.

Thomson, Joseph. *To the Central Lakes and Back: The Narrative of the Royal Geographical Society's East Central African Expedition, 1878–80.* Vol. 1. London: Sampson Low, 1881.

Toby, Ronald P. *State and Diplomacy in Early Modern Japan: Asia in the Development of the Tokugawa Bakufu.* Princeton: Princeton University Press, 1984.

Tosh, John. 'The Northern Interlacustrine Region.' *Pre-colonial African Trade: Essays on Trade in Eastern and Central Africa.* R. Gray and D. Birmingham, eds. London: Oxford University Press, 1970, 102–18.

Toussaint, Auguste. *History of Mauritius.* London: Macmillan, 1977.

———. *Port Louis, deux siècles d'histoire, 1735–1935.* Port Louis: La Typographie Moderne, 1936.

Tschoegl, Adrian. 'Maria Theresa's Thaler: A Case of International Money.' *Eastern Economic Journal.* 27:4 (2001, Fall) 443–62.

Twitchett, Denis and Janice Stargardt. 'Chinese Silver Bullion in a Tenth-century Indonesian Shipwreck.' *Asia Major.* 3rd Series. 15:1 (2004), 23–72

d'Unienville, Baron. *Statistique de l'Ile Maurice et ses Dépendances. Tome premier.* Paris: Gustave Barba, 1830.

Uzoigwe, Godfrey N. 'Pre-colonial Markets in Bunyoro-Kitara.' *Comparative Studies in Society and History.* 14 (1972) 422–55.

Valette, Jean. *Études sur le règne de Radama Ier.* Tananarive: Imprimerie Nationale, 1962.

———. 'Deux documents français sur Madagascar en 1825: les rapports Duhaut-Cilly et Frère.' *Bulletin de l'Académie Malgache.* 16:1–2 (1968) 71–86.

Vaughan, Megan. *Creating the Creole Island. Slavery in Eighteenth Century Mauritius.* Durham: Duke University Press, 2005.

Verghese, S.K. 'International Monetary Crises and the Indian Rupee.' *Economic and Political Weekly.* 8:30 (1973, July 28): 1342–8.

Vogel, Hans Ulrich. 'Chinese Central Monetary Policy, 1644–1800.' *Late Imperial China.* 8:2 (1987) 1–52.

———. 'Cowry Trade and its Role in the Economy of Yunnan: From the Ninth to the Mid-Seventeenth century.' *Journal of the Economic and Social History of the Orient.* 36:3 (1993) 211–52.

Volterra, Alessandro. *Sudditi Coloniali: Ascari Eritrei 1935–1941.* Milan: FrancoAngeli, 2005.

Von Glahn, Richard. *Fountain of Fortune: Money and Monetary Policy in China, 1000–1700.* London: University of California, 1996.

———. 'Monies of Account and Monetary Transition in China, Twelfth to Fourteenth Centuries.' *Journal of the Economic and Social History of the Orient.* 53 (2010) 463–505.

———. 'Myth and Reality of China's Seventeenth-Century Monetary Crisis.' *The Journal of Economic History.* 56:2 (1996) 429–54.

———. 'The Ningbo-Hakata Merchant Network and the Reorientation of East Asian Maritime Trade, 1150–1350.' *Harvard Journal of Asiatic Studies.* 74:2 (2014), 249–79.

von Slatin, Rudolph. *Fire and Sword in the Sudan: A Personal Narrative of Fighting and Serving the Dervishes, 1879–1895.* Translated by F. R. Wingate. London: Edward Arnold, 1896.

Wagoner, Phillip B. '"Lord of the Eastern and Western Oceans": Unguents, Politics and the Indian Ocean Trade in Medieval South India.' *From Local to Global: Papers in Asian History and Culture.* Vol. 1. Kamal Sheel, Charles Willemen, and Kenneth Zysk, eds. Delhi: Buddhist World Press, 2017. 310–33.

———. 'Money Use in the Deccan, c. 1350–1687: The Role of Vijayanagara Hons in the Bahmani Currency System.' *The Indian Economic and Social History Review.* 51:4 (2014) 457–80.

Wallach, Yair. 'Creating a Country through Currency and Stamps: State Symbols and Nation-Building in British-Ruled Palestine.' *Nations and Nationalism.* 17:1 (2011) 129–47.

Wang, Helen, Michael Cowell, Joe Cribb, and Sheridan Bowman. 'Metallurgical Analysis of Chinese Coins at the British Museum.' *British Museum Research Publication Number* 152 (2005).

Warburg, Gabriel. *The Sudan Under Wingate; Administration in the Anglo-Egyptian Sudan, 1899–1916.* London: Frank Cass, 1971.

Wicks, Robert S. *Money, Markets, and Trade in Early Southeast Asia. The Development of Indigenous Monetary Systems to A.D. 1400.* New York: Cornell Southeast Asia Program, 1992.

Wilkinson, J.C. 'The Zanzibar Delimitation Commission 1885–1886.' *Geopolitics and International Boundaries.* 1:2 (1996) 130–58.

Wills, John E. 'China's Farther Shores: Continuities and Changes in the Destination Ports of China's Maritime Trade, 1680–1690.' *Emporia, Commodities and Entrepreneurs in Asian Maritime Trade, c. 1400–1750.* Roderich Ptak and Dietmar Rothermund, eds. Stuttgart: Franz Steiner Verlag, 1991. 53–77.

Wingate, Francis Reginald. *Ten Years' Captivity in the Mahdi's Camp 1882–1892.* London: Sampson, Low, Marston and Co, 1892.

Wink, André. *Al-Hind: the Making of the Indo-Islamic World. Vol. II, The Slave Kings and the Islamic Conquest 11th–13th Centuries.* Leiden: Brill, 1997.

———. *Al-Hind: the Making of the Indo-Islamic World. Vol. III, Indo-Islamic Society, 14th-15th Centuries.* Leiden: Brill, 2004.

Wray, L. Randall and Stephanie Bell. 'Introduction.' *Credit and State Theories of Money: The Contribution of A. Mitchell Innes.* L. Randall Wray, ed. Cheltenham, UK: Edward Elgar, 2004. 1–13.

Wright, H. Nelson. *The Coinage and Metrology of the Sultans of Delhi*. Delhi: Oxford University Press, 1936.

Wubneh, Mulatu and Yohannis Abate. *Ethiopia: Transition and Development in the Horn of Africa*. Boulder, CO: Westview Press, 1988.

Wynne-Jones, Stephanie and Jeffrey Fleisher. 'Coins and other Currencies on the Swahili Coast.' *The Archaeology of Money*. C. Haselkgrove and S. Krmnicek, eds. Leicester: Leicester University Press, 2016, 115–36.

Yan Zhongping 嚴中平. *Qingdai Yunnan tongzheng kao* 清代雲南銅政考. Beijing: Zhonghua shuju, 1957.

Yang, Lien-sheng. *Money and Credit in China: A Short History*. Cambridge, MA: Harvard University Press, 1952.

Yang, Bin. 'The Bay of Bengal Connections to Yunnan.' *Pelagic Passageways: The Northern Bay of Bengal before Colonialism*. Rila Mukherjee, ed. Delhi: Primus, 2011. 317–42.

———. *Between Wind and Clouds: the Making of Yunnan (Second century BCE to Twentieth Century CE*. New York: Columbia University Press, 2009.

Yokkaichi Yasuhiro 四日市康博. 'Chinese and Muslim Diasporas and the Indian Ocean Trade Network under Mongol Hegemony.' *The East Asian Mediterranean—Maritime Crossroads of Culture, Commerce, and Human Migration*. Angela Schottenhammer, ed. Wiesbaden: Otto Harrassowitz, 2008. 73–102.

Young, Richard J. C. *Colonial Desire: Hybridity in Theory, Culture and Race*. London: Routledge, 1995.

Yule, Henry, ed., trans. *The Book of Ser Marco Polo the Venetian, Concerning the Kingdoms and Marvels of the East*. Vol. II. London: Murray, 1871.

Zainie, Carla M. 'The Sinan Shipwreck and Early Muromachi Art Collections.' *Oriental Art*. 25:1 (1979) 103–14.

Zysow, A. 'Ṣarf.' *Encyclopedia of Islam. Volume XII: Supplement*. Leiden: Brill, 2004. 706.

Index[1]

[1] Note: Page numbers followed by 'n' refer to notes.

S. Serels, G. Campbell (eds.), *Currencies of the Indian Ocean World*, Palgrave Series in Indian Ocean World Studies, https://doi.org/10.1007/978-3-030-20973-5

I

J

K

N

O

The manufacturer's authorised representative in the EU is Springer Nature Customer Service Centre GmbH, Europaplatz 3, 69115 Heidelberg, Germany. If you have any concerns regarding our products, please contact ProductSafety@springernature.com

Printed and bound by CPI Group (UK) Ltd, Croydon, CR0 4YY
25/09/2026
02222863-0001